# INSIDE THE KREMLIN DURING THE YOM KIPPUR WAR

# VICTOR ISRAELYAN

# INSIDE THE KREMLIN DURING THE YOM KIPPUR WAR

Foreword by
ALVIN Z. RUBINSTEIN

The Pennsylvania State University Press
University Park, Pennsylvania

Library of Congress Cataloging-in-Publication Data

Israèlīan Viktor Levonovich, 1919–
    Inside the Kremlin during the Yom Kippur War / Victor Israelyan.

    p.   cm.
    Includes bibliographical references and index.

    1. Israel-Arab War, 1973—Diplomatic history.  2. Soviet Union—Foreign relations—Middle East.  3. Middle East—Foreign relations—Soviet Union.  4. Soviet Union—Foreign relations—1953–1975.  I. Title.
DS128.13.S64I84   1995
327.47056'09'047—dc20                                      95–13306
ISBN 978-0-271-01737-2                                            CIP

Copyright © 1995 The Pennsylvania State University
All rights reserved

It is the policy of The Pennsylvania State University Press to use acid-free paper for the first printing of all clothbound books. Publications on uncoated stock satisfy the minimum requirements of American National Standard for Information Sciences—Permanence of Paper for Printed Library Materials, ANSI Z39.48-1992.

*To my wife, Alla*

# CONTENTS

| | |
|---|---|
| Foreword by Alvin Z. Rubinstein | ix |
| Introduction | xv |
| Key Soviet Officials Named in the Book | xxi |
| Map of Middle East in October 1973 | xxii |
| 1  On the Eve of the War | 1 |
| 2  Searching for an Early Cease-Fire | 21 |
| 3  "We Have to Help Our Arab Brothers" | 53 |
| 4  Kosygin's Visit to Cairo | 87 |
| 5  Kissinger in Moscow | 115 |
| 6  The Escalation | 151 |
| 7  The De-escalation | 177 |
| 8  Conclusion | 211 |
| Notes | 221 |
| Index | 227 |
| About the Author | 239 |

# FOREWORD
# BY ALVIN Z. RUBINSTEIN

On October 6, 1973, at 2:00 P.M. Middle East time, Egyptian and Syrian armies attacked the Israeli forces that were occupying Sinai and the Golan Heights. During the next three weeks the most intense fighting since the Second World War took place. Not only were more battle tanks, for example, deployed in Sinai by the Egyptians and Israelis than at the decisive battle of Kursk in 1943, when the Soviet Union crushed Nazi Germany's lingering hopes of victory, but Arab losses of Soviet-supplied combat aircraft and tanks approximated the total frontline strength of all the nations of Western Europe. Israel's losses were comparably high. Indeed, without a major U.S. airlift and resupply by sea, Israel would have run out of critical weapons and ammunition. Certainly developments on the battlefield transformed the political dynamics of the Arab-Israeli conflict.

Egyptian and Syrian forces performed well in the early days of the fighting, making impressive advances. But the inability of Egyptian President Anwar Sadat and Syrian President Hafiz Assad to coordinate political strategy or military offensives (their decision to start the war at 2:00 P.M., for example, being a last-minute compromise between Egypt's desire for a later hour and Syria's for an earlier start) led to reversals on the battlefield and ultimately forced them to look again to Moscow to bail them out. The Israelis initially seemed paralyzed by their strategic error in having assumed that the Arabs would not dare attack as long as Israel maintained air superiority, but once they regained their equilibrium and their audacity on the battlefield, they exploited the Egyptian military's mistake in advancing ahead of its protective missile umbrella and rolled back the Egyptian forces. Their counterattack on the Golan Heights proved a tough slog. Arms were used with profligate disregard for cost. Each actor calculated, correctly, that its superpower patron would not permit it to be defeated and would do logistically whatever was necessary.

The oil weapon came of age during the Yom Kippur War (also known as the October War). An oil embargo imposed by the Organization of Arab Petroleum Exporting Countries (OAPEC) against the United States and other countries in an effort to exact support for the Arab cause quadrupled the price of oil once in the year after the war, and once again over the course of the decade. This brought the Arabs international prominence and considerable influence in the United Nations. Ironically, the effect on the Soviet Union was disastrous: as a prime beneficiary of the higher oil prices (both through its exports of oil for hard currency and its sales of weapons to oil-rich Arab states or to clients whose purchases of weapons were subsidized by these states), Moscow indulged in wasteful military spending and overly generous support for other Third World clients, such as Cuba, Vietnam, and Ethiopia, thus aggravating the economic stagnation that Gorbachev sought ineffectually to reverse in the late 1980s. In the process of pushing reform, Gorbachev precipitated the collapse of the entire Soviet system.

Relations between the United States and the Soviet Union were profoundly affected. The war destroyed the budding détente that President Richard Nixon and Soviet leader Leonid Brezhnev had started with the signing of the first strategic arms limitation agreement (SALT I) in Moscow in May 1972, and that they had worked to deepen with a "code of conduct" agreed to during Brezhnev's visit to the United States in late June 1973, the gist of which was a commitment to consult in the event of a threat of war and to cooperate in preventing it from jeopardizing their détente relationship. But détente was just not strong enough to bring the Yom Kippur War to a halt before it enmeshed the two superpowers in a dangerous confrontation. When the fighting in the Middle East stopped, a "new" Cold War ensued with rapidly escalating spirals of weapons deployments and regional crises. Not until the mid-1980s would another Soviet leader try to improve relations with the United States.

The Yom Kippur War was significant because for the first time both superpowers regarded one crisis with equal seriousness, not only in regard to their respective client states but also to their relationship with each other. It was the first time that the United States and the Soviet Union were locked in a direct confrontation over a Middle East issue, the first time that they found themselves in the midst of a crisis that had broken out while they were trying to stabilize their global rivalry in a setting of incipient détente. And it was the first crisis to erupt when the Soviet Union enjoyed military equivalence, both nuclear and conventional. Unlike the 1956 Suez crisis or the 1967 Six-Day War, in 1973 Moscow had a potent power projection capability that it was prepared to use on behalf of beleaguered clients. Neither superpower was distracted by pressing problems elsewhere (the United States had disengaged from Vietnam, the Soviet border with China was quiet, and the unrest in Eastern Europe had been temporarily suppressed), and the oil factor had become part of the consciousness of decision-makers in both countries.

By the end of the October War, the United States and the Soviet Union had moved from being fledgling partners in a dawning détente to being adversarial patrons intent on safeguarding their respective warring clients. Their divergent aims, different policy assumptions, and misperceptions of each other's actions took on enormous significance. Nowhere was this more evident, as Victor Israelyan shows, than in the United States' rush to nuclear confrontation, an escalation that shocked the Kremlin. For the first time, accurate comparisons of the Cold War's two nuclear crises—Cuba in October 1962 and the Middle East in October 1973—are possible, precisely because of Israelyan's insider information and insights.

In analyzing U.S. and Soviet behavior in October 1973, we now have an evidential basis for examining the considerations that prompted each superpower's moves; for assessing how accurately they perceived events and the diplomatic-military actions of the other; for better understanding the assumptions that dominated the thinking of the decision-makers concerning battlefield developments, national interests, deterrence, risk-taking, and domestic politics; for factoring in the bureaucratic rivalries at work and how they affected decisions; and for evaluating the dynamics—personal and bureaucratic—that drove each side's decision-making process. Are there lessons to be learned from the crisis? Is each crisis sui generis? These questions have long fascinated Western analysts of crisis decision-making. Research in comparative foreign policy assumes commonalities and linkages. In this ongoing intellectual and policy-relevant endeavor, Victor Israelyan's seminal work will find a welcome reception, valuable as it is both for hypothesis-testing and for comparative foreign policy analysis.

On the American scene, we know a great deal. Although most of the official documents and memoranda remain classified, there is a rich memoir literature from participants on Washington's side of the crisis. Institutionally, the discussions centered in the State Department's Washington Special Action Group (WSAG), established in 1969 to operate in crisis situations. The crucial decisions, however, were made elsewhere, at the level of the President and the Secretary of State. The WSAG functioned under Secretary of State Henry Kissinger. Its principals were: General Brent Scowcroft, Kissinger's deputy; Secretary of Defense

James Schlesinger; Admiral Thomas Moorer, chairman of the Joint Chiefs of Staff; CIA Director William Colby; Deputy Secretary of State Kenneth Rush; Deputy Assistant Secretary of State for Near East Affairs Alfred Atherton; Deputy Assistant Secretary of Defense for International Affairs James Noyes; and several staff members from the White House's National Security Council, including General Alexander Haig Jr., who was Nixon's Chief of Staff, Harold Saunders, and William Quandt.

The accounts from these insiders make possible an accurate reconstruction of what the chief players in the Nixon administration thought and did during the Yom Kippur War. That there are discrepancies is to be expected, because each memoir, it may be presumed in the absence of the full documentary record, is presenting a perspective in which the writer appears in a commendable light. William Quandt has observed: "There was very little controversy or argument during any of the [WSAG] meetings" (*Decade of Decisions*, p. 170). This suggests a certain "groupthink" mind-set and that the main decisions were made elsewhere.

The key works written by members of the October 1973 crisis-management team are President Richard Nixon's *RN: The Memoirs of Richard Nixon;* Henry Kissinger's *Years of Upheaval,* which contributes more detail of the day-to-day process and assessment and is the most important American perspective to date; Alexander M. Haig Jr.'s *Inner Circles;* and William B. Quandt's *Decade of Decisions* and two essays in the British journal *International Affairs* (1977). Other perspectives are to be found in articles and speeches published over the years by such participants as Brent Scowcroft, James Schlesinger, Admiral Thomas Moorer, Roy Atherton, Harold Saunders, and Admiral Elmo Zumwalt. Also useful are the writings of scholars and journalists who have interviewed many of the participants at various times.

Until Victor Israelyan's extraordinary memoir, the decision-making process in the Kremlin during the October 1973 crisis was virtually unknown. Snippets in secondary works and in post-perestroika interviews with Soviet analysts and diplomats yielded information, but it was incomplete and not always accurate, and none of the Russian/Soviet experts interviewed had been an actual participant in Brezhnev's equivalent of Kissinger's WSAG. But as we shall learn from this book, a clue for understanding the way foreign-policy decisions were made in Moscow was given by Winston S. Churchill, when he said in a broadcast on October 1, 1939, apropos of the Soviet Union's collusion with Nazi

Germany to dismember Poland: "I cannot forecast to you the action of Russia. It is a riddle wrapped in a mystery inside of an enigma; but perhaps there is a key. That key is Russian national interest."

*Inside the Kremlin During the Yom Kippur War* is the first insider's account of what went on in the Kremlin during those three critical and dangerous weeks in October 1973. The narrative is straightforward and revealing. It will require a searching new look at many of the implicit and sometimes faulty assumptions that permeated American assessments of Soviet decision-making—for example, that Marxist-Leninist ideology was an important determinant; that Moscow's top diplomats in the United States were scrupulous in keeping their assessments of U.S. policy free of dogma, in not "cooking the books," so to speak; and that no notes were kept of Kremlin deliberations.

Unlike the abstruse, self-serving, ideologically generalized memoirs of such important Soviet political figures as Mikhail Gorbachev, Alexander Yakovlev, and Eduard Shevardnadze, who write about foreign-policy decisions made during the 1985 to 1991 period, and Andrei Gromyko, who covers a much broader span, Israelyan's account is focused, candid, rich in detail, and analytical—and it is not out to defend or to discredit anyone. Not since Leon Trotsky's writings in the 1930s has a witness to the foreign-policy-making decision process of the Communist Party's top leadership provided us with so substantive a work. (Yegor Ligachev, a member of the Politburo under Gorbachev, has written a valuable account of Kremlin infighting, but he deals solely with domestic issues.)

Victor Israelyan graduated from medical school in 1941 and served as a doctor in the Soviet army during the Second World War. After the war, encouraged to change careers, he earned his doctorate in history and politics at the Moscow Institute of International Relations. His career as a diplomat was meteoric. Rising rapidly to the rank of ambassador, he served for forty-five years in important posts: in disarmament negotiations in Geneva, at the United Nations in New York, at the Ministry of Foreign Affairs, and at the Diplomatic Academy.

Nothing in his experience, however, had prepared him—as he relates in his memoir—for what was to happen starting on the evening of October 4, 1973, when he was summoned to the office of Foreign Minister Andrei Gromyko and assigned to a four-man ad hoc task force that was to take notes and prepare memoranda for the Politburo during the crisis that was expected to erupt on October 6, when, as Gromyko already knew, the Arabs would go to war.

Israelyan's book is a unique and fascinating record. It offers us telling vignettes of Politburo members and other top Soviet leaders, evidence of how nonideological and ideological determinants commingled in the assessments and positions of individuals trying to fashion a sound policy consistent with the Soviet Union's national interest, and a thorough day-by-day account of what went on in Moscow. Writing from his notes, his recollections, and extensive interviews with other Soviet diplomats, Israelyan has opened a window on the Kremlin's past. His descriptions give us a feeling for the human element and for the impulses and calculations that shaped the Kremlin's policy during this crisis.

Although recourse to what we call primary sources is limited because Israelyan did not have access to Kremlin archives when he wrote, his book is very definitely scholarly and authoritative. It should be approached as a memoir that is as close to the truth of events as they were seen at the time by the leaders in the Kremlin as any account we are likely to get, short of open access to the Kremlin's secret memoranda—memoranda prepared by Victor Israelyan.

*Inside the Kremlin During the Yom Kippur War* is a classic whose value will increase with the passage of time. Many of the Kremlin participants in the October crisis are no longer living, and those who are do not seem interested in writing about the event. Israelyan is of the aging generation that served the rulers of the former Soviet Union. Judging by the superficial recollections of the past that we have had to date from this cohort, we shall not see many memoirs from former Communist oligarchs that meet the tests of credibility and candor. We are in Israelyan's debt for having given us this richly textured study of a crisis that may well have been more dangerous than the Cuban missile crisis and that certainly had far greater consequences for U.S.-Soviet relations, and indeed for the fate of the Soviet Union itself.

# INTRODUCTION

The Middle East situation heated up again when on October 6, 1973, Egypt and Syria attacked the Israelis. Egypt crossed the Suez Canal, invading the Sinai Peninsula, while Syria crossed into the Golan Heights. Caught off-guard—because the attack occurred on the Jewish holy Day of Atonement, or Yom Kippur—Israel bounced back quickly, though, forcing the Arabs to retreat from the gains they had made. The war was over three weeks later, but for such a short conflict the costs to all sides were great.

The Soviet Union, along with the United States, played a decisive role in the course and the outcome of the conflict. This book describes and analyzes the Soviet Union's policies during the war from the inside, tries to reconstruct the political vision and partisan perceptions of the Kremlin leaders in an acute international crisis, and examines the implications for past and future conflict management. During the war, which has come to be known as the Yom Kippur War, I was one member of a four-man task force set up in Moscow by the Kremlin leaders. We were charged with providing the Politburo with necessary data and materials and preparing drafts of Politburo decisions, instructions, and other documents. The members of the task force attended almost all meetings of the Soviet leadership, participated in some negotiations, and played the role of liaison officers in maintaining the Politburo's communications with Soviet ministries, agencies, and embassies dealing with the war. Membership in the task force gave me the opportunity to examine the objective and subjective factors that affected the perceptions and thinking of the Soviet leaders.

I hope I do not belong to the unfortunately large group of former Soviet officials (Communist Party *apparatchiks,* high-ranking bureaucrats, diplomats, and other functionaries) who try to convince those who read their memoirs and other writings that throughout their sometimes spectacular careers in the Soviet Union they were aware of the mistakes, lapses, and blunders of the Soviet system and had been (so they said) opposed to certain fundamental decisions of the Kremlin leaders and tried to change the course of events—in vain, of course. Their alleged criticism seems to have gone unnoticed and did not prevent their being promoted to membership in the Central Committee of the Communist Party of the Soviet Union (CPSU) or their being nominated as deputies of the Supreme Soviet of the USSR and to other prestigious and important posts.

Unlike them, I have to confess that I was a typical product of the Soviet system, and its obedient servant. I joined the Ministry of Foreign Affairs (or Foreign Ministry) of the Soviet Union in 1944. After serving as a lecturer and professor of international diplomacy at the Diplomatic Academy during the 1950s and most of the 1960s, I was appointed First Deputy Permanent Representative of the Soviet Union to the United Nations. Later I served as director of the Department of International Organizations in the Foreign Ministry. The Soviet government trusted me to lead several Soviet delegations to many important bilateral and multilateral conferences dealing with political and arms-control issues. I was granted the rank of Ambassador Extraordinary and Plenipotentiary of the USSR, and for twelve years I served as a member of the Collegium of the Foreign Ministry, its principal advisory and decision-making body. Throughout my almost forty-five years of service in the Ministry of Foreign Affairs, I did not have any serious conflicts with my boss, Andrei Gromyko, and I tried to carry out my duties to the best of my knowledge and abilities. I hope I was a good Soviet diplomat, respected by colleagues and partners. This, however, did not prevent my forced resignation in the late 1980s as a result of a trivial Soviet slander against me. That was also a part of the system. Otherwise I could not be a typical Soviet.

Then, why did I write this book? To curse the system I once served, or to justify and glorify it? Neither. The collapse of the Soviet Union was a unique phenomenon in history. It resulted not from war or intervention, and not from an uprising or conspiracy. It was a total bankruptcy of the system, including its foreign policy and diplomacy. Almost overnight the Soviet Union—and later its successor, Russia—lost its numerous allies, and just as quickly a large number of multilateral political, military, and economic organizations initiated by the Soviet Union went to pieces and evaporated. The mighty monolithic Commonwealth of Socialist States, the socialist camp headed by the Soviet superpower, ceased to exist. The special character of the relationship between the Soviet Union and the majority of developing and nonaligned countries, based on a common fight against colonialism and imperialism, became history. Onetime allies became adversaries seeking protection from their former "elder brother." Former enemies, while praising

Russia's inclinations and blueprints for democracy, did not become her allies. Despite the popular character of the Soviet Union's proclaimed international goals—peace, security, disarmament, cooperation—and a huge, experienced diplomatic service, the fiasco of Soviet foreign policy was stunning.

This book is not intended to be a comprehensive analysis of the character and downfall of the foreign policy and diplomacy of the Soviet Union, but rather to provide a close look at the actions of the Soviet Union in a time of international crisis so that the nature of the fiasco can be more clearly understood. The Yom Kippur War was an important episode in international relations and in the foreign policy of the Soviet Union. The Middle East, a region of sharp confrontation between the two superpowers, had always been fraught with the threat of nuclear war. In October 1973 a nuclear confrontation threatened to become reality. The Soviet-American confrontation during the Yom Kippur War was different in many important ways from the other superpower collision, the Cuban crisis. The latter was actually a purely bilateral affair, provoked by Soviet action in or toward Cuba, but superpower policy in October 1973 was heavily dependent on developments in the war between the Arab states and Israel. The growing threat of nuclear confrontation was complex and multifaceted. The client states of both superpowers threatened to involve the United States and the Soviet Union in a military conflict in which their own interests were not always clearly defined and involved.

The Yom Kippur War demonstrates how the cumbersome Soviet policy-making mechanism, headed by the Politburo, functioned in a tense international situation. Almost every day during the war, meetings of senior Communist Party and Soviet government officials were chaired by the Soviet leader, General Secretary Leonid Brezhnev. The first of these meetings took place the day the war broke out, October 6, 1973.

Many meetings in the Kremlin focused on the range of international and domestic issues that fueled the crisis. At one such meeting, in the midst of the crisis, the following issues were the subject of lengthy discussion among Politburo members: the future of Soviet-American relations, the Soviet stand toward the Arab world (assessment of past policy, perspectives for future cooperation), the peace settlement in the Middle East, and the "anti-imperialist" policy and the principle of "peaceful coexistence."

During the war, Soviet leaders conducted many important international negotiations and corresponded with leaders of a large number of states (the Arab states, the United States, other Western states, leading nonaligned countries, and socialist states). An analysis of these negotiations and correspondence highlights typical features of the Soviet/Russian negotiating style.

The discussions in the Kremlin reveal specific interests of different Soviet agencies—the Ministry of Foreign Affairs, the Ministry of Defense, the KGB, and the International Department of the CPSU—and their role in the decision-making process. One important element in this process was the information that reached Moscow from embassies and intelligence agencies. Soviet representatives in Washington, New York, Cairo, Damascus, and other capitals reported to the Kremlin. Having known many of these representatives personally, I tried to determine the quality of the decision-making process from the consequences of the flow and content of their reports. I was acquainted with the members of the Politburo as well—with some of them more, with others less. Their personalities and especially their relationships influenced the process, sometimes significantly.

Although Soviet policy-making mechanisms headed by the highest body of the Communist Party, the Politburo, no longer exist in Russia or in other members of the Commonwealth of Independent States, understanding the thinking and decisions of the senior leadership during the Yom Kippur War is valuable. Russia is still a major power with nuclear capability, and some of the perceptions of the past Soviet leadership have a traditional Russian character that will continue to influence policy-making in Russia now and in the future.

In addition, the Yom Kippur War provides an excellent case study of escalation and de-escalation of an international conflict, as well as an opportunity to evaluate the impact of policy-making mechanisms, negotiating styles, and partisan perception on conflict management.

Despite the variety of accounts of the Yom Kippur War, many questions remain unanswered. When and how did the Kremlin learn the date of the Arab attack against Israel? What was the Soviet leaders' attitude toward this decision? Why did the idea of an early cease-fire fail? How did Brezhnev interpret President Nixon's message, which Secretary of State Henry Kissinger delivered to him in Moscow? What did the Soviet leaders have to say about the "Understanding" initialed by Gromyko and Kissinger on October 21? How did the Kremlin react to the American nuclear alert? What role did the World Congress of Peace Forces, held in Moscow in late October 1973, play in Soviet decisions concerning the war in the Middle East? Who ordered the firing of the SCUD missiles? What effect did the war have on the balance of power in the top Soviet leadership? All these and other questions I have tried to answer, but a number of diplomatic mysteries remain to be solved.

This book is based mainly on documents and notes collected and made by me when I was a member of the task force. I made some of the notes at meetings in the Kremlin and other offices, to use for drafting different kinds of documents. These drafts and many documents were kept in my files in case I should want to use them in my diplomatic activities. I never thought of using them to write a book. It was the irresistible desire to understand the Soviet Union's foreign-policy fiasco that led me to write this book.

Many of my colleagues and friends who participated in the policy-making process in Moscow in October 1973—ambassadors, generals, former functionaries of the CPSU—were kind enough to share with me their reminiscences, thoughts, and observations and to show me documents they had. I would like to express my deep gratitude to them. Their roles in the political drama in the fall of 1973 differed, and so did their recollections. But in their sincere desire to help me by answering questions related to the ups and downs of Soviet foreign policy, all my colleagues were equal. They had the same concerns I had. The reader will find their names in the pages of this book. Russia's Ministry of Foreign Affairs was also cooperative, but the law in Russia still does not give researchers access to the archives related to the Yom Kippur War.

I also want to thank the United States Institute of Peace for the grant that enabled me to write the book, the Earhart Foundation for its kind assistance in the final stage of my research, and of course the Department of History of The Pennsylvania State University, where I had the pleasure to proceed with my manuscript and to teach. This is the first book I have written in English. Therefore, my special gratitude goes to my editors, J. D. Shuchter, who helped at the earliest stages, and especially Peter J. Potter and Peggy Hoover at Penn State Press, whose friendly assistance was invaluable.

In my story of Kremlin policy regarding the Yom Kippur War, I tried to be as objective and as evenhanded as possible, although I myself was a participant—a dancer in the corps de ballet, so to speak—in this grand political and diplomatic performance. I do not know whether I have been successful in that effort, but I know that writing this book has helped me answer some of my questions relating to the bankruptcy of the system I served for several decades.

# KEY SOVIET OFFICIALS NAMED IN THE BOOK

Achromeev, Sergei F.   Deputy Chief of General Staff
Andropov, Yuri V.   Chairman of the KGB; Member of Politburo
Brezhnev, Leonid I.   General Secretary of the Communist Party; Member of Politburo
Dobrynin, Anatolii F.   Soviet Ambassador to the United States
Grechko, Andrei A.   Minister of Defense; Member of Politburo
Gromyko, Andrei A.   Minister of Foreign Affairs; Member of Politburo
Israelyan, Victor L.   Director, Department of International Organizations, Ministry of Foreign Affairs; Member of the Task Force
Katushev, Konstantin F.   Secretary of the Central Committee of the CPSU
Kirilenko, Andrei P.   Secretary of the Central Committee of the CPSU; Member of Politburo
Kornienko, Georgii M.   Director, Department of the U.S., Ministry of Foreign Affairs; Member of the Task Force
Kosygin, Aleksei N.   Prime Minister; Member of Politburo
Kulikov, Victor G.   Chief of General Staff of the Soviet Armed Forces
Kuznetsov, Vasilii V.   First Deputy Minister of Foreign Affairs; Member of the Task Force
Malik, Yakov A.   Permanent Representative of the Soviet Union to the United Nations
Mukhitdinov, Nuritdin   Soviet Ambassador to Syria
Podgorny, Nikolai V.   Chairman of the Presidium of the Supreme Soviet of the Soviet Union; Member of Politburo
Ponomarev, Boris N.   Secretary of the Central Committee of the CPSU
Shelepin, Alexandr N.   Chairman of the Trade Unions; Member of Politburo
Suslov, Mikhail A.   Secretary of the Central Committee of the CPSU; Member of Politburo
Sytenko, Mikhail D.   Director, Department of the Middle East, Ministry of Foreign Affairs; Member of the Task Force
Ustinov, Dmitrii F.   Secretary of the Central Committee of the CPSU
Vinogradov, Vladimir M.   Soviet Ambassador to Egypt

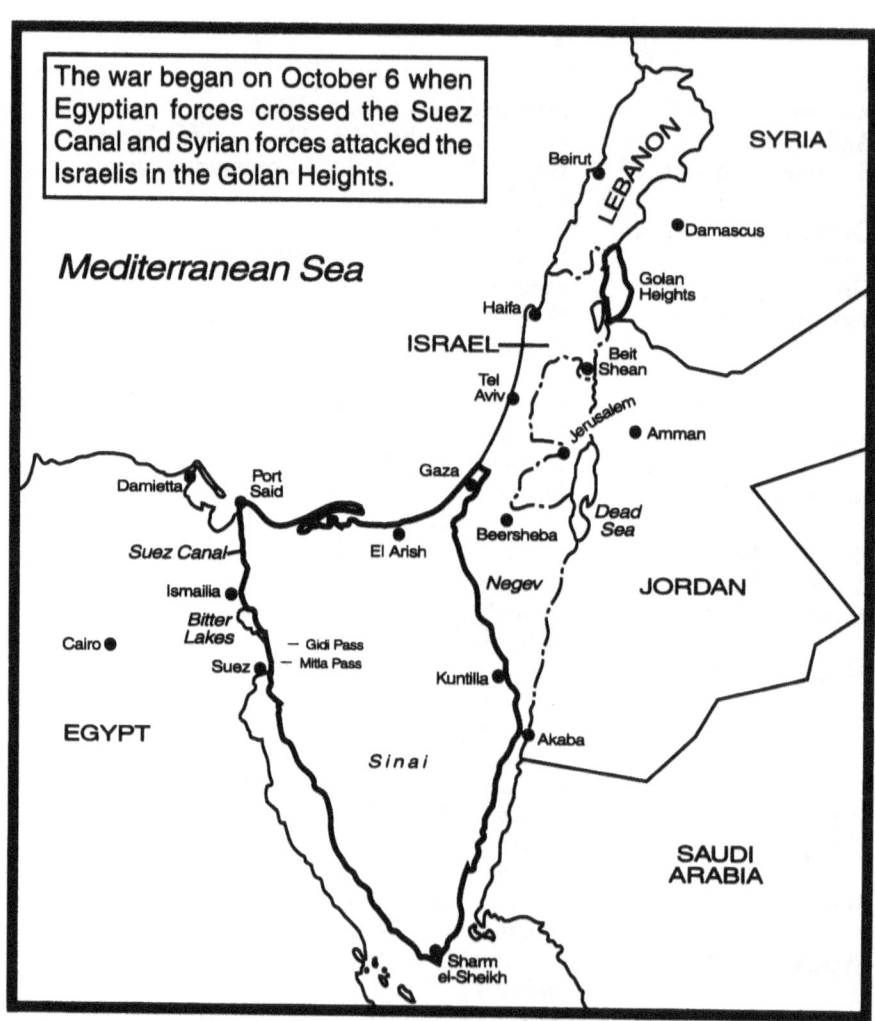

The Middle East in 1973.

# CHAPTER 1

## ON THE EVE OF THE WAR

**THE WAR WILL START AT 2:00 P.M., OCTOBER 6**

Everything began for me on Thursday, October 4, 1973. It was an ordinary weekday full of the usual bureaucratic fuss. My third month in office as director of one of the most important and prestigious Foreign Ministry departments in charge of Soviet policy in international organizations and at disarmament negotiations was rather dull. My boss, Foreign Minister Andrei Gromyko, was in New York and Washington most of the time, and all the issues arising from his talks at the United Nations and in the American capital were settled either by him or in his direct communications with the Kremlin. Our role was limited to collecting the incoming information.

From the embassy cables and other information I received that day, I expected nothing out of the ordinary. Yet at 7:00 P.M., as I was about to leave the Foreign Ministry's high-rise building on Moscow's Smolenskaya Square, I was summoned to the foreign minister's study on the seventh floor, where I found Gromyko; his first deputy, Vasilii Kuznetsov; and the head of the USA Department, Georgii Kornienko, already seated. The head of the Middle East Department, Mikhail Sytenko, soon joined us.

Throughout my long diplomatic career, I found myself in the foreign minister's study many times for different kinds of meetings—important and routine, pleasant, encouraging and displeasing, even sad, including the one at which Eduard Schevardnadze would advise me to resign. But the meeting on October 4 was one of the most remarkable I ever attended in this familiar room.

It was evident that Gromyko had been talking for some time, but bureaucratic etiquette did not permit me to ask him to repeat what had already been said. Although I had begun my new assignment in the Foreign Ministry only recently, I already knew the rules. It was not long, however, before I realized why the meeting had been called. The Egyptian and Syrian leaders had made their final decision to attack Israel. Gromyko repeated several times that the war would start on Saturday, October 6, at 2:00 P.M.

Here it is important to note that the time differences between Moscow, Washington, New York, Cairo, and Damascus played an important role in the political developments of the Yom Kippur War. At noon in Moscow, it was 11:00 A.M. in Cairo and Damascus, and 4:00 A.M. in Washington and New York. As it turned out, Gromyko had Cairo time in mind when he referred to the time of the forthcoming Arab attack. In connection with the decision of the Arab leaders, Gromyko also informed us that steps were being taken to evacuate Soviet civilian personnel and their families from Egypt and Syria. As he talked, he stressed that what he said was to be kept absolutely confidential, especially the time of the planned Arab attack. The matter had already been discussed at the "highest level" in the Kremlin, Gromyko said, but he did not reveal whether the regular meeting of the Politburo that day had taken up the issue, or whether General Secretary Leonid Brezhnev and his closest collaborators had come to any conclusions. It was clear, however, that neither Gromyko nor Brezhnev supported the Arabs' decision. What is more, the foreign minister noted that the Soviet leadership had done everything it could to talk Sadat and Assad out of launching a military attack.

According to Gromyko, negotiations between Brezhnev and President Nixon in the summer of 1973 had created a good foundation for a political solution to the Middle East problem and a military conflict would, in his opinion, ruin these chances. He had warned that an

Arab military action would have a negative effect on Soviet-American relations, and emphasized that a durable peace settlement in the Middle East could not be achieved on the battlefield, but only through negotiations. He also informed us of his recent meetings in New York with the Egyptian and Syrian foreign ministers, during which he had stressed the enormous advantages the Arabs would derive from détente. Several times during our discussion, Gromyko expressed skepticism about the chances for a successful Arab military campaign, although he acknowledged that a surprise attack at the beginning of the war would give the Arabs a certain advantage. Usually an emotionless, impassive person, the foreign minister was clearly annoyed.

The news that the war in the Middle East would start in less than two days was a big surprise to us, and although we shared Gromyko's assessments and his dismay concerning the Arab plans, the results and decisions that came from "the highest level" in the Kremlin were not clear to us. However, we did not dare ask Gromyko about them—that would be against bureaucratic etiquette. When one of us expressed concern about the sudden evacuation of Soviet citizens, which would put the Israelis and the Americans on guard, Gromyko responded bluntly: "The lives of Soviet people are dearer to us."

The Soviet ambassador in Cairo, Vladimir Vinogradov, later told me that the same question had worried him. On October 4 he received a cable from Moscow, signed by Prime Minister Aleksei Kosygin, instructing him to evacuate the families and dependents of Soviet diplomats and advisers in Egypt. Realizing that the sudden evacuation of Soviet citizens could have negative consequences for the Arab plans, he tried to telephone Brezhnev, but in vain. After having learned the reason for Vinogradov's call, Brezhnev's aide, Andrei Alexandrov, refused to connect the ambassador with Brezhnev, saying that such apprehensions had been thoroughly considered by the Politburo before the decision was made.

One other important question was raised at the meeting in Gromyko's office that day: "If the Americans approach the Foreign Ministry, how should we explain the evacuation of Soviet personnel?" Gromyko did not like the question and advised us not to get ahead of ourselves. At the end of the meeting, he recommended that we not stay too late at work that evening and wished us a good night. "You will need your energy and strength very soon," he said. Gromyko's kindliness was quite extraordinary. Normally no one at the top cared much how late subordinates stayed in their offices—in fact, the longer the better. Did Gromyko's advice indicate he had serious concerns over the dangerous consequences of the coming days?

## DID THE AMERICANS KNOW OF THE ARAB PLANS?

The meeting ended at about nine o'clock in the evening. In spite of Gromyko's advice, I returned to my office and tried to find out the sources of the minister's information regarding the date of the Arab attack. There was nothing in the latest cables from Cairo and Damascus, so I checked with Sytenko—but he confirmed that no pertinent information had been received from Soviet embassies in Egypt and Syria. In short, there was nothing to explain how the Soviet leaders knew by at least midday October 4 the date of the forthcoming Arab attack. I believed that the information had come through some special channels.

The next day, Friday, October 5, was relatively quiet, although I myself was in a state of alarm and tense expectancy. During a diplomatic reception that day, I chatted with the Egyptian and Syrian diplomats, but they did not show any awareness of the approaching war. Either they were keeping a strict code of secrecy or they had not been informed. I remained uneasy.

In the evening Kuznetsov summoned me to his office and confirmed what the foreign minister had said the day before. He acquainted me with the latest reports from Cairo and Damascus, which dealt mainly with the evacuation issue. According to the reports, everything was going as planned. Having started on October 4, the evacuation of Soviet families from Egypt and Syria would be carried out within several days. From Egypt alone more than 2,700 children and women, and about 1,000 members of diplomats' families from the embassies of the Soviet Union and other socialist states, were ordered to leave for their homelands. Roughly the same number of Soviet dependents were evacuated from Syria.

Although Moscow instructed the Soviet embassies to carry out the evacuation without any "unnecessary ado," the whole world noticed this unusual move. Reports that Soviet passenger planes had landed in Syria and Egypt and that they were there to evacuate the Soviet families could only fuel suspicions that Egypt and Syria were about to launch a war.

My greatest concern was how we would explain this whole matter at the United Nations, where some representatives might approach the Soviet delegation. The issue of a possible American inquiry came up again. The permanent missions of the two superpowers, the Soviet Union and the United States, in New York maintained extensive contacts at that time. I expected that the Americans would ask their Soviet colleagues to explain the developments in the Middle East, but Kuznetsov's remark—"Do you seriously think the Americans are not aware of the Arab plans?"—surprised me. "There is so much evidence of the Arab military preparations that only a stone-blind person could miss it," Kuznetsov added. In his opinion (and Kuznetsov's opinions were usually shared by Gromyko), the Americans wanted to see the situation in the Middle East heat up. "This is why the Americans aren't asking us for an explanation," he said. As the Americans saw it (and they were very likely right, Kuznetsov believed), the war—which the Arabs would start and most probably lose very quickly—would lead to a much more important role for the United States in the Middle East. "Aren't you reading Malik's reports about the hectic activity of Kissinger and Sisco with the Arabs in New York? Is this not proof that the Americans are eager to play first violin in the Middle East?" he asked me. (Yakov Malik was the Soviet permanent representative to the United Nations then.) It was difficult to argue with Kuznetsov. I took note of what he said, and many times in the future I asked myself whether the experienced diplomat was correct in his judgment.

I had another revealing conversation on October 5. An old friend of mine, who worked for *Pravda*, called me and apologized for not being able to publish an article on disarmament written by a member of my department. He told me the article was very good but that he did not have room for it, because the editorial board had received an order from Old Square (where the offices of the Central Committee of the Communist Party of the Soviet Union [CPSU] were located in Moscow) to keep space available for stories on the Middle East. Consequently, in the last two or three days before the outbreak of the war, Soviet broadcasts and the press had been disseminating an increasing number of reports of an alleged Israeli military buildup. Soviet correspondents from all over the world, instigated by the Kremlin, issued stories accusing Israel of inflaming the situation in the Middle East. On October 5 a Soviet broadcast spoke of stepped-up war preparations by the Israelis.[1] In his October 6 article, "Tel-Aviv Is Whipping up Tension," Yuri Gluchov, *Pravda* correspondent in Egypt, claimed that Israel was preparing a massive attack, concentrating tanks and heavy artillery on the borders with Arab states, and so on and on.[2] Warnings of imminent Israeli aggression appeared in *Izvestia*, *Krasnaya Zvezda*, and other Soviet papers. The denunciation of Israel was based mainly on the Arab interpretation of the developments in the area.

I was not surprised by this hostile propaganda campaign against Israel, which surfaced periodically in the Soviet media, reflecting the Kremlin's propaganda agenda. However, in the month of September 1973 the Soviet press had been relatively quiet on the Middle East issue. Looking back on these events, some analysts suggest that this meant the Kremlin was debating the merits of the position it would adopt in the coming conflict. As Alvin Rubinstein has pointed out, however, there is no evidence to support such a conclusion.[3] In fact, there could be a much simpler explanation for the silence: In September 1973 the Soviet media were preoccupied with Chile: the coup, the downfall of Allende's government, and his assassination. To some degree, the events in Chile had preempted reports on other international problems, so it is not surprising that little mention was made of the Middle East that month.

From the conversation with my colleague at *Pravda*, and the propaganda campaign launched in the Soviet media, I became more and more persuaded that Old Square had begun to prepare the Soviet public for a war in the Middle East. I assumed that the character of the broadcasts and the commentaries in the press indicated that the Kremlin had reason to trust the information that the war would start on October 6 at 2:00 P.M. Cairo time.

## MOSCOW'S CONTACTS WITH CAIRO

As of late Friday, October 5, I still could not find any information concerning the date of the Arab attack in the reports from Soviet embassies in Cairo and Damascus. So where did Moscow get the information? Some have claimed that top-level consultations took place between the Soviet leaders and Egyptian and Syrian leaders in the weeks preceding the war. For example, *Agence France Presse*, citing a Lebanese newspaper, told of a secret meeting between Brezhnev and Sadat at an undisclosed site sometime in the middle of September. Others reported that the "undisclosed site" was in Bulgaria, where Brezhnev had been on an official visit from September 18 to 21, and asserted that Sadat had informed Brezhnev as early as September 22 that the war would begin on October 6. This information was allegedly contained in a message to Brezhnev, which Sadat handed over to Soviet Ambassador Vinogradov during their meeting in Egypt.

The most widespread assertion concerning the Soviet sources of information, however, was that the Soviet leaders had been informed of the date on many occasions by Egyptian President Anwar al-Sadat and Syrian President Hafiz al-Assad themselves during their encounters with Soviet ambassadors in Cairo and Damascus, and that therefore the Kremlin did not need to receive information on the subject from its own intelligence operatives.[4] Various dates in connection with these encounters were mentioned, from September 22 to October 5.

In reality, there were no top-level meetings or consultations of any significance between Soviet leaders and Egyptian and Syrian leaders in September or early October. The only meetings worth mentioning were Gromyko's talks with Egyptian Foreign Minister Mohammed al-Zayyat (on September 29) and the Syrian Vice Prime Minister and Foreign Minister Abd al-Khaddam (on September 30) in New York. But these talks were routine consultations of heads of delegations to the United Nations General Assembly. Gromyko had more than thirty such encounters in the fall of 1973, and his talks with Zayyat and Khaddam were essentially no different from the rest.

According to the information about Gromyko's encounters with Zayyat and Khaddam received from New York, after giving a general assessment of the world situation and some Soviet foreign-policy actions, Gromyko repeated the well-known Soviet stand on the Middle East problem. His Arab partners, while agreeing with some of the Soviet assessments, expressed dissatisfaction and extreme disappointment with the deadlock in the Middle East. They mentioned the need to look at the problem in new ways, and they expressed hope for continuing cooperation with the Soviet Union. There was no hint of the date of the forthcoming Arab attack. I remember that when we in the Department of International Organizations read Gromyko's cables about his talks with the Egyptian and Syrian ministers, we classified the information as unimportant, secondary. In the fall of 1973 the daily contacts among the Soviet, Egyptian, and Syrian representatives in the three capitals were maintained primarily on an ambassadorial level.

The Soviet ambassador to Cairo, Vladimir Vinogradov, did, however, play a significant role in the Soviet political play during the Yom Kippur War. His contacts in Cairo were extensive, and he later claimed that he had thirty-five encounters with Sadat on the eve of and during the Yom Kippur War.

A chemist by education, Vinogradov worked for the Ministry of Foreign Trade before joining the Soviet foreign service in 1962. He was experienced in international affairs, having been ambassador to Japan and Soviet deputy foreign minister in charge of Middle East affairs for several years. Throughout the decades of his service in the Foreign Ministry, his energy, knowledge, and experience made him one of the best Soviet diplomats.

Vinogradov was appointed to Cairo in 1970 and by the time of the Yom Kippur War was well acquainted with the political and economic situation in Egypt. Very sociable, a good pianist, active, and intelligent, he was popular in the Cairo diplomatic community. His contacts with the Kremlin were very good, and sometimes he dared to communicate with Brezhnev directly, bypassing the foreign minister, which invariably angered Gromyko, as one might expect. I remember that once, after learning from Brezhnev about the contents of Vinogradov's cable addressed personally to the general secretary, Gromyko issued an order strictly prohibiting Soviet ambassadors from communicating with any addressee except through the Foreign Ministry.

Vinogradov's relationship with Egyptian President Sadat, however, was far from being frank and friendly. He tried his best to establish the same kind of relationship with Sadat that his predecessor had with Nasser, but with little success. Although he had direct access to Sadat, Vinogradov failed to maintain close relationships with some of the president's favorites. I can attest that Ismail Fahmy, who became Egypt's foreign minister in October 1973, was one of those who disliked Vinogradov. This became obvious during an encounter I witnessed between Gromyko and Fahmy in Geneva in December 1973.

Vinogradov was convinced that Egypt had a vital interest in maintaining and developing close cooperation with the Soviet Union, and that Sadat would never depart from Nasser's friendly stand toward the USSR and other socialist states. He did not realize that moving to the West suited Sadat's conservative mentality and gave him another opportunity to establish a separate identity, disregarding the international connections established by his predecessor. Nevertheless, the ambassador's reports to Moscow painted a rosy picture of his contacts with Sadat and of Soviet-Egyptian relations in general.

The head of the Soviet Military Mission in Egypt, General Vasilii Okunev, shared Vinogradov's views. The general reported to Moscow that as long as the Egyptian army was totally dependent on Soviet weapons and training there was no reason to worry about Egypt's stand. Because the Soviet Union had provided Egyptian armed forces with the kinds of weapons Israel did not possess, Okunev believed, the Egyptian military was bound to the Soviet army forever. But Soviet intelligence in Egypt, headed by Vadim Kirpichenko, was sending a different message to Moscow. Kirpichenko was drawing the Kremlin's attention to Sadat's growing departure from Nasser's line as well as to the cooling of Soviet-Egyptian relations and Sadat's widening contacts with the Americans.

This disparity in Soviet assessments of Egypt's policy was clear at a Politburo meeting as early as 1971 and played an important role in Kremlin discussions during the Yom Kippur War. In the period preceding the war, the "optimistic" line—aimed at developing "brotherly" relations with Sadat, "educating" him—prevailed. Vinogradov was glad to carry out this mission.

During most of September 1973, Vinogradov was on leave in the Soviet Union. After he returned to Cairo, he was received by President Sadat at Bourg al-Arab, not far from Alexandria, on September 22. Vinogradov was disconcerted. He was in time for the appointment, but he had to wait while Sadat continued his negotiations with a group of Americans headed by Nelson Rockefeller. When he was finally invited into Sadat's office, he recalled later, he had a feeling Sadat was really thinking about something else—perhaps the previous meeting with the Americans. When the discussion turned to the situation in the Middle East, Sadat described Arab-Israeli relations as unbearable and suggested that the situation might be on the verge of blowing up. What would others think of that? he asked Vinogradov. But Sadat spoke only in vague terms, not mentioning any of Egypt's military plans or preparations. The ambassador was puzzled. If Egypt had really decided to start a war, Sadat was obliged in accordance with the Soviet-Egyptian treaty of 1971 to consult or at least to inform the Soviet government of such a decision well in advance. Sadat, however, gave no hint of Egypt's immediate political and military plans. The ambassador was not happy, because he realized that an obscure, indefinite report to Moscow after his long absence from Cairo would only embarrass him and disappoint the Kremlin.

The next meeting between Sadat and Vinogradov, on October 3, was clearly more substantial and informative. In his report to Moscow, Vinogradov emphasized Sadat's concern about the situation in the

Middle East. During the meeting, Sadat had spoken at length about Israel's military preparations and continuing provocations, after which he confessed to the ambassador that he could no longer put up with such arrogance. Sadat then admitted that the Arab states would be forced to retaliate in order to break the deadlock in the Middle East situation.

But the Egyptian president apparently did not elaborate on the nature of the planned Arab action, nor did he say anything about a scheduled date. When Vinogradov asked specifically about the scale and timing of the "retaliatory" military operations of the Arabs, Sadat answered only that, if necessary, he would inform the ambassador without fail "in due time." He then advised Vinogradov not to leave Cairo for the time being. According to what Sadat later reported, the only information he conveyed to the Soviet Union on Wednesday, October 3, was the following: "Egypt and Syria have decided to embark on a military operation to put an end to the no peace, no war situation."[5] He did not claim that he had informed Vinogradov about the date of the Arab attack either on October 3 or later. Likewise, Vinogradov's cable to Moscow reported about Egypt's extensive military preparations but did not refer to any precise time for an eventual Egyptian attack.

## BREZHNEV'S MESSAGE TO SADAT

At the same meeting, on October 3, between President Sadat and Vinogradov, Sadat urged the Soviet government to accelerate the delivery of military supplies and stressed the utmost importance of implementing the appropriate bilateral agreements in a timely manner. While giving Moscow his assessment of the situation in the Middle East and of the possibility that Egypt might take military action, Sadat asked what the Soviet Union's stand toward such a development would be.

The answer came from Moscow the next day, Thursday, October 4, when Vinogradov met with Sadat and delivered a message from Brezhnev. The Soviet leader emphasized that the decision regarding such a vital issue as whether to start a war against Israel would be left completely to the Egyptian leadership, but that the decision would have to be preceded by careful and comprehensive preparatory work because any failure in such an important venture would set back the Middle East settlement indefinitely. Brezhnev then reiterated the Soviet government's position on the Middle East and its emphasis on political means toward a solution.

Brezhnev's message also informed Sadat of the decision to evacuate Soviet families from Egypt and Syria. According to Vinogradov, Sadat reacted calmly. "It is your business," he remarked. Some have suggested that Brezhnev asked Sadat for "permission" to withdraw Russian civilian advisers and their families and that the Egyptian president "reluctantly" agreed to it, but that is not accurate.[6] Vinogradov's aide, Pogos Akopov, who participated in many encounters between the ambassador and Egyptian leaders, confirmed Cairo's calm response to the Soviet decision and strongly denied that there had been a Soviet request for "permission" to withdraw Russian civilians.

Thus the official Soviet reaction to Sadat's information regarding the planned Egyptian and Syrian attack was cautious and restrained. It is true that Brezhnev did not try to dissuade the Arabs from their decision, because a firm negative stand against the Arab plans from the Kremlin would, in Moscow's eyes, only ruin already shaky "brotherly" relations with the Arabs. But neither did Brezhnev encourage the Arabs to go ahead with their military plans. There is no reason to conclude, as Marvin and Bernard Kalb have, that Brezhnev "raised no objections" to the Egyptian plan and that, from his point of view, the plan "had obvious advantages."[7] This conclusion derives from a basic misunderstanding of Sadat's and Brezhnev's mentality and the nature of their political relationship. Sadat did not ask and did not need the Soviet leader's permission to go ahead with the Egyptian plan. Brezhnev, in his message to Sadat, emphasized the obvious advantages of a political settlement of the crisis, not the military plan, but the decision was ultimately Sadat's.

On Saturday, October 6, Vinogradov talked with Sadat several times at the Egyptian's initiative. The first conversation took place in the morning in Sadat's palace, Tahra, where the president informed him that the situation was in "constant development" and warned the ambassador to "expect events . . . in four hours." He did not specify the character of the "events," though, and all Vinogradov's attempts to gain more concrete information failed. Vinogradov told Sadat about Moscow's "positive reply" to the president's request regarding military supplies. Sadat expressed his gratitude and said he would be happy to have Vinogradov stay with him—but that was impossible because the ambassador had to be in the embassy to maintain constant communications with Moscow. Vinogradov was disappointed that on the eve of the war Sadat had still not given him precise information on Egypt's military plans.

In a few hours, Sadat telephoned Vinogradov at the Soviet embassy and declared triumphantly: "Safir! We are on the eastern bank of the Canal! The Egyptian flag is on the eastern bank! We crossed the Canal!" Mohamed Heikal's book asserts that Sadat said in the same conversation, "Tell Brezhnev that it is Soviet arms which achieved the miracle of the crossing."[8] I wish Sadat had said that, and perhaps he did, but, in any case, one can appreciate the noble attempts of Heikal, the Soviet Union's friend of long standing, to magnify Soviet-Egyptian relations in a flattering way.

Moscow learned of the outbreak of war from the radio broadcast and from Vinogradov, who cabled Moscow from the Soviet embassy in Cairo. Vinogradov reported that at 3:00 P.M. Cairo time Sadat had informed him that the Israelis had started military operations against Egypt at 2:30 and that, in response, Egyptian forces had crossed the Suez Canal. That, unfortunately, is how the Soviet embassy in Cairo informed Moscow that the war had started. Many years later, Vinogradov recalled bitterly: "Why did Sadat, a friend and representative of a friendly country, tell me such an obvious untruth."

## MOSCOW'S CONTACTS WITH DAMASCUS

Developments in Cairo, of course, tell only part of the story. Sadat's ally in the war was President Assad of Syria, and for the Soviet role in Damascus we must turn to Nuritdin Mukhitdinov, the Soviet ambassador to Syria, who, like Vinogradov, played an important role in the diplomatic developments during the Yom Kippur War. Mukhitdinov's background was quite different from Vinogradov's. An ethnic Uzbek who started his career as a Communist Party functionary in Uzbekistan, he became leader of the republic within a short time. His speedy rise to power continued in Moscow, where he was elected secretary of the Central Committee of the CPSU and member of the Politburo in 1957. His political downfall came in 1961. For several years thereafter, he occupied a secondary bureaucratic post in Moscow, and in 1968 he left for Damascus as the Soviet ambassador.

Mukhitdinov had no previous experience in international affairs, although he had been Uzbekistan's foreign minister. In the Soviet

Union, however, such a post did not in any way broaden one's vision of foreign affairs because no Soviet republic maintained diplomatic relations with any foreign state. The Supreme Soviet's decree of 1944 creating Ministries of Foreign Affairs in the republics turned out to be a farce. The staffs of the ministries consisted of fewer than ten people, and the occasional briefings on various international subjects prepared by these ministries were usually not taken into account in Moscow. The rare initiatives the republic diplomats took elicited only annoyance or even outcries from Moscow. I recall that one of Gromyko's deputies, in a rush of frankness in an informal situation, once amicably advised a republic's foreign minister: "Never stick your neck out. Keep quiet if you want to be successful and attain an ambassadorship." Mukhitdinov probably followed that advice when he was Uzbekistan's foreign minister.

The new ambassador to Syria did not maintain the same contacts with the Kremlin as Vinogradov did, but he was much more familiar with the labyrinths of power in Moscow. He knew how to please and play up to Old Square. One story I've heard tells how Mukhitdinov "edited" one of his reports to Moscow. After an encounter with a Syrian V.I.P., he asked his interpreter to read out the record of the conversation, made some changes in the text, and to the great surprise of the interpreter, named the person he talked to as Assad, not specifying the position of the latter. The interpreter humbly noted "But Comrade Ambassador, you talked not to President Assad but to his brother." "It doesn't make any difference," the ambassador replied. "This Assad or the other one. Leave it as it stands."

Mukhitdinov's aide, Veniamin Popov, who later became Soviet ambassador to several Arab states, recalled that in difficult times, such as the Yom Kippur War, however, Mukhitdinov acted calmly and with confidence, informing Moscow accurately and promptly of the Syrian president's views. He did not have as many encounters with Assad as Vinogradov had with Sadat, but the encounters were more friendly and open. Perhaps Mukhitdinov's Asian background played a part in that.

## ASSAD EXPLAINS SYRIA'S STRATEGY

Among the meetings the Soviet ambassador to Syria had with President Assad, the most important was undoubtedly the meeting on Thursday,

October 4, when the Syrian president spoke at length on the imminent war with Israel. At this meeting Mukhitdinov learned more from Assad than Vinogradov had learned from Sadat. Assad said that the decision to attack Israel had been approved by the leaders of Syria and Egypt and that the war would start in the next few days. He did not, however, refer to any precise date—day or hour—for the forthcoming attack. The main subject of the conversation was Syrian strategy in the war. Assad stressed that Syria's goal was the complete and unconditional withdrawal of Israeli armed forces from all Arab territories occupied by Israel, and restoration of the legitimate rights of the Palestinians. This could be achieved, as he saw it, by means of a shattering military blow to Israel. Such a blow should be carried out with a massive surprise attack executed in a short period of time. According to Assad, after this initial blow and the Arab's first military success, the war should be stopped. The rest of the plan—complete liberation of Arab land and restoration of the 1967 borders—should be achieved by political means. In his view, the military phase of the overall strategic plan should take only one or two days.

Assad informed Mukhitdinov that Syria had prepared its armed forces for the war against Israel based on this strategic timetable. He emphasized that the massive concentration of Syrian armed forces was aimed at a complete or near complete liberation of the Golan Heights in the first few days of the war. The Syrian president thus acknowledged that Syrian forces were not ready for a protracted campaign, that their main goal was to prevent the Israeli army from recovering and launching a counteroffensive. For this very reason it was of utmost importance for Syria that there be a cease-fire immediately after the initial stage of the war.

When Mukhitdinov asked how the cease-fire was to be achieved, Assad answered unequivocally: With the help of Syria's friend, the Soviet Union. The president said that, after the initial victories of the Arabs, the Soviet Union should promptly initiate a cease-fire resolution in the United Nations Security Council and, with the support of nonaligned states, urge a vote. The resolution should include a demand for immediate withdrawal of Israeli troops from all Arab territories occupied by Israel. Assad expressed his confidence that nobody, including the United States, would dare to vote against a cease-fire resolution.

Heikal's portrayal of the Assad-Mukhitdinov talk is not entirely accurate.[9] Contrary to what he reports in *The Road to Ramadan*, the issue of a cease-fire was raised by Assad, not by Mukhitdinov. Heikal also claims that Mukhitdinov asked Assad if he wanted the Soviets to "take any action in the Security Council." But Mukhitdinov was an experienced bureaucrat who would never ask such a question without first getting clearance from Moscow. Popov, who accompanied Mukhitdinov during that encounter with Assad, strongly denies Heikal's version of this episode. Neither is it confirmed by the official record of the Assad-Mukhitdinov talk.

In sum, Mukhitdinov learned from Assad that he had a strategic plan for the war. Whether this plan had been agreed on jointly by Egypt and Syria, Assad did not say. The plan, as related to Mukhitdinov, consisted of two stages. The first, the military stage, would last a few days and be carried out by the Syrian armed forces. The effectiveness of the second, political, stage would depend mainly on the Soviet Union's diplomatic activity and persistence in the United Nations. From what Assad said, it is clear that Syria was prepared only to launch a short-term "blitzkrieg." Mukhitdinov promised to report Assad's thinking to Moscow, and he did so immediately.

The next meeting between Assad and Mukhitdinov took place on Saturday, October 6, early in the morning, when Assad announced that Syrian and Egyptian leaders had decided to launch a joint attack against Israel later that day at 2:00 P.M. The decision had been made on October 4, he said. Once again he reiterated the two-stage strategy and said he was relying on the Soviet Union's understanding and support.

Thus the precise date of the Arab attack on Israel (which, judging from the conversation with Gromyko, the Kremlin had been informed of at least by October 4) did not come initially from Sadat or Assad. I was therefore greatly surprised to read the following assertion of Hafiz Ismail, Sadat's national security adviser and participant in many important Soviet-Egyptian talks, made twenty years after the Yom Kippur War: "They [the Russians] knew that we were going to war, *but they did not know the date, nor the time of the attack*" (emphasis added).[10] How could the national security adviser have been so poorly informed? The Russians did know the date and time of the attack! The question is, who among the Egyptian or Syrian V.I.P.'s provided the Kremlin with this information?

According to Egyptian and Syrian sources, the date of the attack Sadat and Assad finally agreed on was known only to a few of the closest associates of the Egyptian and Syrian presidents. Other sources claimed that the Palestinian leaders might have been aware of the date too. In any case, the information did not come through diplomatic channels.

At the same time, one should totally discount the notion that KGB representatives in Cairo or Damascus reported the date of the eventual Arab attack to Moscow without informing the ambassadors in Egypt and Syria. Whatever Moscow's source of information, its "special connection" in Cairo or Damascus remains undisclosed.

The issue, however, is not whether the Kremlin was aware of the plan by Cairo and Damascus to launch a war against Israel in 1973, but rather what the Kremlin's attitude toward such a plan was. The answer to this question is not simple. Certainly Moscow knew about the military preparations and activities going on in Egypt and Syria. Soviet intelligence had gathered enough information to show the serious nature of the Arab preparation. For example, the KGB resident in Cairo, Vadim Kirpichenko, claimed that intelligence had predicted the outbreak of a war in the first days of October. But there were also serious doubts regarding Arab intentions. I recall a conversation in September 1973 with a high-ranking official of the Central Committee in charge of the Middle East, who expressed skepticism about Arab threats to use force against Israel. From his point of view, this was a "typical" Arab bluff, no different from all the others since 1967. It seemed to me that such disbelief and skepticism—which, to be honest, I shared too—was widespread throughout Moscow up to October 4.

## THE NO WAR, NO PEACE POLICY

In my opinion, the Soviet position regarding Arab plans to launch a war against Israel was not consistent. In fact, it was at times rather two-faced, ambiguous, and contradictory, as was the foreign policy of the Soviet Union in general. The Soviet Union had been supplying Egypt and Syria with increasing amounts of weaponry, including the newest, modern types, among them SCUD missiles, without which a war against Israel would have been impossible. For years, Egypt, Syria, and other Arab states had enjoyed the full political and diplomatic support of the Soviet Union. As a Soviet representative at the United Nations, I can confirm that our instructions on any Middle East issue were often to coordinate our stand with that of the Arabs, and especially the Egyptians. Soviet propaganda was one-sided, based on Arab information and sometimes on obvious disinformation. The goal was to manifest "proletarian internationalism" and support of "anti-imperialist forces" all over the world—slogans that conveyed Soviet global aspirations.

At the same time, the Kremlin wanted to maintain and develop cooperation with the West—which in view of the Soviet Union's shaky economy and backward technology was a necessity. A military confrontation with the West, and in particular with the United States, was by no means on the Kremlin's political agenda. A war in the Middle East could only worsen relations with the West, which is why the Soviet leadership tried to steer the Arabs toward a political solution to the problem. Down to his last message to Sadat just before the outbreak of the war, Brezhnev warned that a defeat would set back a Middle East settlement. But there was great skepticism in Washington that the Kremlin genuinely wanted such a settlement, at least one that would satisfy both the Arabs and Israel. Hence President Nixon's assertion that "it was hard to believe that the Egyptians and Syrians would have moved without the knowledge of the Soviets, if not without their direct encouragement."[11] In my judgment, however, this is a misperception of Soviet objectives in the Middle East.

Throughout 1973 many Soviet leaders spoke out about the extreme threat a war in the Middle East posed to world peace. In their talks with Nixon, Brezhnev and Gromyko both stressed the danger of a war. "We could all wake up one day and find there is a real conflagration in that area," Gromyko told Nixon, according to Henry Kissinger.[12] The Kremlin apparently was seeking a joint Soviet-American action to prevent an outbreak of war. At the initiative of the Soviet delegation, a paragraph on the Middle East was inserted into the communiqué on the Brezhnev-Nixon 1973 summit. Perhaps, therefore, the deliberate decision to evacuate Soviet dependents from Cairo and Damascus was meant to be read by the West as a call for joint preventive action. If so, the decision can be seen as a reflection of the other basic, and contradictory, principle of Soviet foreign policy: "peaceful coexistence and cooperation" between states with different social systems.

Arming Egypt and Syria with all kinds of technical means for waging a war, while at the same time trying to talk the Arab leaders out of a military solution to the Middle East conflict—that was the Soviet position on the eve of the Yom Kippur War. What could the Soviet Union gain from a war? If the Arabs won (which from what Gromyko said at our October 4 meeting the Kremlin did not think they could do), the victory would lead only to their greater independence from the Soviet Union. Relations with Egypt, which had eased in recent years, would become more strained, anti-sovietism would become more open, and contacts with the West would become more extensive. Given Egypt's influence in the Arab world, such a prospect was not welcomed in Moscow.

If the Arabs lost, the Soviet Union would be blamed and its prestige would surely decline. Finally, few in the Kremlin truly believed that any "anti-imperialist" Arab unity would result from a war. The "no war, no peace" policy was probably the most acceptable to the Kremlin, at least in the fall of 1973. The fact that Brezhnev, Kosygin, and Gromyko said they wanted a Middle East settlement does not mean they wanted an immediate settlement. It was, rather, a long-term goal.

The relationship among the Soviet, Egyptian, and Syrian leaders on the eve of the war was far from open and trusting. As I have shown, the Soviet government could not have learned of the decision to start the war from the presidents of Egypt and Syria. Assad delivered the belated information to Mukhitdinov only a few hours before the war, by which time Moscow already knew of it. In Egypt, meanwhile, Sadat never told Vinogradov the exact time of the planned attack at all. According to Vinogradov's report to Moscow, Sadat also claimed that the outbreak of war was the result of a military action by Israeli armed forces.

Egypt and Syria, therefore, did not officially consult with Moscow on either military or political strategy. When Sadat met with Vinogradov, he spoke only in very general terms of Egypt's final goal of liberating the Occupied Territories. Assad was more concrete in his talks with Mukhitdinov, but he merely informed the Kremlin of his vision of the war. From its diplomatic channels, Moscow did not even know whether the Egyptians and Syrians had agreed on a joint strategy, not to speak of what that strategy was. Therefore, Moscow's information on the date and time of the war must have come from another source. Who that source was I do not know.

Perhaps the many questions regarding Arab intentions had caused Brezhnev to avoid mentioning the Middle East in his two public speeches in September in Sofia and in Tashkent. The same uncertainties might have prevented the Soviet leaders from formulating a strategy of their own in the event that a war broke out. Yes, Prime Minister Kosygin in Yugoslavia, and especially Gromyko in his address to the United Nations General Assembly in September, did deal at length with the Middle East. But did anything happen in the Kremlin after it became obvious that the Arabs were going to launch a war against Israel? Did Soviet leaders assess the potential impact of a new Middle East crisis on the world situation in general, and on the Soviet Union's foreign policy in particular? Alas, the answer is no, they did not. At least, when the war in the Middle East started, the Kremlin was not provided with a list of possibilities or scenarios, with implications of each for Soviet policy and position, despite a large number of experts on the Middle East in the Central Committee, the Foreign Ministry, the Defense Ministry, and the KGB. Kremlin leaders merely restated the unshakable dogmas of the Leninist foreign policy: the incompatible principles of "proletarian internationalism" and "peaceful coexistence."

# CHAPTER 2

## SEARCHING FOR AN EARLY CEASE-FIRE

### THE BAD NEWS

Early in the morning of Saturday, October 6, I listened to various broadcasts and read cables and newspapers. Only the Soviet papers continued the propaganda campaign started a few days ago and sounded the call to arms. Otherwise, it seemed that the whole world was quiet. I even thought our fears might be groundless. We at the Foreign Ministry could not believe that neither U.S. nor Israeli intelligence, nor the journalist corps in the Middle East, had noticed the unusual military preparations in Egypt and Syria, the gathering of forces that were meant to strike a shattering blow to Israel in a couple of hours.

Soon after 3:00 P.M., however, word about the start of military action began to come in. A broadcast from Cairo reported that the Israeli navy had attacked Egyptian troops in the vicinity of the Suez Canal, and one from Damascus reported that Israeli armed forces had attacked Syrian positions near the Golan Heights. Both broadcasts were based on what later became the official Arab version of the outbreak of the war.

But the first serious alarm heard in Moscow was sounded from Washington. At 2:45 P.M. Moscow time, Anatolii Dobrynin, the Soviet ambassador to the United States, reported that Secretary of State Henry Kissinger had just called him from New York and asked him to notify the Soviet government that, based on information from Israeli government sources, Syria and Egypt intended to attack Israel on the Golan Heights and on the Sinai within the next few hours. On behalf of Israel's leadership, Kissinger assured Moscow that Israel would not strike first against the Arabs but that Israel's response "would be very strong" if attacked. The seriousness and urgency of Kissinger's message was emphasized in the way Dobrynin chose to send it to Moscow. He used the fastest method: the White House telephone system. "Since he had to assume that we would read his message, this was undoubtedly designed to show, once again, that Dobrynin had nothing to hide," Kissinger wrote in his memoirs.[1] The ambassador's report of the conversation with Kissinger came by open communication, which Dobrynin had never used before. Soon after Dobrynin's cable came in, reports from Vinogradov and Mukhitdinov with news of the outbreak of war reached Moscow.

I was lecturing at the Diplomatic Academy when at around 3:30 P.M. I was interrupted by a telephone call from the Foreign Ministry urging me to come to Gromyko's office immediately. It took some twenty to twenty-five minutes to reach the ministry, and when I arrived Gromyko's aide informed me that the foreign minister had already left for the Kremlin, accompanied by First Deputy Kuznetsov, Head of the USA Department Kornienko, and Head of the Middle East Department Sytenko. Brezhnev had summoned members of the Politburo to discuss the developments in the Middle East. "What shall I do?" I asked the aide. "You'd better deliver lectures," he answered with irony and malicious pleasure. This was typical of my bureaucratic colleagues, who never looked favorably on the fact that I continued my academic activity while simultaneously holding the post of a high-ranking diplomat. Such anti-academic sentiment, indeed one could call it anti-intellectualism, was typical in quite a number of my Foreign Ministry colleagues. In the Soviet Union the field of political science did not contribute much to policy-making and was not respected much. There were, of course, academic people who were interesting and thoughtful, but there were also many others who were not knowledgeable and who were, quite frankly, shallow in their judgments. I remember that when Malik became angry with me he would address me not by name, as usual, but as "Comrade Professor." "Comrade Professor," he would say, "you are now acting in the field of diplomacy, and here thinking is indispensable"—implying, of course, that in my previous academic activity intellect was not necessary. In spite of these anti-academic sentiments, I tried throughout my entire diplomatic career to continue my professorship, which gave me a little independence.

So, having arrived at the Foreign Ministry after Gromyko and the others had already left for the Kremlin, I waited nervously in my office for hours and hours while the meeting took place in Brezhnev's office. My account of this first Politburo meeting dealing with the war is therefore based on information Gromyko and other members of the task force shared with me later. Before reconstructing the meeting, however, a few words are in order about the nature of the Politburo at the time, and about its members and the way it considered international issues.

## THE POLITBURO IN FALL 1973

In October 1973 the Politburo, headed by General Secretary Leonid Brezhnev, consisted of sixteen full members and five candidate members. Since 1964, when he followed Nikita Khrushchev as the CPSU leader, Brezhnev had succeeded in making some personnel changes in the Politburo, securing a number of strategic positions on the Central Committee for his closest associates (Andrei Kirilenko, Konstantin Chernenko, Nikolai Shchelokov). The latest change in the Politburo was made in the spring of 1973, when KGB Chief Yuri Andropov, Minister of Defense Andrei Grechko, and Foreign Minister Andrei Gromyko were promoted to full membership. But some of Brezhnev's opponents (Alexandr Shelepin, Nikolai Podgorny, Aleksei Kosygin) still opposed his efforts to promote his personal cult as a means of increasing his influence and power over his colleagues. Not until the mid-1970s was Brezhnev finally able to start removing his adversaries. He took full advantage of the Yom Kippur War for this purpose.

Participants in foreign-policy discussions were usually Brezhnev, Prime Minister Kosygin, Chairman of the Presidium of the Supreme Soviet Podgorny, Gromyko, Andropov, Grechko, and Secretaries of the Central Committee of the CPSU Mikhail Suslov, Konstantin Katushev, and Boris Ponomarev. Katushev and Ponomarev were not members of the Politburo, but as heads of the two International Departments of the Central Committee they took part in Politburo meetings. Other members of the Soviet ruling elite in charge of domestic, economic, and administrative matters did not usually participate in discussions of international issues, or else they limited themselves to occasional comments.

Brezhnev's role in formulating and implementing Soviet foreign policy was gradually increasing by 1973. At the beginning of his leadership, in the fall of 1964, and for several years thereafter, his image as foreign-policy spokesman was poor and he was forced to share this function with the two other members of the leading "Troika": the formal head of state, Podgorny, and Prime Minister Kosygin. Brezhnev did not like to yield the international spotlight to either of them. He was jealous of the publicity that resulted from Kosygin's activity in arranging the Tashkent Agreement between Pakistan and India in 1965, his meeting with U.S. President Lyndon Johnson in Glassboro in 1967, his participation in the Special Session of the United Nations General Assembly on the Middle East the same year, and some of Kosygin's other diplomatic missions. Podgorny's activity in foreign policy was less impressive. It was limited to ceremonial visits, mainly to socialist and developing countries, but Podgorny's treatment abroad as head of the Soviet Union irritated Brezhnev.

I remember an episode that illustrates Brezhnev's eagerness at the time to change the allocation of external responsibilities. In 1969–70 I was the Soviet representative on the Committee for the Commemoration of the 25th Anniversary of the United Nations. Among other measures and activities suggested in connection with the anniversary, I strongly supported the proposal that the heads of states or governments participate in the jubilee session of the General Assembly. I sent reports to Moscow outlining the advantages of this proposal, but when Gromyko and I next met in person he expressed his discontent with the idea and with my activity on its behalf. In a rather obscure way, he hinted that because the proposal did not mean that the actual world leaders would participate it was therefore meaningless. Gromyko's closeness to Brezhnev was well known. I got the message and immediately stopped supporting the proposal, but it was adopted by a majority at the United Nations. As a result, many heads of states and governments participated in the jubilee session, but the Soviet delegation was headed by Gromyko. In short, by the time of the Yom Kippur War, Brezhnev was taking an increasingly active role in Soviet foreign policy. Consequently, one could see that he was creating distance between himself and anyone who might threaten his ascendancy. Any failure in performance or unacceptable suggestion from his adversaries was promptly used against them.

From my point of view, there were neither hawks nor doves in the Politburo. It was simply a group of people clustered around a leader whose point of view invariably prevailed. They had the ability, characteristic of Soviet party bosses ever since Stalin's time, to guess and grasp the leader's opinion and immediately back it. This by no means meant that they were sharing some noble common ideas or philosophy, or that they would not engage in a conspiracy against the leader when they felt the time was ripe. They were a team of political chameleons, adaptable, guided primarily by the desire to keep their positions, which guaranteed them exceptional power and privileges. Not by accident, after the collapse of the Soviet Union, many leading figures of the Communist Party of the Soviet Union became presidents of anti-Communist states striving to construct Western-style market-oriented economies, Boris Yeltsin being the prime example.

Brezhnev was certainly the Politburo's superstar. He knew what he wanted, orchestrated the discussions, succeeded in finding a consensus, and was always fairly well acquainted with the subject. The first time I met him was in December 1967 on the eve of my departure for New York as Deputy Permanent Representative to the United Nations. In our conversation, he mentioned the importance of the Middle East problem only briefly, without any specifics—which he probably did not know. In October 1973, however, he not only followed a definite political line but also demonstrated a certain knowledge of details, often referred to Security Council Resolution 242, knew the attitudes of different Arab states with respect to the resolution, remembered Soviet-American discussions on the Middle East, and so on. In the early 1970s, before his health declined, Brezhnev was still a dynamic, lively, energetic, agile man in the Kremlin. Those who viewed him as a transitional political figure proved to be wrong. He brought stability to the traditional Soviet bureaucracy, which had been weakened by Khrushchev.

In the 1960s and 1970s, Kosygin was one of the most respected and powerful Soviet politicians. He had started his career in Leningrad and soon became a leading specialist in Soviet economic structure. I met him several times—once while I spent a couple of weeks in a sanatorium, where he was also staying. He was always very serious, even sullen, businesslike, and in private life rather modest. He was also a pragmatist and did not like to be involved in ideological discussions. Kosygin participated in the United Nations Special Session on the Middle East after the Six-Day War and conducted a series of negotiations with a number of statesmen in New York on the subject. Kosygin was present at Nasser's funeral and several times met Arab leaders in Moscow and other capitals. To me he seemed the Soviet leader most knowledgeable about the Middle East. His influence and authority, however, gradually decreased, and after his visit to Cairo in October 1973 he played almost no significant role in the discussions. Brezhnev contributed considerably to his downfall.

Nikolai Podgorny, Brezhnev's former ally and one of his main opponents in the 1970s, tried to be active and important in foreign affairs. The fact that he signed the Soviet-Egyptian Treaty of Friendship and Cooperation in 1971 during his visit to Cairo convinced him that he was the architect of the relations between the two countries. But a lack of sometimes elementary knowledge of the situation, and his taste for ideological stereotypes, made his participation in the discussion practically useless. I remember one occasion when Brezhnev, angered by Podgorny's remarks, said to Gromyko, "This old fool [he used a much more abusive word] only hampers our work."

And now for the Politburo's "freshmen": Yuri Andropov, Andrei Grechko, and Andrei Gromyko. I met Yuri Andropov for the first time in 1956 when I was a lecturer at the Diplomatic Academy in Moscow. My master of science degree in history was devoted to the prewar foreign policy of Hungary. I taught Hungarian history and spoke Hungarian fairly well, so one can imagine my delight when in early December 1956 I learned that the Soviet ambassador to Budapest, Andropov, was coming to the academy to deliver a lecture on the 1956 "counterrevolution" in Hungary. I had heard much about the ambassador's unusual style. Unlike Soviet ambassadors in other socialist states, who preferred to learn about the countries to which they were accredited mainly from the reports of their subordinates, Andropov had taken many trips around Hungary, talked with workers, peasants, and intellectuals, was a very courteous host, and enjoyed sports, music, and the arts. He even took lessons in Hungarian. His lecture at the academy was a great success, and I was pleasantly surprised by his knowledge of Hungarian history and literature. He quoted Sandor Petoefi's verses, told Hungarian anecdotes, and spoke at length about the tragic events in Hungary in the fall of 1956, explaining that the uprising was mainly a result of the mistakes and blunders of the former Hungarian Communist leadership.

During a chat after the lecture, I asked Andropov about the decisive role of "American imperialism" in organizing the Hungarian "counterrevolution"—the main thesis of Soviet propaganda at the time. "That's nonsense," he said, laughing. "The events in Hungary took the Americans by surprise. They came to the Soviet embassy and asked *us* what was going on in Budapest. No, they played no role whatsoever." I was astonished by such frankness from the young ambassador. But many years later I learned that, in one of his secret reports to the Central Committee soon after the Hungarian uprising, the same Andropov had taken a different position. He favored connecting the "treacherous group of Imre Nagy" (the leader of the uprising) to the "imperialists," whom he wished to implicate in the "counterrevolution."[2] That was Andropov! He knew better than any other Soviet leader the real situation within the Soviet Union and abroad, but if and when the truth did not fit into the political or ideological perception of the Communist leadership, he was quick to ignore it.

Andropov regularly used this tactic, and the Middle East crisis was no exception. Whenever the issues of Egypt's or Syria's efforts to build socialism, and their desire to strengthen their relationship with the Soviet Union, came up at the meetings, he preferred to keep silent. From the numerous reports of KGB agents in the region, he knew perfectly well that quite the opposite was taking place, at least in Egypt. One of his former subordinates later explained Andropov's silence as an unwillingness to argue with those in the Politburo who considered the world developments "in favor of socialism" irreversible, the relationship with Egypt and Syria stable, and their leaders reliable. Besides, Grechko and Gromyko, who shared those views, had much closer personal relationships with Brezhnev, and Andropov did not want to jeopardize his position in the Politburo by opposing the influential colleagues. He was very cautious and successfully avoided extreme positions.

I had never met Andrei Grechko before October 1973, although I had heard of his self-will, capriciousness, roughness, and rudeness, very common among the Soviet—only to the Soviet?—military command. Typical was his suggestion to his boss and friend Nikita Khrushchev in the early 1960s, when he was the commander of Soviet Land Forces, that the Soviet Union should conquer Western Europe in seven days. The rebuff he received from Khrushchev made him more cautious, and when he became minister of defense under Brezhnev, he did not express similar unreasonable ideas. But Grechko would not hesitate to demonstrate the superiority and might of the Soviet armed forces. He had a number of meetings with the political and military leaders of the

Arab states and considered the Middle East a region of special strategic interest to the Soviet Union. When Sadat decided to remove the Soviet military advisers in 1972, Grechko took personal offense. During the Kremlin discussions in October 1973, his attitude was in my view marked by a good deal of emotionalism. Grechko's position was far from consistent. He wanted the Arabs, and especially the Egyptians, to be punished during the war for their disobedience, but he would not permit a weakening of the Soviet military position in the Middle East. I do not believe he knew how to reach that dual goal. Sometimes he would wave his fists, threatening to liquidate imperialism and Zionism, and although the gesture was impressive (Grechko stood six and a half feet tall), nobody took it seriously. He usually calmed down quickly, no doubt remembering the rebuff he had received a decade earlier for his plans to conquer Europe.

Andrei Gromyko was unique. He was the only member of the Politburo who had lived for many years in the West, in the United States and England. I think he liked America, and he was acquainted with American literature, arts, music, and movies, especially Westerns. Once, though, I made trouble for myself when I ordered a viewing of "The Last Tango in Paris" for him when he was in New York. In the midst of the film Gromyko became furious, left the hall, and said to me: "Don't you dare show me porno films ever again!" After that, I always consulted with his wife, Lydia, before choosing a film for him.

By 1973 he had already occupied the post of Soviet foreign minister for sixteen years (and he was to stay in this position another twelve), much longer than Andropov and Grechko had been heading their offices. Unlike Andropov and Grechko, however, Gromyko faced certain problems that were unique to his position as head of the Foreign Ministry. Whereas the Defense Ministry and the KGB held full sway in defense and intelligence matters (though, of course, under the general supervision of the Central Committee of CPSU), the Soviet Foreign Ministry shared the responsibility for international policy with the International Departments of the Central Committee of the CPSU, which supervised and administered relations with a large number of socialist states, some developing countries, and contacts with Communist parties of the West. Therefore, the main interests and responsibilities of Gromyko and the Foreign Ministry were limited to the Soviet Union's relations with the West. Gromyko's own favorite subjects were Soviet-American relations, disarmament, European security, relations with Western Europe, and the United Nations. He rarely touched on Third

World problems, economic and social issues, or regional conflicts, including the Middle East—except as they influenced, or had an impact on, the larger framework of international security and Soviet-American relations. Perhaps more than anyone else in the Politburo, Gromyko understood the possible devastating consequences of the Yom Kippur War for détente.

By character, Gromyko was not a troubleshooter, though neither was he a troublemaker. He did not like to go to international hot-spots, and he usually delegated negotiation of international conflicts to his first deputy, Kuznetsov. Perhaps it was Gromyko's cautiousness that allowed him to remain as foreign minister for twenty-eight years.

I do not think Gromyko knew the Arab world well or understood the Arab mentality. "Where Nasser was a fighter for Egypt's security and for the Arabs' legitimate interests, Sadat demonstrated a truly astounding ability to ignore both factors," Gromyko recalled later.[3] He did not like Sadat, who according to Gromyko had an extraordinary ability to distort facts and to blatantly contradict himself. He also felt that Sadat suffered from megalomania. Many in the Kremlin shared this assessment by the foreign minister, whose views were usually respected. I had the privilege of working for Gromyko for almost twenty years and will always pay tribute to this extraordinary man and remarkable diplomat of the Soviet era.

Among the other participants, more familiar with the Middle East was Boris Ponomarev. A longtime Communist Party *apparatchik* and ideologist who started his career in the 1930s in the Comintern, he knew well the national liberation movements and different Communist and pro-Soviet groups in the Middle East and provided them with financial support. Because he knew so much about the differences, arguments, and weaknesses of these groups, he was sometimes inclined toward assessments that were more measured than those of some of his colleagues.

Some may notice that I have not mentioned Alexandr Shelepin, one of Brezhnev's chief adversaries. This is because in October 1973 he was absent from Moscow most of the time and did not participate in the proceedings.

Formal meetings of the Politburo were usually recorded in shorthand, and on the basis of those verbatim reports the secretariat prepared summary records that were circulated among the members of the Politburo as official top-secret documents. These documents enumerated the views and proposals made at the meeting and the decisions approved, never disclosing the authors of the proposals or how the decision was made (by vote, consensus, acclamation, etc.). Suffice it to say that there were no stenographers present at informal meetings in Brezhnev's office or at the meetings of numerous task forces and commissions. Unlike Nixon, Brezhnev and his colleagues did not face consequences of tape-recording—there were no tapes. Therefore, to reconstruct the Politburo proceedings will be a difficult task for future historians.

## KREMLIN LEADERS' MEETINGS ASK: WHAT SHOULD BE DONE?

Meetings of the Kremlin leaders during the Yom Kippur War were convened either in Brezhnev's office or in the Politburo's conference room in the Kremlin. These rooms have been described by many visitors and authors: big halls, high ceilings, pale silk wall coverings, portraits of Marx and Lenin staring down at long tables, which were covered with green or red baize and surrounded by twenty to twenty-four chairs. Frankly, I do not remember these details, not even the color of the baize, but I do remember the row of chairs along the walls. They were reserved for us—experts, advisers, aides—those who had to keep the files, make notes, find necessary documents, and so on. However, no tables were made ready for our use. While the members of the Politburo and the secretaries of the Central Committee had the privilege of being seated around the large conference table, our knees were our table, and consequently we were never very comfortable. I remember also that every twenty or thirty minutes a charming waitress would enter the hall and ask the participants in the meeting if they wanted a cup of tea (coffee was not a favorite drink in the Kremlin in those days) or a sandwich. Of course, only those seated around the table were asked. To be honest, though, I have to admit that we were well compensated after the meetings, when we got plenty of tea and sandwiches.

Most of the Politburo meetings in October 1973 were presided over by Brezhnev, but in his absence two other senior party secretaries, Mikhail Suslov and Andrei Kirilenko, chaired the meetings. Brezhnev usually had a long working day, especially during the Yom Kippur War. Once, when asked how long it was, he answered: "A terribly large figure." Therefore at the meeting on October 12 he expressed dissatisfaction with the fact that some of the members were enjoying time at their dachas while he had to stay in the Kremlin and work late into the night. "This is unfair," he complained, and suggested that a Politburo commission headed by Suslov, with Andropov, Gromyko, Grechko, Ponomarev, and Katushev, be set up and charged with preparing draft decisions on the war in the Middle East for the Politburo. The Suslov Commission had several meetings, but to my knowledge it did not play any significant role during the war. All major decisons were made in Brezhnev's presence—that was the rule of the game in the Kremlin.

The strongest memory of my almost month-long presence in the Kremlin was, however, the atmosphere, the spirit of the Kremlin. The moment I passed through one of the gates, I felt significant and anxious, important and diffident, proud and fearful—all at the same time. There were actually few people around. I passed through long corridors and would meet almost no one except the guards. The closer one got to Brezhnev's office, the more guards there were. And there was the solemn silence. People even spoke softly, without full voice. I soon got used to it, though when I left the Kremlin I always relaxed.

The main participants in the first meeting during the Yom Kippur War—on Saturday, October 6, starting around 5:00 P.M.—were Gromyko, Grechko, Andropov, and Ponomarev. Others—Kosygin and Kirilenko—joined later. Though I was not present, I learned later that General Secretary Brezhnev started the discussion by expressing his disappointment that war had broken out. He said the Arab action would whip up international tensions and complicate the Soviet Union's relations with the West, especially with the United States. According to Brezhnev, the decision of Sadat and Assad to go to war was a gross miscalculation and a major political error. He predicted certain and speedy defeat of the Arabs. Others fully shared Brezhnev's belief that there was no chance for an Arab victory. Some participants even believed that in a few hours Israel would begin a counterattack that would result in the surrender of Egypt and Syria and the fall of their governments. The Arabs would be sorry they had not followed the advice of the Soviet leadership, Brezhnev concluded.

The Kremlin leaders were unanimous in favoring strict implementation of the principal Leninist foreign policy of the Soviet Union, which called for support "of the national liberation movements and peoples fighting to end colonial oppression" and opposing "the policy of the U.S. imperialist circles that is a threat to peace," as proclaimed in numerous party documents. Many spoke in favor of helping Egypt and Syria give a resolute rebuff to Israel and lashed out at the "Israeli invaders," who had provoked another crisis in the Middle East. Some participants were disposed to believe the Arab version of the outbreak of the war. In their view, Egypt and Syria had embarked on the road of noncapitalist, socialist development, and their "progressive" leaders, Sadat and Assad, had no other choice but to break away from the capitalist world. These were the views usually expressed at such meetings by those who knew little about the Middle East: Podgorny, Kirilenko, Suslov, Katushev, and some others.

The next question to be raised was the one clearly weighing most heavily on the minds of everyone in the room. In truly Russian fashion, that question was: "What has to be done?" In response, Gromyko drew attention to the strategy Assad had related to Ambassador Mukhitdinov during their meeting on Thursday. Gromyko's remarks were free from ideological stereotypes, and his analytical assessment was based on Realpolitik. Comments regarding Assad's early cease-fire idea were unequivocally positive, although the participants had several different reasons and arguments for supporting a cease-fire. Grechko believed that the Arabs could not win back by military means all the territories occupied by Israel and wage a protracted war. A new defeat of the Arabs, who were armed with Soviet weapons, could be viewed as a challenge to Soviet military might. Therefore an early cease-fire during the initial Arab offensive would be the best solution. As Gromyko saw the situation, an early cease-fire resolution in the Security Council might even breathe new life into the process of securing a political settlement of the Middle East conflict and open the door for talks aimed at establishing a durable peace in the region on the basis of United Nations Security Council Resolution 242. In this process, according to Gromyko, the Soviet Union would continue to play a decisive role. The champions of "proletarian internationalism," supporters of the Soviet Union's "unconditional backing" of the just struggle against Israeli aggressors and "those external reactionary circles" that constantly support Israel, also favored the idea of an early cease-fire. They assumed that a Soviet peace initiative at the United Nations would consolidate the success of the Arabs and elevate the Soviet Union's international standing and prestige. That in turn would establish better conditions for another powerful assault "by revolutionary forces on imperialist positions all over the world."

Finally, the proponents of the Soviet-American détente, Brezhnev and Kosygin among them, saw in an early cease-fire a real chance to avoid any deterioration of the superpower relationship. Indeed, they envisioned some kind of cooperation with the United States at the

United Nations and on a bilateral level. In other words, they were looking for a way to salvage something positive for Soviet-American relations from an otherwise destructive war. Brezhnev concluded the discussion of this issue by stating that an early cease-fire was in the interests of both the Soviet Union and the Arabs. The sooner it could be achieved, the better, he noted.

However, since Mukhitdinov's cable did not make clear whether Assad had expressed the views of Syria alone or the common strategy of the two Arab states agreed on by their leaders, it was decided that the first step should be to get clarification of Sadat's position. Some participants considered this step unnecessary, claiming that Egypt and Syria were fighting a coalition war and that therefore the strategy Assad referred to in his talks with Mukhitdinov must have been cleared by Sadat. Nevertheless, Vinogradov was instructed to meet Sadat immediately and clarify the issue.

The question of direct Soviet military involvement in the war never came up at the meeting. On the contrary, Grechko reported that Soviet naval units had already left the Egyptian ports of Alexandria and Port Said and moved west in accordance with a previous understanding. The appeal Sadat and Assad made for a speedy and urgent increase of Soviet military supplies did not become a big issue. When Brezhnev stated that the Soviet Union should strictly comply with its obligations and help "our Arab friends," nobody raised any objection. The idea that the new military conflict should be prevented from turning into a large-scale international crisis was emphasized throughout the meeting, and the decision was made to publish a statement by the Soviet government concerning the outbreak of war in the Middle East. The Foreign Ministry was entrusted with drafting the statement.

The meeting ended very late in the evening, after which Gromyko returned to the Foreign Ministry with Kuznetsov, Kornienko, and Sytenko. They gathered in Gromyko's office, where the foreign minister briefly summed up the meeting. When I heard that they had returned, I rushed to join them. I entered the room as Gromyko was speaking, and he told us that in the future the four of us could either attend meetings or stand by. Our task, he explained, would be to prepare draft documents (messages, instructions, resolutions), supply correct dates, maintain contacts with various government agencies and departments, and so on. I'll call our group the "task force," although we had no particular designation.

Senior among us was Vasilii Kuznetsov, whose career was already a distinguished one. In the 1930s he worked for more than one year as an engineer in the United States, so he spoke English and understood the American way of life. During World War II he headed the Soviet Trade Unions, and in 1952, shortly before Stalin's death, he was promoted to full membership in the Presidium (Politburo) of the Communist Party. For reasons not known to me, however, Kuznetsov failed to keep his position in the party's highest body in Khrushchev's time and was appointed first deputy foreign minister. In 1957, when Foreign Minister Shepilov was fired, as a member of the "Anti-Party Opposition Group," there were actually two candidates for the post: two first deputies of the foreign minister, Gromyko and Kuznetsov. The story goes that during the decisive meeting of the Politburo when the question of who would be the next Soviet foreign minister was considered, neither of the two candidates was invited. They were sitting in their studios next door to each other, waiting for the news. Late in the night, a messenger brought the good news and congratulations to Gromyko. Gromyko's aide recalled that it was a great surprise to the new minister, who had believed that Kuznetsov would be appointed because of his past record. After Gromyko got the news, the story continues, he went to Kuznetsov's office, expressed his friendly feelings, and promised closest cooperation with him. I am glad to confirm that Gromyko kept his promise. During Kuznetsov's twenty years as first deputy foreign minister, Gromyko kept the other post, of first deputy, vacant. He did not want to offend Kuznetsov, maintaining his sole position as number two in the foreign service. Kuznetsov was much liked in the Foreign Ministry for he was a decent, knowledgeable, and easily accessible person. The British permanent representative to the United Nations, Lord Caradon, composed the following lines about Kuznetsov:

> When prospects are dark and dim,
> We know that we must send for him;
> When storms and tempers fill the sky
> "Bring on Kuznetsov," is the cry.
> He comes like a dove from the Communist ark,
> And light appears where all was dark,
> His coming quickly turns the tide,
> The propaganda floods subside.[4]

Unfortunately, Kuznetsov played a secondary role during the Yom Kippur War, unlike the days of the Cuban crisis.

Georgii Kornienko was an expert on Soviet-American affairs, arms control, and many other international issues. He was also a workaholic and a man with a computer memory. His devotion to Soviet foreign policy was genuine. No one of us members of the task force could represent the ideas and perceptions of the Kremlin leaders better than he. During the Yom Kippur War, Kornienko drafted many documents, followed the Moscow-Washington correspondence closely, and participated in the Brezhnev-Kissinger talks.

Mikhail Sytenko, head of the Middle East Department for several years, knew the situation in the region better than other members of the task force. He provided necessary dates and documents and was personally acquainted with a great number of Arab officials. Was he pro-Arab? Did he like and trust the Arab world? I do not know, but I doubt it. One saying passed around the Foreign Ministry was that if you wanted to destroy the Soviet Union's relations with any state, all you needed to do was appoint Sytenko ambassador to that state. The source of this saying can be traced back to Sytenko's years as ambassador to Ghana and Indonesia when Soviet relations with each country deteriorated during his respective tenures. Unfortunately, relations with the Arab world were far from improving during Sytenko's tenure as head of the Middle East Department. This was probably a coincidence but could to some extent be explained by the fact that he was too good a servant of the Soviet system.

Having just returned from New York in July, I was the member of the task force who had the least experience in the art of bureaucracy. However, I did know the Middle East from the United Nations angle, having participated in the Four-Power Talks in New York and having close, friendly relations with the Arab representatives at the United Nations, Mohammed al-Zayyat and Abdel Meguid of Egypt, Muhammed al-Farra of Jordan, and Georges Tomeh of Syria. In general, relations within the task force were friendly and businesslike and I do not remember any serious differences among us. I think all of us understood the limited task we had to carry out.

After the meeting in Gromyko's office ended late in the evening of October 6, the task force remained for another couple of hours, double-checking the notes and drafting cables to Washington, New York, and Cairo.

## THE SOVIET-AMERICAN DIALOGUE BEGINS

In the late afternoon of that same day, Saturday, October 6, messages from Washington began to reach Moscow. Cables from the Soviet embassy in Washington always attracted special attention because the Kremlin attached greatest importance to Soviet-American relations.

The Soviet Union was represented in Washington by one of its best diplomats, Anatolii Dobrynin. Ambassador to the United States since 1962, Dobrynin was at that time already a well-known and respected figure in the world diplomatic community. From his appointment to Washington until the late 1980s, there was hardly a single international crisis during which the Soviet leaders did not take his opinion into account. The Yom Kippur War was no exception. His almost daily contacts with U.S. Secretary of State Kissinger, and his excellent knowledge of political life in the American capital, made his reports to Moscow a main component of the Kremlin's decision-making mechanism.

I had known Dobrynin since 1944, when we were schoolmates at the Diplomatic Academy in Moscow. An engineer by education, he had worked for a few years in the aviation industry. After graduating from the academy in 1946, he stayed on as a postdoctoral student and in a year earned a master of science degree in history. His dissertation on the Portsmouth Treaty of 1905 was published in Moscow. Dobrynin joined the Foreign Ministry in 1947, working in the Department of Personnel and as an aide to Deputy Foreign Minister Valerian Zorin. Later, as United Nations under-secretary general, he lived in New York, then returned to Moscow and became a special favorite of Gromyko, who appointed him director of the USA Department. Since then his long career had progressed primarily in the field of superpower relations.

Dobrynin was very professional. To read his cables was a pleasure—he had his own, very convincing style. In addition, he was a masterful courtier. Brezhnev liked him and made him a member of the Central Committee. Although we chatted a good deal throughout the many years of our acquaintance, I am not able to say whether Dobrynin really approved of all the Soviet Union's international actions, but he was superb at helping to carry them out.

On October 6, Secretary Kissinger talked to Dobrynin by telephone several times. He claimed in his memoirs that the ambassador, following his advice, called Moscow to clarify the situation in the Middle East. I do not remember, however, any of Dobrynin's telephone talks with Moscow on that day, nor does Dobrynin. In his cables, Dobrynin conveyed to Moscow the White House's assessment of the situation, its disappointment with the Soviet Union's stand, and, at the same time, America's readiness to cooperate with the Soviet Union to end the hostilities in the Middle East.

On Saturday evening, October 6, the first Yom Kippur War message from President Nixon to Brezhnev arrived and was distributed to the participants at the Kremlin meeting. Nixon expressed his indignation over the Arab attack, urged the Soviet leader to use his influence to force the Arabs to stop the aggression, and stated his unhappiness with the Soviet Union for not having informed the United States in advance of the Arab plan to attack Israel. He also appealed for a cease-fire and a commitment to end the fighting. From the American point of view, elaborated by Kissinger in his talks with Dobrynin, the Security Council's cease-fire resolution would return the armed forces to the status quo ante.

The very fact that Nixon had appealed to Brezhnev was welcomed in the Kremlin. The Soviet leader was glad that the American President was so prompt in doing so. Brezhnev considered himself a founder of détente and was proud of his summits with President Nixon in 1972 and 1973. Witnesses recall that Brezhnev had tears of joy in his eyes when he was standing on the lawn of the White House in 1973. Listening to him on many occasions, I had the impression that he sincerely believed he could be a champion of Soviet-American détente and at the same time a supporter of anti-imperialist, anti-American forces and movements all over the world. The Soviet leader saw Nixon's message as an omen of Soviet-American cooperation during the crisis and an indication of U.S. interest in maintaining détente.

The idea of a cease-fire was well received in Moscow, but nobody in the Kremlin took Nixon's proposal of a cease-fire that advocated a return to the status quo ante seriously. Later, Kissinger himself confessed: "There was no hope for a cease-fire status quo ante, but I wanted to get the Israelis to sign on to the principle so we could use it against them if they turned the war around."[5]

Although Brezhnev liked the idea of an urgent joint Soviet-American action in the Security Council aimed at stopping the war, he did not want to commit himself without consulting the Arabs. As Kuznetsov later recalled, "some comrades," participants in the October 6 meeting (he did not give any names), believed that such an action without formal Arab consent would contradict the principle of "proletarian internationalism." I asked Kuznetsov, "If we and the Americans just go ahead and get a cease-fire favorable to the Arabs, how could that seem to be a blow to proletarian internationalism?" Kuznetsov replied, "Can you imagine what would happen if some of the Arabs oppose our joint step with the Americans, and the Chinese consequently veto the resolution? Do you want the Chinese to become leaders of the national liberation, anti-imperialist forces?" That was it. For the first time during the October war, the "Chinese syndrome" came up and influenced Soviet decision-making.

When I learned of the Kremlin's positive response to the idea of a joint Soviet-American action in the Security Council, I was happy. I even hoped that, perhaps tomorrow, the war that had started so unexpectedly would draw to an end. But that did not happen. Since then I have sometimes wondered what would have happened if the Kremlin had agreed with Washington's genuine or tactical suggestion aimed at a joint cease-fire resolution in the first days of the war. Would the Arabs, the Israelis, or the superpowers suffer? I do not think so. But certainly thousands and thousands of Arabs and Israelis would not have lost their lives.

Instead, Moscow decided to urge the Soviet ambassadors in Cairo and Damascus to meet with Sadat and Assad and show them Nixon's letter to Brezhnev. Their opinion and advice concerning the cease-fire idea had to be sought. At the same time, the Soviet representative on the United Nations Security Council was instructed on October 6 to vote against any draft resolution on a cease-fire if the representatives of Egypt and Syria asked the Soviet Union to veto the draft. This instruction, cleared by the Kremlin leaders, was peculiar in another way. It read: "In case their positions [those of Egypt and Syria] would differ, you should act in accordance with the position of Egypt." This sentence was important. It revealed the real thinking of the "champion" of equal relations with "brotherly" countries and forecast many Soviet miscalculations and political blunders during the Yom Kippur War.

Brezhnev responded to the American complaints and proposals on October 6 and 7. Explaining the character of his messages to Nixon, Brezhnev joked that they reminded him of a Russian saying: The message should say neither yes nor no, but it should sound very friendly. Brezhnev claimed that the "Soviet Union learned about the outbreak of war in the Middle East at the same time the United States did." This was an obvious half-truth. The news of the actual Arab attack reached the Kremlin and the White House at the same time, but as noted earlier, Moscow had information about impending military operations a couple of days before they started. Brezhnev did not reject the idea of a cease-fire and promised to get in touch with President Nixon shortly in order to coordinate the actions of the Soviet Union and the United

States. "We need to gain time," he noted, while informing his colleagues about the content of the messages.


## VINOGRADOV TALKS WITH SADAT

After the idea of an early cease-fire was blessed by the Kremlin and encouraging news from Washington came in, I immediately instructed my colleagues from the Foreign Ministry's Department of International Organizations to draft a United Nations Security Council resolution on a cease-fire in the Middle East. Late in the evening of October 6 the first draft was written. Subsequently, a great number of working papers and drafts on that issue were generated by our task force before the joint Soviet-American draft was finally submitted to the Security Council two weeks later. I had in my files a whole collection of those drafts.

On the evening of October 6, however, any diplomatic move on the cease-fire issue was linked to Cairo's stand. We were waiting impatiently for news from the Egyptian capital. In the meantime, at 8:00 P.M. Cairo time, Vinogradov met with President Sadat at the president's palace. On behalf of Brezhnev, he conveyed to Sadat the Soviet leadership's congratulations on the successful crossing of the Suez Canal. He then informed Sadat of Assad's views regarding the Syrian strategy and said Moscow wanted to know whether these views, including the early cease-fire proposal, were shared by Sadat. Sadat answered that Assad's strategy had not been agreed to by him and did not reflect the Egyptian position. He strongly rejected the idea of an early cease-fire and said he would get in touch with Assad to convince him of this.

In the course of the talks, Ambassador Vinogradov told Sadat about Nixon's message to Brezhnev and asked his opinion about what Moscow's eventual response to that message should be. Sadat, quite irritated by Nixon's presumption that the Soviet Union could put pressure on Cairo, said the United States must be told that the responsibility for the conflict in the Middle East was Israel's alone, that the United States had to be advised to use its influence on Israel to give up her policy. Egypt might participate in a peace process with Israel, but only after the withdrawal of all Israeli troops to the 1967 borders. Sadat concluded by saying that only under those circumstances would he welcome a Soviet initiative on a cease-fire and convening a peace conference on the Middle East.

Vinogradov was impressed by Sadat's self-confidence and spirit. He did not believe that Sadat, being in such high spirits, would be ready for a cease-fire. The ambassador's report of this meeting with Sadat, however, caused great disappointment in the Kremlin. Chatting with our task force, Gromyko accused Sadat of being shortsighted. "He can't see farther than his nose," he grumbled. Hopes of an early, advantageous cease-fire and a speedy end to the war were fading.

Sadat's tough stand created some problems in Soviet-American relations. The Kissinger-Dobrynin consultations aimed at joint action at the United Nations were being jeopardized by Sadat's opposition to the idea of a cease-fire. The Kremlin, however, did not want to turn down the proposal to cooperate with the United States on a cease-fire. Besides, Soviet and U.S. leaders had pledged in two documents signed by them—in May 1972 in Moscow, and in June 1973 in Washington—to do everything in their power to avoid conflicts or situations that would increase international tension. Washington did not fail to refer to this pledge.[6] For his part, Gromyko, at the meeting with the task force on October 7, in discussing chances for cooperating with Washington, referred to the superpowers' commitment to exercise restraint in their mutual relations and to negotiate and settle differences by peaceful means, as declared in the "Basic Principles of Mutual Relations Between the USSR and the USA," signed in 1972.

But how could the Soviet leaders act against the will of their "Arab friends," who were fighting "imperialism and international Zionism"? On October 7, Brezhnev had no indication that the Arabs were ready to stop the fighting, but he still hoped that Assad would succeed in convincing Sadat to go along with his strategy, which would benefit all Arabs. The opposite happened. But first, in the evening of that day, Sadat informed Vinogradov that the differences between Assad and himself regarding the cease-fire issue had been resolved in his telephone talk with the Syrian president. According to Sadat, Assad now fully shared the Egyptian opposition to a cease-fire.

On Sunday, October 7, the Soviet Foreign Ministry was in constant contact with the General Staff. Since the tide was expected to turn at any moment, our task force had to be well informed about the military situation. The latter was surprising—the Egyptians and Syrians were continuing their offensive. Was it a miracle? Perhaps we were mistaken in our assessment of the military potential of the Arabs?

Arab success and Sadat's firm position changed the Kremlin leaders' mood to some degree. "We shall wait a while and see," Gromyko said, summing up a telephone conversation he had had with Brezhnev that evening. In accordance with such a strategy, Brezhnev's second message to Nixon was drafted. Its very vague language did not contain any concrete suggestions, making it clear that the Kremlin was not ready for a joint action in the Security Council. The message was limited to a general description of Soviet policies in the Middle East. It repeated the "principled policy" of the Soviet Union and expressed the hope that the fighting in the Middle East could be contained. Brezhnev fully agreed with the American view that the two powers should act in cooperation.

Kissinger was right in assuming that the position taken by the Kremlin leaders could be explained by reasons beyond their control. Moscow did not have as much influence with its Arab friends as it had sought, and as Washington thought it had.[7] Brezhnev's stand actually differed very little from that of Nixon, who later confessed that he saw no point in trying to impose a diplomatic cease-fire that neither side wanted or could be expected to observe.[8]

## THE KREMLIN SPEAKS

Early in the morning on Sunday, October 7, I went to the Foreign Ministry. Gromyko came to his office from his dacha too. Our task force devoted a great deal of time composing the text of the Soviet government's statement. Although the Kremlin knew perfectly well that military operations had been initiated by the Arabs, Gromyko instructed us to formulate the statement in such a way that the blame would be on Israel. At the same time, however, he advised us to use "mild and calm language" in our draft. "The statement has to be convincing," he stressed. It took us a long time to find what seemed to be an appropriate formula: "As a result of the absence of political settlement, a new military confrontation has broken out in the Middle East, which entails loss of human lives, calamities, and devastation." We avoided the issue of who started the war. Following Gromyko's instructions, we prepared a text in which Israel was accused both of obstinacy and of provocation, which had culminated in a concentration of Israeli forces along the existing cease-fire lines with Egypt and Syria "in recent days" and calling up reservists. We stated the Soviet Union's commitment to the Arabs and warned Israel in the following general way:

> The Soviet Union, true to its principled policy of support for peoples striving for liberation and independence, consistently acts as a reliable friend of the Arab states. Condemning Israel's annexationist policy, the Soviet Union resolutely supports the legitimate demands of the Arab states for the liberation of all Arab territories occupied by Israel since 1967.[9]

Our draft went on to say that if the government of Israel remained deaf to the voice of reason, and continued to pursue its annexationist policy by holding on to the occupied Arab lands, this could cost the people of Israel dearly. Responsibility for the consequences of this unreasonable course, the draft concluded, would be fully borne by the leaders of Israel.

Our draft did not contain any references to the U.S. policy of supporting Israel. The text composed was comparatively mild, but I do not think it was convincing. Most of the world understood very well who had provoked a military confrontation in the Middle East this time. Gromyko liked our draft, made minor editorial corrections, and inserted the following statement: "Israel finally unleashed military operations." We did not dare to argue with him. We understood that this obvious lie would manifest the Soviet Union's "principled support for peoples striving for liberation." Gromyko said he would clear the text with Brezhnev and other Kremlin leaders himself. The next day, when the statement was published in the papers, I found more new sentences in it. The new passage read:

> For several years now, Israel, enjoying the support and patronage of imperialist circles, has constantly effected a fomentation of the situation in the Middle East by its reckless, aggressive actions, [and therefore] the responsibility for the present developments in the Middle East and their consequences rests fairly and squarely on Israel and those external reactionary circles which have constantly encouraged Israel in its aggressive ambitions.[10]

The author of these sentences remains unknown to me, but I have no doubt that it was someone from the International Department of the Central Committee.

Within the next few days, several Soviet nongovernmental public organizations—the All-Union Central Council of Trade Unions, the Solidarity Committee of Peoples of Asia and Africa, and others—came out with their own statements. None differed much from the one issued by the Soviet government, because all of them were cleared at the same place—Old Square, where the headquarters of the Central Committee were located. Typical of the system, however, was the desire of every "independent" Soviet organization to demonstrate its toughness and arrogance. The more hawkish it appeared, the more reliable the Kremlin considered that organization to be—that was an unwritten law of the system. The Solidarity Committee, for example, placed special emphasis on Israel's systematic violations of United Nations resolutions. Even the failure of the Jarring mission was mentioned in this connection. On behalf of "the whole world" (!) the Council of Trade Unions expressed "indignation" over the "new criminal act of the Israeli government circles" and singled out the destructive role of the "external imperialist forces and international Zionist circles."[11] Others followed suit.

## ASSAD'S APPEAL FOR A CEASE-FIRE

At 4:00 A.M. on Monday, October 8, I was awakened by a call from Kuznetsov, who asked me to come to the Foreign Ministry immediately. There he showed me a cable from Damascus in which Ambassador Mukhitdinov reported that during his talk with Syrian President Assad late at night on October 7 Assad had described the situation at the Syrian-Israeli front as critical. He explained that the successful Syrian offensive was coming to an end and that an Israeli counteroffensive could be expected at any moment. Therefore, he asked the Soviet government to urge an extraordinary meeting of the United Nations Security Council aimed at approving a cease-fire resolution that would include a provision for Israel's withdrawal to the 1967 borders. My impression was that Assad was beginning to panic. We were shocked by the cable. How could the Syrians, after gaining an evident initial success and maintaining an obvious superiority in tanks and some other armaments, now be seeking an immediate end to the fighting? One of Kuznetsov's aides called the General Staff to check the current situation on the Syrian-Israeli front. The colonel from the Staff said that the

Syrians were continuing the offensive started on October 6 and that there was no reason to worry about the situation. We were even more puzzled.

Actually, we suspected that what Moscow had received from Damascus was not an accurate reflection of Assad's message but rather an interpretation of it—very free perhaps—by Mukhitdinov, who wanted to please and play up to the Kremlin. The profound difference between Assad's appeal and the way Sadat described his attitude toward the cease-fire in his talk with Vinogradov, at almost the same time, caused surprise and, as it turned out, unjust suspicion toward the Soviet ambassador in Damascus. Later, the trustworthiness of Mukhitdinov's report was confirmed by another Soviet diplomat, Veniamin Popov, who had attended the Assad-Mukhitdinov talk. Popov was struck by Assad's anxiety and alarm about the future of the military operation and by his urgent appeal to the Soviet Union to initiate a cease-fire in the Middle East. Indeed, throughout the Yom Kippur War and even after it, Assad continued to reproach the Kremlin for not having responded to his appeal for an early cease-fire. His latest appeal was in full conformity with the strategy he spoke about on October 4.

After reading Mukhitdinov's cable, our task force decided that we had to prepare all necessary documents for an urgent meeting of the United Nations Security Council. I drafted instructions for our permanent representative in New York, Yakov Malik, with a text of a cease-fire resolution that reflected Assad's views. My colleagues did the same for our ambassadors in Cairo and Damascus. When we had everything ready, about 8:00 A.M. on October 8, Gromyko appeared. He did not like the hasty actions we had suggested and thought it necessary to limit our activities to instructing Vinogradov to meet with Egytian President Sadat, informing him of Assad's formal appeal, and securing Sadat's support for a Soviet initiative in the Security Council. Gromyko wanted his position to be cleared with Brezhnev. When Brezhnev read Mukhitdinov's cable and the instructions for Vinogradov, he agreed with Gromyko's approach. "Vinogradov ought to be very persistent," he noted while reading the instruction.

All of us on the task force were disappointed with Gromyko's and Brezhnev's decision and were convinced that the Soviet Union had to act on its own. The constant attempts to please everybody could only obstruct and weaken our own position. I don't know whether Kusnetzov conveyed our doubts to Brezhnev or Gromyko, but nothing changed in the Soviet attempt to implement incompatible principles. I was under no illusion about Sadat's eventual flexibility, and I believe some of my colleagues shared my pessimism.

While waiting for Vinogradov's report, I was busy answering a number of telephone calls from many ambassadors accredited in Moscow. Their efforts to see or talk to Gromyko, Kuznetsov, or some of Gromyko's other deputies had failed, so they had no choice but to try talking to department heads. Their questions were standard: Had the Soviet Union known in advance of the planned Arab attack? What was the Soviet attitude toward the American proposal for a cease-fire? Had the Soviet Union started an airlift to Egypt and Syria? And so on. Of course, none of us dared to answer these questions. Instead, I quoted the statement of the Soviet government that had been published in the papers—causing outrage and offense to my distinguished colleagues. I was hoping they would understand the reasons for my evasive comments.

Late that evening, October 8, Vinogradov's cabled report of his meeting with Sadat came in. Vinogradov wrote that he had informed Sadat of Assad's formal appeal to the Soviet government asking for an urgent meeting of the United Nations Security Council in order to offer a cease-fire resolution. The ambassador had stressed that Moscow favored a cease-fire-in-place, especially in view of Syria's deteriorating military situation, and asked what Sadat thought about such a move by the Soviet Union. According to the report, Sadat expressed surprise at Assad's position and said that if Assad wanted to end the war that was his business—but that Egypt would continue it. In response to Vinogradov's question, Sadat stated that Egypt's strategic goal in the war was to exhaust Israel, that its territorial goal was to seize the Gidi and Mitla passes, and that its political goal was to unblock the crisis and secure a peaceful settlement of the Middle East conflict. Sadat further claimed that the military situation on the Egyptian-Israeli front, as well as on the Syrian-Israeli front, was excellent at the time, and he spoke at length about the Arab victories. Finally, according to Vinogradov, Sadat asked the Soviet Union not to urge a meeting of the Security Council and not to propose a cease-fire. There was no hint that Sadat was willing to meet the Soviet proposal halfway. That was the depressing news from Cairo.

In Damascus, Mukhitdinov was informed about the Sadat-Vinogradov talk, and he in turn confirmed Syria's interest in an early cease-fire.

## THE LAST ATTEMPT AT AN EARLY CEASE-FIRE

A new attempt to persuade Sadat to agree to a Soviet initiative in the Security Council was made the next day, Tuesday, October 9. I was present at an ad hoc meeting Brezhnev held with Gromyko, Andropov, and Grechko the morning after Vinogradov's report on his talk with Sadat reached Moscow. The Kremlin leaders were furious at Sadat's "stubbornness." I remember hearing remarks such as "We have to teach him!" and "His position is ridiculous!" coming from Brezhnev, Grechko, and others.

After a short discussion of Sadat's stand, our group was instructed to draft another urgent appeal from Brezhnev to Sadat. The new message emphasized the need to secure military success in the first days of the war, so that an immediate cease-fire-in-place would guarantee an Arab victory. Brezhnev explained that the intent was not to freeze the situation but simply to set up new front lines for the next steps aimed at liberating all Arab territories. He wanted to draw Sadat's attention especially to the utmost importance of unity and harmony in the policy of the Soviet Union, Egypt, and Syria. This was, in Moscow's view, a prerequisite for success in the war, since discord among these states would only weaken the common cause. That is why the message stressed the necessity of meeting Assad's appeal. Finally, the Kremlin assured Sadat that the Soviet Union would continue its support of the Arabs, but at the same time warned that, if the situation should worsen, the whole posture would become more complicated.

Ambassador Vinogradov was ordered to see Sadat immediately and discuss with him again an eventual Soviet proposal in the Security Council for a cease-fire-in-place. At the meeting with the Egyptian president on October 9, Vinogradov used two new arguments. First, the tide of war on the Golan Heights had begun to turn and the Israelis had started their offensive—and the Syrians had already lost 600 tanks, which made Assad's appeal even more justifiable. Second, the ambassador referred to the United Nations Security Council meeting in New York, which at the request of the United States had begun to consider the situation in the Middle East. Vinogradov asked Sadat what he advised the Soviet Union to do if a resolution on a cease-fire sought by Syria should be put to a vote by some of the members of the Security Council. Should our representative veto it?

Sadat was not impressed by these arguments. He stated that the situation on the Syrian-Israeli front would improve once the Iraqi forces came in, and that an Egyptian offensive in the Sinai would develop. He did not comment on Vinogradov's questions regarding the Security Council meeting, and he indignantly rebuffed the misinterpretation of Assad's position. Sadat claimed that he was in full harmony with Assad and that he was quite unhappy that the Soviet Union had, as he thought, some kind of special contacts with the Syrian president. As far as relations between Egypt and the Soviet Union were concerned, Sadat believed they should be (as reported by Vinogradov) based on three principles: the character of the relations should not be disclosed, Soviet military assistance should continue, and joint efforts to liberate Arab territories occupied by Israel in 1967 should be undertaken.

Sadat then turned to another important issue: He was not happy with the quantity and speed of Soviet military supplies going to Egypt, and pointed out how much military assistance the United States had already given Israel. At one point he said to Vinogradov, "You'd better answer my question. When will the promised airlift start?"

At the end of the conversation, when Vinogradov again mentioned Assad's stand on the cease-fire issue, Sadat interrupted him and suggested that the Soviet ambassador in Damascus, Mukhitdinov, be punished for lies and disinformation. It is interesting to note that, according to Heikal, Assad was likewise unhappy with Vinogradov and puzzled by his language.[12] Thus the Egyptian and Syrian presidents tried to put the blame for their serious differences in military and political strategy and perceptions on the Soviet ambassadors. Unfortunately, in the history of diplomacy such conversions are not unusual. The Sadat-Vinogradov encounter on October 9 was as unsuccessful as the previous one.

Late that day, after the Kremlin leaders had heard the substance of Vinogradov's talk with Sadat and the latter's reaction to Brezhnev's message, a consensus emerged: The idea of an early cease-fire should be dropped. Once again I had to set aside the different draft resolutions for the Security Council on the cease-fire, which we had prepared for our delegation in New York.

It is regrettable that some confusion exists about the substance of the Sadat-Vinogradov meetings dedicated to the cease-fire issue at the beginning of the war. Sadat himself has partly contributed to this confusion. In his memoirs he described his meeting with Vinogradov on October 6 in the following way:

> He [Vinogradov] said he had come to tell me that President Hafiz al-Assad of Syria had summoned him to a meeting on

October 4th and had told him that war would be launched on the 6th. I said I knew about it, as it was done with our prior agreement. The Ambassador went on to say that Syria had asked the Soviet Union, at the same meeting of October 4th, to work for a cease-fire forty-eight hours at most from the start of military operations on the 6th. It was on the basis of this that he now called to inform me of this request, officially, and to demand my approval of it.[13]

First, Sadat is mistaken when he says that Assad had summoned Vinogradov to meet with him. Vinogradov was not summoned on October 4 or on any other day to meet with the president of Syria. He was in Egypt. Second, Vinogradov could not "demand" that President Sadat approve on October 6 a request by President Assad that in fact was made later—on October 7. Third, the Sadat-Vinogradov meeting devoted to an eventual Soviet cease-fire initiative in the United Nations Security Council took place not on October 7—as many authors have claimed, referring to Vinogradov's interview with the Beirut daily *Al-Safir*—but only after Vinogradov had received the Kremlin's instruction of October 8 containing news of Assad's formal appeal. The ambassador explained later that the wrong date attributed to him by the Beirut paper was a mistake, which he discovered after the interview was published. Fourth, Vinogradov's talks with Sadat on October 6, 8, and 9 about the cease-fire issue were quite different. On October 6 the ambassador had limited himself simply to informing Sadat of Assad's views. On October 8 and 9, however, he was instructed to secure Egypt's support for the Soviet Union's action in the Security Council.

For a comprehensive view of the failure of the Soviet government to get an initiative for an early cease-fire in place, one must keep in mind that Syrian President Assad, throughout all the talks concerning his strategy, always linked a cease-fire to the unconditional withdrawal of Israel from all territories occupied by her. As Assad saw it, that was a precondition of any settlement. But the Kremlin had torn apart this linkage. It knew that a cease-fire resolution, which included a provision that Israel immediately withdraw to the 1967 borders, would inevitably cause a confrontation with the United States and its veto. Therefore, the instruction Vinogradov received from Moscow did not even mention the withdrawal part of Assad's formula. Gromyko had said to those of us who were drafting the instruction for Vinogradov and trying to describe Assad's position in full, "Don't make our life more complicated, please." Consequently, Sadat did not get the correct picture of Assad's position and was naturally angered by the apparent defeatism of the Syrian president. This detail was another manifestation of the Kremlin's desire to please its "Arab friends" while at the same time maintaining friendly cooperation with its superpower partner.

## HEADACHES FROM THE DISCUSSIONS IN NEW YORK

The news from New York was also discouraging. The American permanent representative to the United Nations, Ambassador John Scali, had asked in a letter dated October 7 that a Security Council meeting be convened so that it "might be seized of the grave situation which has arisen."[14] Shortly thereafter, Dobrynin conveyed to Moscow Kissinger's assurances that, for the time being, the United States did not intend to introduce any draft resolution in the Security Council. A cease-fire status quo ante, proposed informally by Kissinger, had no chance of being passed in the Security Council. It was totally unacceptable to the Arabs and would have been opposed by the nonaligned members of the council and vetoed by the Chinese. We learned from the Soviet delegation in New York that Kissinger's idea was not very popular, even among some Western delegations.

Unfortunately, we had our own problems to contend with at the United Nations. Aware of the differences between Assad and Sadat on the cease-fire issue, the Soviet Union was forced to refrain from taking any active role in the debate in the Security Council. Although the Soviet representative on the Security Council had instructions to support the Egyptian position if it differed from that of the Syrians, Moscow wanted very much to avoid the appearance of a split between Egypt and Syria. We limited ourselves to preparing instructions for Malik to refrain from any polemics with Scali and to maintain close contacts with the Arab delegations.

To make matters worse, there was one additional problem: the Soviet permanent representative to the United Nations, Yakov Malik himself. Along with other Soviet participants in the diplomatic play of October 1973, Malik, needs an introduction. As his colleague in the United Nations, George W. Bush, put it, "Malik was one of the early Cold War Russian diplomats who made the word '*nyet*' known to the English-speaking world."[15]

I had known Malik for a very long time. I was his deputy in New York for more than five years, and afterward we had continued working together in my capacity as director of the Foreign Ministry's department in charge of the United Nations. Malik was a remarkable representative of the "Stalinist school" of Soviet diplomats—an orthodox Communist, well-educated, intelligent, companionable, and very experienced. During his long career he served as deputy, first deputy foreign minister of the Soviet Union, Soviet ambassador to Japan and to Great Britain, and twice as the Soviet representative at the United Nations. In confrontational diplomacy he was a star, and many speeches Malik delivered at the United Nations were exciting shows. In the annals of diplomacy he was known for having walked out on a Security Council meeting during the Korean War, in 1950. He liked his "cold warrior" popularity. I remember that once in the late 1960s the *New York Times* compared Malik's performance at a Security Council meeting to that of a lion growling in a cage. Malik liked that very much and asked me to insert the story into the delegation's report to Moscow.

At the same time, one has to admit that Malik was occasionally cooperative. His contacts with colleagues in the West made it possible to reopen, quite informally, negotiations on the Berlin blockade, to resolve on a package-deal basis the problem of admitting a large group of states to the United Nations, and so on.

In the present case, however, our uneasiness about Malik's eventual performance proved to be justified, as when we learned of the Security Council meeting on October 8. On the one hand, we were pleased to learn that Scali's speech that day had been of a very general character, expressing hope that in the days ahead the Security Council could "restore its historic role of constructive ameliorator in the most critical and explosive area in the world."[16] Not a single word on the cease-fire! However, when we learned of Malik's speech, we were dismayed by his statements that "it was inappropriate to convene the Council" and that "without a clear statement by Israel that it is prepared to withdraw all its troops from the occupied territories, *the Security Council cannot make a single constructive decision in the present circumstances in the Middle East*" (emphasis added).[17] Malik had not been authorized to make such statements. When I drew Kuznetsov's attention to Malik's improvisations, his reaction was: "Forget it. The conflict will not be settled in New York." Gromyko decided not to show the delegation's report to Brezhnev.

Although some disharmony had been manifested in the Security

Council, the Kremlin was satisfied that an understanding not to let the war in the Middle East seriously damage Soviet-American relations or lead to confrontation seemed to have developed between Moscow and Washington. This was reflected in a very moderate speech by General Secretary Brezhnev at a luncheon in honor of the visiting Moscow Japanese Premier Kakuei Tanaka on October 8.

The Soviet leader put special emphasis on the importance of relaxing East-West tensions. An early draft of Brezhnev's speech had contained a call for an end to the fighting, but because of Sadat's position and the Arab victories of the previous days, that passage was deleted. Likewise, a sentence that had repeated the Arab version of the outbreak of the war was removed. At one point, Brezhnev almost appeared to admit that Egypt and Syria, as aggrieved parties, were the original movers in the fighting. As a result of joint efforts by the Foreign Ministry task force and Brezhnev's aides, the following formula was decided upon: "What is taking place there is a battle between Israel—the aggressor—and Egypt and Syria, the victims of aggression, which strive to liberate their lands."[18] It is interesting to note that Defense Minister Grechko, in an article published in *Pravda* on October 8, also did not support the Arab version of the outbreak of the war, which according to him was a result of "the militant policy of Israel."[19]

In Brezhnev's speech at the luncheon, he depicted the Soviet Union as a convinced supporter of a just and stable peace in the Middle East and of guaranteed security for all countries and peoples of the area. Brezhnev reiterated the Soviet Union's readiness to contribute toward such a peace. The word "guaranteed" was inserted into the text by Brezhnev himself, who explained that he wanted to emphasize the role of the great powers—the Soviet Union and the United States—in setting up peace in the region. Brezhnev's moderate tonality in his judgment of the war in the Middle East was welcomed in the West. Our task force had prepared a special file of the comments on the Brezhnev speech. It opened with Dobrynin's report, which contained Kissinger's satisfaction with the mild tone of Brezhnev's speech. Similar assessments were found in the cables from Soviet ambassadors in Paris, London, Bonn, and other capitals. The General Secretary was pleased with the comments.

Summing up the first days of the Yom Kippur War, Brezhnev noted during one Kremlin meeting that the most important result thus far had been that Moscow and Washington had confirmed their mutual desire to maintain cooperation.

But that was only one side of the coin.

# CHAPTER 3

# "WE HAVE TO HELP OUR ARAB BROTHERS"

## "CAN THE ARABS WIN THE WAR THE WAY THEY'RE WAGING IT?"

The successful Arab offensive at the start of the Yom Kippur War was a big surprise to the Kremlin. The apparent failure of Israel to strike back puzzled Soviet experts on the Middle East, and Sadat's tough stand against a cease-fire was unexpected as well.

The first days of the war seemed to disprove the Soviet military's pessimistic prediction, which was shared by the Kremlin leadership. Defense Minister Grechko, Chief of the General Staff Victor Kulikov, and other military leaders had been sure that without the broad assistance of Soviet advisers and their direct participation in the planning and implementation of military operations, Egypt and Syria would not succeed in crossing the Canal and mounting an offensive in the Sinai or on the Golan Heights.

Before the war, Sadat had reduced military cooperation with the Soviet Union—a fact that clearly irritated the Soviet military. Consequently, our military leaders rejoiced at the expected misfortune of the Arabs. This might also explain, at least partly, their pessimistic analyses of the fighting in the Middle East almost from the very first days of the war. Reports were usually submitted by Grechko, or more frequently by Kulikov. The latter was also an important player in the Kremlin during the war. A professional soldier, Kulikov had entered the Soviet Army at the age of eighteen and remained in the armed forces for more than half a century. He was a tanker in World War II and held various army command positions after the war, including commander-in-chief of the Soviet Group of Forces in Germany. In 1971 he became chief of the General Staff of the Soviet armed forces and first deputy to Grechko. Kulikov's presentations at the Politburo were usually well grounded, not very "ideological," and sometimes boring—Brezhnev advised him to shorten them. Among the military, Kulikov did not have the reputation and authority of some of his predecessors (Vasilii Sokolowsky) or successors (Nikolai Ogarkov).

On October 9, three days after the outbreak of the war, Marshal Kulikov presented his analysis to the Politburo at a meeting in the Kremlin. He admitted that the initial operations of the Egyptians and the Syrians had been successful and that the Israelis, taken by surprise, had not put up the expected resistance. As a result, in four to five hours the Egyptians had crossed the Suez Canal with several mechanized divisions, reinforced by infantry and a large number of tanks. The Syrians were also on the offensive, with three mechanized divisions and two armored divisions with almost 1,200 tanks. Kulikov stressed the importance of Soviet weapons in the Arab offensive—for example, the successful crossing of the Canal, attributed mainly to the effectiveness of Soviet anti-aircraft missiles, and the Syrian attack on the Golan Heights, attributed to the Soviet self-propelled guns and T-62 tanks. He spoke with pride about the extreme accuracy of the mobile surface-to-air missiles Kvadrat (SA-6) and Strela (SA-7) and the sophisticated personal infantry RPG rockets. Soviet surface-to-air missiles were tumbling Israeli combat aircraft out of the sky like ninepins, Kulikov noted with satisfaction, referring to reports from Soviet military representatives in Cairo and Damascus. These missiles soon acquired a reputation for destroying their targets no matter what the latter tried in the way of maneuvers or electronic countermeasures.

The Soviet military attaché in Egypt, Nikolai Ievlev, later recalled the great effectiveness of the Soviet infantry-operated antitank weapons, Maliutka (AT-3, Sagger), in the first days of the war, which turned out to be a complete surprise to the Israelis. Usually, two-man teams of Egyptian infantry opened what looked like small suitcases and inflicted casualties on Israeli battle tanks the likes of which had seldom been seen on any battlefield. The Soviet Union supplied Egypt with almost 600 such antitank weapons, and the Egyptian troops had been highly trained in the use of the Maliutka by Soviet instructors.

During a break in the meeting, I heard Kosygin saying to Kulikov that the Maliutkas would downgrade the importance of tanks in future wars, but Kulikov, who had served in tank units for decades, disagreed. He said that tanks, supported by mechanized light infantry and by aircraft, would still rule the battlefield.

In his presentation, Kulikov complained that the Arabs did not have a clear-cut, solid military doctrine. He pointed out that while armored and mechanized divisions of Egypt and Syria had developed a surprise attack in a coordinated thrust and had advanced into the Israeli defense system, the airborne divisions and paratroopers of the Arab states did not attack the enemy's rear flank. This was, in Kulikov's words, a gross mistake. He also stated that neither the Egyptians nor the Syrians had tried to gain supremacy in the air, although the Arabs had a mighty air force and well-trained pilots. The initial coordination and contacts between the Egyptian and Syrian armed forces, he claimed, had already been lost at the very beginning of the war.

The tactical success of the Syrians on the Golan Heights, according to Kulikov, could have been turned into a decisive military and political victory if they had continued the offensive on land and in the air. He claimed that the Israeli command had been forced to concentrate more than a third of its brigades at the comparatively narrow Syrian-Israeli front.[1] Kulikov estimated that Israeli losses on the Syrian front had been considerably higher than on the Egyptian front. The Soviet anti-aircraft missile systems, which had been deployed in Syria shortly before the war, could effectively protect the airspace of Syria and the Golan Heights, but the Syrians had stopped the intense activity displayed during the first days of the war, for reasons he could not explain. When one participant in the meeting interrupted Kulikov and asked him why the Soviet military advisers to Assad did not correct the Syrian military conduct, Kulikov answered, "They do not listen to us. They pretend to be their own military strategists."

Kulikov was rather critical of the military leadership of Egypt as well. After the Egyptian armed forces crossed the Canal, he said, they wasted time in clearing the Bar-Lev Line. From Kulikov's point of view, the fact that the Egyptians entrenched themselves on the narrow strip they seized on the Sinai and had not continued the offensive was a fatal mistake.

Grechko and Kulikov supplied statistical data that demonstrated not only how large the battle had become but also how enormous were the losses of personnel, weapons, and equipment for both Egypt and Syria. Yet when Kosygin asked Kulikov what the Israeli losses were, he could not answer. The military emphasized for the Politburo the instances of Syrians and Egyptians abandoning undamaged tanks and other equipment on the battlefield, which created the impression among those listening that the military leadership of Egypt and Syria was not up to the task. The comments of Grechko and Kulikov were clear: The Arabs were now paying the price for rejecting close military cooperation with the Soviet Union. "Can the Arabs win the war the way they are waging it?" Grechko asked his colleagues with irony at a meeting in the Kremlin on October 9.

As I listened to Grechko and Kulikov, I gradually came to realize how poor the military cooperation of the Soviet Union with Egypt and Syria was. The Soviet military leaders had only vague ideas about the strategy of the war Egypt and Syria were planning to conduct. Although a large number of Egyptian and Syrian officers had been trained in Soviet military academies, Soviet military doctrine was not applied in the Egyptian and Syrian armies. More than 8,000 Egyptian officers, including many generals, had graduated from war colleges in the Soviet Union, and more than 11,000 Soviet advisers were working in Egypt before the war. But this unfortunately did not lead to a mutual understanding of vital problems of strategy and tactics. Finally, the Soviet military leaders were surprised by the spirit and motivation shown by Egyptian and Syrian soldiers in the first days of the war. I have to confess that most of the experts and advisers, including myself, had been lulled into believing that the Arab soldier not only was insufficiently trained technically but also lacked courage under battle conditions. In short, we had underrated the Arab armies. These thoughts went through my mind at the time I was listening to the depressing but, as it turned out, largely correct reports of Grechko and Kulikov to the Politburo.

These reports strengthened the skepticism of the Kremlin leaders, who believed that in the near future—at almost any moment—the tide would turn. Once again, some participants of the gatherings in Brezhnev's office criticized Sadat and Assad for "irresponsibility" and "unwillingness to listen" to the opinion of their friends in the Kremlin.

## THE DECISION TO RESUPPLY THE ARABS

I do not remember any specific meeting in the Kremlin during the Yom Kippur War fully devoted to the issue of supplying the Egyptians and

Syrians with weapons, although this topic came up at almost every meeting in one way or another. During the discussion on October 6, the Kremlin leaders decided that the Soviet Union should resupply its "Arab brothers," which, they believed, would comply with the Soviet Union's international commitments and obligations affixed in several treaties and agreements with Egypt and Syria. Moreover, Brezhnev and his colleagues were convinced that, in resupplying the Arabs, the Soviet Union was fulfilling its "historical mission" as leader of the socialist camp and of the "whole progressive mankind," so they never argued about whether to supply the Arabs with military equipment. As Brezhnev frequently repeated on different occasions, the Soviet Union "had to resupply" the Arabs.

However, the amounts, specifications, and frequency of the supplies were not discussed at the Politburo. Sometimes when a participant in the Politburo meeting would offer a proposal or comment on a specific issue related to supplies, Brezhnev would interrupt him, noting that the issue was not a political one and should therefore be dealt with by the appropriate government agencies. The understanding was that decisions concerning the quantity and content of the supplies would depend on the course of the military operations and the judgment of the military as to what was needed.

I believe that the decision to start an airlift to Egypt and Syria was made on either October 6 or October 7. Sometimes, important resolutions were cleared by telephone communication and formalized afterward by the Politburo's Secretariat. In any case, early in the afternoon of October 7, Vinogradov and Mukhitdinov were instructed to inform Sadat and Assad immediately that the Soviet Union would begin an airlift to Egypt and Syria starting the next day, October 8.

The ambassadors carried out the instructions from Moscow in the evening of that day. Both Arab leaders expressed their gratitude. Sadat, according to Heikal, believed the Kremlin leaders decided to start the airlift because "they saw the situation moving in a very favorable direction and felt this was their chance to regain most or all of their lost prestige in the Middle East."[2] On the other hand, many accounts of the war, incorrectly referring to October 10 as the date the Soviet airlift began, claimed that the bombing of Damascus on the morning of October 9 could have had an effect on the timing of the start of the airlift.[3] But this was only part of the truth. The main reason for the Kremlin's decision to send military supplies to the Arabs was, as I mentioned above, the principal concept of Soviet foreign policy—the support of "peoples struggling against imperialism." This is why the Soviet Union, in Brezhnev's words, "had to resupply" the Arabs.

There were no serious problems with the opening of the airlift because, according to military authorities, all necessary preparatory work had been done well in advance. But the first Soviet airplanes with military equipment did not arrive in Egypt and Syria on October 8, as expected. This was why the Egyptian and Syrian leaders approached the Soviet ambassadors in Cairo and Damascus and asked for an explanation for the delay. The apparent delay of the Soviet airlift has been explained by some writers as a hesitation in implementation of the Soviet airlift pledge and by others as evidence of the Kremlin's hope that an early cease-fire could still be achieved.

The first airplanes did leave the Soviet Union, as promised, on October 8 and 9, but because they had a night stopover in Budapest or Belgrade they began to land in Syria and Egypt the next day—a few on October 9, a larger group on October 10. From then on, a massive airlift from the Soviet Union to Egypt and Syria took place, accompanied by the sealift and inaugurated simultaneously with the airlift. Huge Soviet Antonov transport planes landed at Syrian and Egyptian airfields. Vinogradov later recalled that, on clear days, people in Cairo could see large contrails stretching across the sky from Antonov transports flying at thirty-to-forty-minute intervals, and that this filled him with pride. Soviet Military Attaché Ievlev, attending the arrival of the first transport planes at the Cairo airport, accepted the gratitude of the Egyptian military, who were impressed by the number of the planes and the amount of cargo.

The turning of the tide on the battlefield, especially on the Golan Heights, and the pessimistic account of the events submitted by Grechko and Kulikov provoked varying reactions in the Kremlin, particularly when faced with persistent requests from Sadat and Assad to supply them with equipment they needed to make up for their losses. Discussions concerning Egyptian and Syrian requests generated sometimes sharp arguments. At one Politburo meeting, the chairman of the Supreme Soviet, Podgorny, suggested that the requests of Egypt and Syria be fully met no matter what the military situation. He said the Soviet Union must be generous to its Arab friends and should go beyond the existing bilateral agreements. The KGB head, Andropov, and the secretary of the Central Committee in charge of military-industrial affairs, Dmitrii Ustinov, favored increasing Soviet military supplies to Egypt and Syria. Others—Kosygin and Gromyko among them—had some reservations. Their various arguments were that the Arabs had sufficient weaponry, significantly surpassing the Israeli arsenal, that the growing military aid to the belligerents would prolong the war, and so on, and they referred to the data on Egyptian and Syrian weapons holdings as of October 6, 1973, submitted by the Ministry of Defense. Later, after the war, my military colleagues showed me the Defense Ministry's paper containing the figures. The Egyptian weapons holdings were estimated as follows:

LAND FORCES
| | |
|---|---|
| Surface-to-surface missiles, Luna M (SCUD) | 12 |
| Tanks and self-propelled guns | 2,455 |
| Heavy guns and mortars | 3,605 |
| Antitank weapons, Maliutkas | 557 |
| Antitank guns | 1860 |
| ZSU-23-4 Shilka vehicles | 13 |
| Anti-aircraft weapons | 1,313 |

AIRCRAFT
| | |
|---|---|
| Mig-17 | 174 |
| Mig-21 | 328 |
| SU-7 | 72 |
| SU-17 | 16 |
| SU-20 | 12 |
| IL-28 | 22 |
| TU-16 | 26 |

The document did not specify the anti-aircraft weapons, but mentioned only that Egypt had the Soviet surface-to-air missiles Dvina (SA-2), Desna (SA-2 export), Pechora (SA-3 export), and Kvadrat (SA-6 export). The Syrian weapons holdings were estimated as follows:

LAND FORCES
| | |
|---|---|
| Tanks and self-propelled guns | 2,335 |
| Armored motorcars | 1,265 |
| Heavy guns and mortars | 1,980 |
| Antitank guns | 1,016 |
| Antitank weapons, Maliutka and Shilka | 375 |
| Surface-to-air missile, Strela (SA-2) | 284 |

AIRCRAFT
| | |
|---|---|
| Mig-17 | 111 |
| Mig-21 | 180 |

| | |
|---|---|
| SU-7 | 25 |
| SU-20 | 15 |
| Helicopters | 57 |

The correlation of all kinds of weaponry of both Arab states—Egypt and Syria—and Israel was estimated as 1.6 : 1 or 1.7 : 1 in favor of the Arabs.

The position of the military on the supplies issue was ambivalent. They understood perfectly well that without fresh supplies the Arabs would not be in a position to continue the fighting and would surrender, but they were concerned that Soviet supplies could fall into Israeli hands. Colonel Leonid Medwedko, a member of the Defense Ministry's ad hoc group on the Middle East set up in October 1973, recalled that the issue of supplying the Arabs with modern Soviet weapons was one of the most difficult the group had to deal with throughout the war. Belief that an Arab victory was not possible, and mistrust of the "Arab brothers," often led to rejection of an Arab request for modern Soviet weaponry.

The following episode was typical. During a meeting with Vinogradov in the first days of the war, Sadat urged the Soviet government to give the Egyptian president the exclusive right to make decisions regarding the use of the SCUD missiles deployed on Egyptian territory and the Egyptians to operate them. Vinogradov knew very well that this was a sensitive issue for Moscow, so in response to Sadat's request he said jokingly, "Why do you want to have additional headaches with these missiles, Comrade President? Don't you have enough problems of your own?" Vinogradov reported Sadat's request to Moscow but never received a reply.

The Kremlin leaders had no intention of prolonging the war, but in accordance with the principle of "proletarian internationalism" Moscow decided to assist Egypt and Syria in their war against "the common enemy—imperialism." Although the Soviet Union could use restraint in providing the Arab states with arms, and thus put additional pressure on them aimed at an early cease-fire, the Soviet resupply operations continued throughout the war. Many who have written about the war—Galia Golan, Jon Glassman, Amnon Sella, William Quandt, and others—have dealt specifically with the issue of Soviet arms supplies to the Arab states. Quandt's research contains approximate figures on the Soviet sealift and airlift to the Middle East during the war. They sound reasonable, but I can neither confirm nor challenge them. At the meetings of the Politburo, the tonnage and the specification of deliveries never came up. These were "technical," not political, issues, although nobody in the Kremlin underestimated the enormous importance of the resupply policy of the Soviet Union. General Mahmut Gareyev, deputy chief of staff of the Soviet armed forces, who worked in Egypt for many years, acknowledged that the Soviet Union, in reply to Egypt's request, had airlifted military technology, spare parts, and ammunition in an operation that involved 4,000 military transport planes. In addition to the previously agreed quantity, 1,500 tanks and 109 airplanes were delivered. Before the war, the general recalled, the Soviet Union "provided Egypt—on easy terms—with anti-aircraft missiles, 2,500 tanks, and 1,200 combat aircraft. This was the most advanced weaponry for its time: T-62 tanks, Mig-21 and Mig-23 planes, and the Kvadrat (Square) anti-aircraft-missile complex."[4]

## "ARABS ALL OVER THE WORLD UNITE!"

The other important avenue of Soviet support of the Arabs was political. The idea of encouraging other Arab states to lend support to Egypt and Syria was first voiced at the October 6 meeting in Brezhnev's office by Ponomarev, whose views were approved. Accordingly, several steps were taken to create a united Arab front against Israel. First, Brezhnev would send personal messages to the leaders of the Arab countries. Second, Podgorny, Kosygin, Suslov, Gromyko, and Ponomarev were advised to meet representatives of Arab states who were accredited in or visiting Moscow and to convey to them the Kremlin's views concerning Arab unity. Third, the leaders of the Warsaw Treaty Organization were to be informed of the Soviet Union's attitude toward the war in the Middle East and the importance of Arab solidarity with Egypt and Syria. Finally, the Soviet media were to be instructed to propagate the significance of active and broad aid from "all progressive forces" to and in support of Egypt and Syria. All these actions were carried out throughout the conflict, starting on October 8.

Brezhnev's messages were addressed to a large number of Arab leaders. Drafted by the International Department of the Central Committee in cooperation with the Middle East Department of the Foreign Ministry, they were delivered by the Soviet ambassadors in Arab states in written form or verbally. The message to Yasser Arafat, chairman of the PLO, was handed over by Sarvar Azimov, the Soviet ambassador to Lebanon. The content and form of the messages depended on the character of relations with the appropriate Arab leader and the Soviet assessment of the foreign and domestic policy of his country.

The most straightforward and frank of these messages were addressed to Algerian President Houari Boumedienne and Iraqi President Ahmad Hassan Bakr. Brezhnev urged these Arab leaders to use all means at their disposal to support Egypt and Syria in their struggle "imposed by the Israeli aggressor." He also appealed to Boumedienne and Bakr to take all required steps to help the Egyptian and Syrian armed forces defeat the "treacherous enemy." The political systems and regimes in Egypt and Syria were characterized as "progressive." The message to Bakr was an unambiguous hint of the desirability of direct military assistance to Syria, Iraq's neighbor and ally in the struggle against the common enemy, Zionism.

Concluding his messages, Brezhnev expressed Moscow's firm conviction that the Arab leaders should understand perfectly well "all the peculiarities of the present situation" and that they should be guided by the ideals of fraternal solidarity with Egypt and Syria. In the messages to Arafat, Bakr, and Boumedienne, Brezhnev referred to their "broad and expansive experience in the anti-imperialist struggle," which would contribute to the common victory.

The Soviet ambassadors in the capitals of the Arab states delivered Brezhnev's personal messages immediately and reported that the Arab leaders responded with understanding, interest, and gratitude. Boumedienne's response, however, was rather bizarre. He ordered the publication of Brezhnev's confidential messages in the Algerian press, and they were subsequently reprinted all over the world. When Brezhnev found out he became furious. "How can you do business with such people?" he shouted, outraged, in his office. He had good reason to be chagrined. The same time he was encouraging all Arab states to actively support Egypt and Syria and, guided by the ideals of "fraternal solidarity," to actually expand the war, he was assuring President Nixon and the rest of the world that the Soviet Union was eager to restrict the war, to contribute toward ensuring peace, to continue the policy of relaxing East-West tension, and so on. Such double-dealing!

The appearance of Brezhnev's confidential messages to Boumedienne in the press was not a surprise to some diplomats in the Foreign Ministry who were familiar with Eastern diplomacy. They believed that such delicate messages had to be transmitted verbally, otherwise leakage would be inevitable and Soviet-American relations would be damaged. Some colleagues even teased us members of the task force: How could it happen, they asked jokingly, that one member of the task force (Mikhail Sytenko, head of the Middle East Desk) prepared a document that undermined another member (Georgii Kornienko, head of the American Desk)? It seemed to me that Gromyko himself did not like the idea of delivering Brezhnev's messages in written form but that he was not insistent enough to prevent it. After Brezhnev's messages to Boumedienne were published, we were expecting an American démarche or some kind of protest. Fortunately there was almost no response.

Nevertheless, Brezhnev could not ignore Boumedienne's imprudent behavior. On October 10, the Soviet ambassador in Algeria was ordered to inform the Algerian leader about Moscow's "disappointment" that Brezhnev's personal messages had been published. The ambassador was instructed to convey to Boumedienne that "our common adversaries" had used the published confidential messages "in their interests." Without confidentiality, an exchange of opinions on important and delicate issues through personal messages was, in Moscow's view, useless. It was an unpleasant mission for the ambassador, but he carried it out. Boumedienne got the message.

While Brezhnev's messages were being dispatched to Arab leaders, important meetings were taking place with Arab representatives in Moscow. On October 8, Secretaries Suslov and Ponomarev met with the leaders of the Syrian Communist Party (SCP), Politburo member and secretary of the SCP Y. Feisal, and Politburo member I. Bakri. Chairman Podgorny talked to a member of the Iraqi Revolutionary Command Council, Minister of Foreign Affairs Murtada Abdul Baqi, who was visiting Moscow for consultation pursuant to the Soviet-Iraqi treaty of friendship and cooperation, on October 9. Two days later, on October 11, Gromyko had an encounter in the Foreign Ministry with the ambassadors of Egypt, Y. Abdul Qadr; of Syria, J. Shaya; of Iraq, S. M. Amasha; of Algeria, R. Malek; and of Jordan, K. Hamud. Finally, Premier Kosygin received the ambassador of the People's Democratic Republic of Yemen on October 12.

The notes for the talks with the Arab representatives were prepared in the Soviet Foreign Ministry. Although some specific issues concerning bilateral relations came up during the negotiations with the Iraqis, the Syrians, and the Yemanis, the primary subject was clearly the war in the Middle East. The Foreign Ministry's notes emphasized the following points: the Soviet Union supports the legitimate struggle of the Arab people aimed at liberating their lands seized by Israel; it favors a just and durable peace in the Middle East; the war of Egypt and Syria against Israel is a common cause of all Arab peoples, and therefore the broadest and most varied support had to be given to the two nations fighting the common enemy; and Arab solidarity was an essential prerequisite of victory for Egypt and Syria. No less important were the omissions. The Egyptian and Syrian versions of the outbreak of the war were not repeated, and the cease-fire issue was not mentioned either, because of the differences between Sadat and Assad.

The results of these meetings were not discussed at the Politburo. I do not think there was anything extraordinary in them. The Soviet V.I.P.'s were pleased to hear the gratitude expressed by the Arab representatives for the Soviet Union's "invaluable all-around assistance and support to Arab states fighting imperialist Israeli aggression." The main message was the utmost importance of Arab solidarity. Suslov and Ponomarev stressed the need for unity in the Syrian leadership and urged the Syrian Communist Party bosses to give full support to Assad. Podgorny was straightforward in advising the Iraqi armed forces to participate in the war and to send troops to the Syrian-Israeli front.

Gromyko's meeting with the ambassadors of Egypt, Syria, Iraq, Algeria, and Jordan was held at the Foreign Ministry. A few points from this session are worth mentioning. In referring to Brezhnev's speech at the luncheon in honor of the Japanese prime minister, Gromyko once again asserted that Moscow was determined to continue exerting "all efforts in the interests of safeguarding a durable and just peace in the Middle East and safeguarding the guaranteed security of all states and peoples of the region." The word "guaranteed" reflected the Soviet leader's vision of not only the character of the settlement of the conflict but also the future of the peace in the Middle East in general. This was the expression of the Soviet Union's readiness and willingness to guarantee a "durable and just" peace in the Middle East. Yet at the same time that they were declaring special interest in a guaranteed peace, the Kremlin leaders, in appealing to Arab states, were busy destabilizing the area. It was another example of the contradictory nature of the Soviet Union's policies. Perhaps this was the reason the West did not pay much attention to Soviet declarations regarding the future peace in the Middle East. The *New York Times* dropped the adjective "guaranteed" from its quote from the Tass report.[5]

Gromyko's meeting with the Arab ambassadors was also noteworthy because the ambassadors had been trying for several days to see the Soviet foreign minister. The delay in Gromyko's first wartime meeting with the Arab ambassadors was explained partly by the uncertain and indecisive situation regarding the cease-fire issue. On the eve of the meeting, our task force discussed how the foreign minister should respond if the Arabs should question him about the Soviet attitude toward a cease-fire. We recommended that he emphasize that the Soviet Union would act in harmony with Egypt and Syria. As it turned out, none of the ambassadors touched on the cease-fire issue, perhaps knowing of the differences between Cairo and Damascus.

Gromyko's communication with the ambassadors of Egypt and Syria was typical of the Soviet Union's superpower diplomacy. While the Soviet ambassadors in Cairo and Damascus had unlimited opportunity to communicate not only with the foreign ministers but also with the presidents of Egypt and Syria, their counterparts in Moscow—Ambassador Kader of Egypt and Ambassador Shaya of Syria—could only dream of being granted audiences with the foreign minister. Their usual contact was the head of the Middle East Department or occasionally the deputy foreign minister. To seek a meeting with Brezhnev would have been a daring but hopeless step. During the Yom Kippur War, Gromyko met Kader and Shaya only a couple of times. If one compares Kissinger's almost daily meetings with the Israeli ambassador to Washington, Simcha Dinitz, the differences in the style of the two foreign ministers becomes evident. Gromyko, a consummate bureaucrat, devoted a great deal of time to clearing almost all major Soviet diplomatic steps with the Central Committee. His American counterpart had no such obligation to clear his actions with a "Central Committee" of the Republican party. Therefore he had much more freedom and was more operational.

The Soviet style had never been helpful, and I believe it played a negative role during the Yom Kippur War as well. The Egyptian and Syrian ambassadors, who had limited access to the Kremlin leadership, could not report the Soviet arguments and perceptions to their capitals or receive answers to different questions from appropriate competent Soviet officials. Therefore, for Sadat and Assad the main sources of information on the Soviet position were the Soviet ambassadors in Cairo and Damascus. Unfortunately, the latter were not always trusted much by the presidents, as was the case during the unsuccessful attempts to reach an agreement on the cease-fire issue in the first days of the war. If these attempts had been matched by frank and friendly talks between Brezhnev and the Egyptian and Syrian ambassadors in Moscow, the results might have been different.

However, the main attention of the Soviet leaders was focused on general appeals for Arab solidarity. Robert Freedman might be right in his assessment: "The Russians, perhaps sensing the possibility of finally being able to rally the Arabs into the long advocated 'anti-imperialist' alignment and strike a blow at U.S. interests in the Middle East, moved to increase their involvement in the war, yet at the same time keeping their involvement within limited bounds."[6] To some extent, Soviet efforts to strengthen Arab unity were productive. They encouraged some Arab states to expand their military, financial, and economic aid to Egypt and Syria.

## "THE SOVIET UNION WILL NOT TOLERATE ISRAELI CRIMINAL ACTS"

After the initial successful Arab offensive, the situation began to change gradually and to develop unfavorably for the Arabs. By October 9, after getting over the first shock, Israel launched a counteroffensive on the Golan Heights that caused the Syrian forces to withdraw until Israeli troops recaptured the territories lost in the first days of the war and advanced to the hills overlooking Damascus. On the Sinai, the Egyptian forces, apart from small attacks on Israelis that did not affect the overall military situation, stopped their original successful advance and embarked on an "operational pause" that lasted to the end of the week, October 13.

Throughout this period, there were almost daily meetings in the Kremlin, where the deteriorating military situation of Syria became the main subject. On October 12, Kulikov's analysis before the Politburo (Grechko was on a two-day visit to Warsaw) was even more skeptical than before. He claimed that the initial Syrian success began to disappear when their tanks halted the offensive. The deterioration of the Syrian position could have a very negative impact on the balance of armed forces in the Middle East in general, Kulikov stressed. Likewise, he labeled as shortsighted the Egyptian "operational pause" and delays in capturing the Gidi and Mitla passes in the Sinai. Kulikov said that the inept, unqualified military leadership would bring defeat to the Arabs, and he expressed indignation over the lack of cooperation and coordination between the Egyptian and Syrian high commands.

I remember that when the issue of the danger for Israel of facing two fronts came up at the meeting on October 12, I sent Gromyko a note with a quotation from Israeli Defense Minister Moshe Dayan's press conference on October 9: "It would not be possible to carry out both operations—taking the Syrians out of the war and throwing the Egyptians back across the Canal at the same time."[7] Gromyko did not make use of the note, saying after the meeting that Dayan's opinion was not the right argument at the right place.

Kulikov's critique was reinforced by Ambassador Mukhitdinov's cables from Damascus, which had been circulated among the members of the Politburo. Mukhitdinov reported that the contacts both the Soviet military and he had had with their Syrian counterparts proved that communication between Assad and Sadat, as well as between the Syrian and Egyptian military commands, was far from warm and friendly. According to our reports from Syria, the Egyptian representative at the military headquarters in Damascus delivered to his Syrian colleagues information and data that had already been published in the press. Referring to reliable sources, the ambassador informed Moscow that Sadat had turned down Assad's request to send Egyptian bombers against Israeli cities in retaliation for the Israeli air attacks on several civilian targets deep inside Syria. Mukhitdinov reported that Assad had sent his special representative to Cairo to plead for an immediate Egyptian offensive in the Sinai. Damascus was waiting from hour to hour for a positive response, but the expected Egyptian offensive did not start. The ambassador suggested instructing Vinogradov to talk with Sadat in order to meet the Syrian request.

At this crucial time, the decision of some Arab states to send their troops to the Syrian front was extremely important for Syria. Iraqi, Moroccan, and Jordanian troops had arrived in Syria and started to participate in the fighting against Israel. Several Palestinian brigades fought at the Golan Heights ("Hittin" and "Qadisiya") and in Sinai ("Ain Jalut"). Especially effective were the actions of the Iraqi forces, which succeeded in halting the Israeli advance, and afterward in pushing them back at some points. General V. Mazulenko, a military expert on the Middle East in the Defense Ministry, asserted that in addition to Egypt and Syria, the following Arab states participated in the Yom Kippur War: Jordan, Kuwait, Libya, Iraq, Saudi Arabia, Morocco, and Algeria.[8] Vinogradov claims that King Hussein of Jordan told him, after the war, that he had repeatedly made offers to Sadat and Assad to enter into the war, but that although Assad welcomed the king's intention Sadat flatly rejected it. The report from Mukhitdinov about the arrival of troops in Syria from several Arab states was welcomed by the Kremlin. Podgorny was particularly proud because he had conducted negotiations with the Iraqi foreign minister and regarded the Iraqi action as a result of his efforts.

But Kulikov's main concern was the Israeli provocation against the Soviet Union. On October 9, during their air raid on Syria, Israeli planes had bombed the Soviet Cultural Center in Damascus, and on October 12 a Soviet merchant ship, the *Ilya Mechnikov*, had been sunk in an Israeli raid in the Syrian port of Tartus. By the middle of that week it was clear to Kremlin leaders that the latest military developments, and especially the Israeli challenges, signaled a new stage in the war that required a response. Nobody rejoiced at the military misfortunes of the Arabs anymore. The war had now developed in a way that could jeopardize the Soviet Union's vital interests and prestige. "This would be totally unacceptable to us. Nobody should dare to think of such a development," Brezhnev declared at the meeting on October 12.

The news of the sinking of the *Ilya Mechnikov* aroused indignation and criticism of "aggressive" Israelis and "helpless" Arabs. Some of the participants in the meeting—Podgorny, Kirilenko, Suslov—were inclined to take retaliatory measures against Israel, but Brezhnev and Kosygin were opposed to any military action that could involve the Soviet Union in the war. A decision was made to send a message to President Nixon, in Brezhnev's name, strongly protesting the "barbaric bombing and shooting of civilians" by Israel and stressing that the Soviet Union would not tolerate "such criminal acts" by Israel and would take appropriate measures to defend its ships and other means of transportation. The message also expressed hope that the United States would exert its influence to bring an end to Israeli criminal acts. "This message to Nixon should be a serious warning to the Israelis indeed," noted Brezhnev when he instructed Gromyko to draft it.

The Politburo also decided to issue a special statement from Tass, whose head, Leonid Zamyatin, was charged with preparing it. By evening of that day, October 12, the draft was ready. Rather harsh, it contained numerous references to the criminal role of "certain imperialist circles" supporting Israel, appeals to the "progressive forces" all over the world to defend the Arab case, and so forth. The statement included the remarkable assertion that the Arabs had demonstrated a "humane and merciful attitude" toward the population of Israeli cities.

Our task force made some hasty and primarily editorial changes to the message. After clearing them with Gromyko, we sent the draft back to the Central Committee, and the statement was published by Tass the next morning, October 13. The main part of the statement read:

> The Soviet people resolutely condemn the barbaric bombing and shooting of civilian targets and the peaceful population by the Israeli armed forces. The Soviet Union cannot regard indifferently the criminal acts of the Israeli military, as a result of which there are victims also among Soviet citizens in Syria and Egypt, and demands an immediate stop to the bombings of peaceful towns in Syria and Egypt and strict observance by Israel of the norms of international law, including those regarding the freedom of navigation. The continuation of criminal acts by Israel will lead to grave consequences for Israel itself. The Soviet Union believes that an end of Israeli aggression and of Israel's acts of violence, and the liberation of Israeli-occupied Arab territories, is the basis for establishing a just and lasting peace in the Middle East.[9]

When I read the statement, I was surprised to find that on this occasion the final text was milder than the original draft. I knew that the change had not been introduced by the Foreign Ministry, but because the labyrinths of Soviet power were so complicated there was scant prospect of finding out who had made the change. The softener might well have been one of Brezhnev's aides—perhaps his main foreign-policy aide, Andrei Aleksandrov, who was always able to grasp the latest political mood of his boss.

At any rate, the demands for an end to Israeli aggression were becoming increasingly frequent. The Central Committee orchestrated a number of similar statements from "independent" Soviet nongovernment organizations—the Council of Trade Unions, the Soviet Peace Committee, the All-Union Society of Cultural Relations with Foreign Countries, and some others. As usual, the statements of the "independent" organizations were one step tougher than the official Tass statement. The Council of Trade Unions, for example, called for punishment of the Israeli aggressors for their criminal acts.[10] To justify this claim, the Soviet newspapers *Pravda*, *Izvestia*, and *Trud* published articles from their special correspondents in Cairo and Damascus containing accounts of Israeli "atrocities" and "monstrosities" in the territories occupied by Israel.

But the toughest Soviet response to the Israeli bombing was voiced in New York. At the meetings of the United Nations Security Council, the Soviet permanent representative, Malik, equated the Israeli bombing to the crimes of the Nazis. He claimed that thirty staff members of the Soviet embassy had been killed in the Israeli blow to Damascus and that no less than ten foreign embassies had been destroyed. And he declared that responsibility for these "bloody and villainous acts" rested "fully and entirely" on the Israeli government and personally on Prime Minister Golda Meir and General Dayan, "those international criminals."[11] Malik appealed to all countries and peoples to unite their efforts to curb the Israeli aggressors. In a bitter and angry exchange, typical of the Cold War, with the Israeli permanent representative, Yosef Tekoah, Malik felt he was at his best. When the Israeli representative was expressing condolences for the "innocent civilian victims of the bombing in Damascus," Malik shouted: "The Soviet delegation does not wish to hear excuses from a representative of murderers and international gangsters!"[12] Then he walked out, accompanied by applause in the Security Council chamber. Tekoah responded: "If anyone around this table is continuing meeting after meeting to use Goebbels' methods, it is you!"[13]

When we received the report of our delegation in New York, Gromyko expressed his dissatisfaction with Malik's performance, calling it "a cheap show." He instructed me to advise our press to make no "big stories" of these "shows" and to recommend to Malik that he tone it down. As a result, the Soviet press published only brief reports of Malik's behavior at the Security Council, and, at least for the time being, our permanent representative demonstrated some restraint.

The discussion of the report on the Israeli bombing of Damascus and the sinking of the Soviet merchant ship at the Politburo meeting on October 12 had another consequence. When Kosygin asked whether we could ensure the safety of our transportation to the Arabs, Brezhnev ordered Kulikov to take "necessary steps" to prevent "any repetition" of Israeli attacks on "Soviet targets." Kulikov assured Brezhnev that "necessary steps" would be taken, but he did not elaborate on the character of those steps or on defining the term "Soviet targets." This important issue never came up again, but from later contacts with the military I understood that some air defense missile units under exclusive Soviet control and operation had been deployed in Syria. An increased state of readiness had probably been declared in some Soviet military units as well. At the Kremlin meeting on October 12, however, nobody expanded the issue of the protection of Soviet shipments and transportation to Egypt and Syria or raised the question of direct Soviet involvement in the war.

## EXPANDING MILITARY ASSISTANCE

At several meetings in the Kremlin on October 10, 11, and 12, the idea of giving the Arabs all kinds of additional support and advice prevailed. On October 10 the Politburo had taken note of Kulikov's report that the airlift of weapons and supplies to Syria and Egypt was under way and ordered an increase in supplies. At one of the meetings that followed, Ustinov informed the Politburo that the amount of military supplies sent to the Arabs had been multiplying since October 9. On October 11, Vinogradov and Mukhitdinov were instructed to convey to Sadat and Assad the Kremlin's decision to increase the military deliveries to Egypt and Syria and to emphasize the importance of coordinated action.

Special consideration at these meetings was given to Syrian losses. Kulikov's urgent proposal to send Syria more equipment and missiles to replace the losses from the Israeli air raids was endorsed. For a few days, deliveries to Syria exceeded those to Egypt. The military was charged with looking into Sadat's request to deliver to Egypt the Soviet surface-to-air Volga (SA-5) missiles promised to him. Without these missiles, Sadat had claimed in his encounter with Vinogradov on October 10, Egypt was not in a position to start an offensive.

In those days the Soviet ambassadors and military representatives in Egypt and Syria were instructed to render their "good advice" concerning the conduct of the war to their counterparts in Cairo and Damascus. Kulikov called Vinogradov almost every day, giving him all kinds of arguments for his talks with Egyptian leaders. In accordance with Moscow's instructions and Kulikov's advice, Vinogradov stressed in his talks with Sadat the importance of coordinated action in a coalition war. He said that the prospect of a war on two fronts would be fatal for Israel and that to miss this opportunity would be a great mistake. Referring to the highest Soviet military authorities, he stated that from the military point of view there was no justification for the "operational pause" on the Sinai front. He informed the Egyptian president that the Soviet command had given its approval to an Egyptian offensive and stated that if Egypt wanted to develop the attack in order to recover the Gidi and Mitla passes this should be done immediately. Vinogradov asked Sadat why he was allowing Syria to be bled white. He replied: "Let it go on the defensive and wage guerrilla warfare. Our main goal is to knock out as many enemy forces as possible."

Sadat did not like the advice of the Soviet command—it irritated him, because it conflicted with his plans. Sadat's "stubbornness" in turn made Kulikov furious, although he surely knew that as far back as March 1971 the Egyptian president had made his thinking crystal clear to the Soviet military. He had told the Soviet senior military adviser, General Vasilii Okunev, and his chief of staff, General Mahmut Gareyev: "I am concerned that the world public is losing interest in the Middle East problem. I have to shake up the world and draw its attention to this problem. I need to gain only ten centimeters of land east of Suez. That is all. Thereafter I will seek to end the war on terms acceptable to Egypt."

Unfortunately the Soviet military, following the path of the politicians, had not paid much attention to what Sadat said at that time. Little by little during the war, however, they began to understand that while Sadat was willing to let the Syrians do whatever they liked, he was planning his own action in a very different way. Grechko and Kulikov, followed by many members of the Politburo, voiced their conviction that it was Sadat's duty to inform the Syrians of his plan. In response to Vinogradov's arguments, Sadat only reminded the ambassador about the Soviet supply promises that had not been kept. The talks that the Soviet military attaché in Cairo, Ievlev, had with his Egyptian colleagues had the same result.

There was little advice Mukhitdinov could give to the Syrian leaders. Their hopes of liberating the Golan Heights and changing the regional balance of power were evaporating. The Syrian army was fighting stubbornly, but retreating nonetheless toward Damascus. In these circumstances, to discuss problems of coalition warfare with the Syrians was like rubbing salt on open wounds. Besides, the Soviet failure to meet Assad's request on the cease-fire issue had significantly affected the Syrian president's attitude toward Moscow. Mukhitdinov's aide, who had interpreted for the ambassador during his conversation with

Assad, recalled that Assad had once portrayed the Soviet Union's stance toward his appeal for an early cease-fire as "traitorous."

The large number of Soviet advisers assigned to almost every Syrian military unit tried to be efficient on a day-to-day basis. In addition, Soviet military technicians reassembled the fighter aircraft that were sealifted and airlifted from the Soviet Union to Syria, drove tanks from Syrian ports to Damascus, repaired tanks and military equipment damaged in the fighting, and so on.

And yet in those days I was puzzled by the Kremlin's attitude toward Syria. After Assad's call for help on October 8 and the speedy deterioration of Syria's military situation, one might have expected Moscow to give priority treatment to Syria, but that did not happen. The Kremlin continued to pay primary attention to the situation in Egypt, to its relationship with Sadat. To some extent this was natural, because of Egypt's leading role in the Arab world. Besides, Moscow's perception of Soviet-Egyptian relations was greatly affected by the personality of former President Nasser, who in the early 1960s was even in favor of Egypt's becoming a member of the Warsaw Treaty Organization.

During my stay in New York, I felt the special role that Moscow attached to relations with Egypt very clearly. The permanent missions of the Soviet Union and Egypt were located in the same neighborhood—on Sixty-seventh Street in Manhattan—and the ambassadors, their deputies, and other diplomats were frequent guests at both missions. Our contacts and cooperation in those days were many and great, and, it seems to me, effective.

I maintained friendly relations with the permanent representative of Syria, Georges Tomeh, as well. Both of us had the same academic background. I remember chats when the Syrian ambassador tried to explain to me Syria's negative attitude toward Security Council Resolution 242, an issue on which the positions of our countries had serious differences. These differences, however, could in my view by no means justify the Soviet position toward Syria in October 1973. Therefore I approached Sytenko and his deputy Evgenii Pyrlin and asked them to clarify Moscow's attitude toward Syria and toward Assad personally.

According to my colleagues, the Kremlin's position had deep roots. From the beginning of the Cold War, the Soviet Union had tried to play a dominant role in Syria's development. Sometimes its efforts had been successful: trade programs and joint projects were expanded, political ties and cooperation were intensified, diplomatic support was effectively rendered on many occasions, and so on. However, the Soviet Middle East experts believed that the Soviet Union had made serious mistakes and miscalculations in the assessment of political forces in Syria, especially after the coup by the Arab Socialist Resurrection (Ba'th) Party in 1966. Moscow supported the radical-civilian wing within the Ba'th Party, one of the main leaders of which was Salah Jadid, and did not like the nationalist-military faction headed by Assad. Assad was considered to be a temporary figure, an anti-Communist who was hostile to the Soviet Union. My colleagues put the blame for this miscalculation mainly on the Syrian Communists, who in the late 1960s launched an all-out attack on Assad's wing. The prestige of the leader of the Syrian Communist Party, Khalid Bakdash, was very high in Moscow. Ponomarev, in charge of Communist movements abroad, supported him. Although the Kremlin leaders favored Jadid, Assad's leadership was promptly accepted when Assad finally assumed full power in a coup in November 1970. Nevertheless, their stereotype of Assad, drawn with the assistance of Bakdash, remained in the minds of the Kremlin leaders. This could partly explain the Soviet Union's inconclusive and limited response to Assad's plea for an immediate cease-fire and to the Syrian defeat on the Golan Heights. It seems to me that the sentence in the cable sent to Malik on the first day of the war (to act in accordance with the position of Egypt in case the position of the two Arab states differed) was originated by the same "old thinking" so typical of the Brezhnev era.

The day after my encounter with Sytenko and Pyrlin, I received a copy of a clipping containing Assad's statement regarding the radical Ba'thists' collusion with the Communists, published in Beirut's *Al-Hayat* on October 13, 1968. The anti-Communist and anti-Soviet statement suggested that the Soviet Union was interfering in Syria's domestic affairs. I was sure this statement was well known to the Politburo members too. Many years after these events, I talked with one of the best experts on the Middle East in the Central Committee, Karen Brutenz, who explained the Soviet Union's attitude toward Syria during the Yom Kippur War along the same lines.

Another kind of activity of the Soviet military representatives is worth mentioning. In accordance with an order from the Defense Ministry, the Soviet military attachés and their employees were to collect samples of any equipment and weaponry made or produced in the United States, other Western states, or Israel and captured by the Arabs or left by the Israelis on the battlefields, and send them to Moscow immediately. Ievlev and his colleagues collected about sixty samples of different equipment on the Sinai front, but when they tried to send them to the western bank of the Suez Canal, the Egyptian authorities confiscated the samples as military trophies. The Soviet Defense Ministry had a particular interest in the new American M-60 tanks, a few of which had been captured by the Egyptians. Grechko himself ordered Ievlev to send one of the captured tanks to Moscow, but it took almost a week before the Egyptians agreed to hand the tank over. A special Antonov airplane was sent from Moscow to Cairo to pick it up and bring it to the Soviet Union. After difficult negotiations with the Egyptian military authorities, another trophy—the newest pilotless Israeli fighter, shot down by the Egyptians and exhibited together with other trophies in Cairo—was sent to Moscow. Ievlev succeeded in persuading his Egyptian colleagues to replace the original Israeli fighter with a dummy plane at the trophy exhibition.

In Damascus the Soviet military advisers and technicians took action along the same lines. Moscow was very pleased with the delivery from Syria of sophisticated modern electronic equipment deployed on Mount Hermon in the Golan Heights and captured by the Syrians in the first days of the war. Soviet technicians participated in the dismantling of some installations and acquired valuable information.

## "WE SHOULD NOT BE FOOLED"

During a discussion about Soviet military deliveries to the Arabs at the Politburo meeting on October 12, KGB Chief Andropov, who supported an increase in supplies, stated that according to the information at his disposal the Americans had been resupplying the Israelis from the very beginning of the war. He claimed that President Nixon had given the green light not only to the delivery of equipment and weaponry but also to certain military moves aimed at demonstrating America's strong support of Israel. The Americans were seeking all kinds of roundabout ways to deliver weaponry to Israel, he said, "but we should not be fooled." Referring to the undeniable information and reports published in some foreign newspapers, Andropov asked, "Are we going to put up with secret American supplies?" He was seconded by Kulikov, who said military intelligence had described movements of the American Sixth Fleet aircraft carriers toward the Suez Canal. Andropov advised Brezhnev to let the American President know the Soviets are not "blind kittens" and also suggested that the Soviet media keep the public informed about U.S. support of Israel.

Andropov's position was shared by other participants in the meeting. Brezhnev ordered Andropov, in consultation with Gromyko, to draft a message to Nixon that was "strong and to the point" regarding American military assistance and supplies to Israel. Andropov promised to fill the message with concrete facts. The resulting message, however, was based on stories published in the press and stated that the Soviet Union was aware that the United States was supplying Israel with fighters, tanks, missiles, and bombs. It also repeated rumors that 150 American pilots were going to Israel disguised as tourists. Andropov's statement at the Politburo meeting had sounded much more impressive than the "facts" in Brezhnev's message. Late in the evening, October 12, two messages from Brezhnev were sent to Washington: the one concerning the Israeli bombings, mentioned above, and this other message concerning the U.S. military supplies.

I must say that the October 12 Politburo meeting was perhaps the gloomiest throughout the Yom Kippur War. Being in the Kremlin on that day, I had the feeling that events were slipping out of Soviet control, and I believe some of my colleagues had the same feeling. The anger at the Americans and, especially, the Israelis came out in snide and profane comments by the Politburo members in the conference hall, and even more by their aides outside the hall. I cannot remember any particular person who made such comments, but I can say that the general mood at the meeting was militant. That was alarming. As far as Brezhnev's messages to Nixon were concerned, they did not seem very convincing—particularly the message dealing with American assistance to Israel. Perhaps Andropov did not want to disclose the sources of his information. I do not know.

The Soviet media intensified their reports of U.S. assistance to Israel, and starting on October 13 the reports were dispersed regularly. As a rule, they referred to American and West European sources. On October 14 all leading Soviet newspapers published American press reports of U.S. assistance to Israel. The same day, some papers quoted a statement by Arab ambassadors in Paris who claimed that American pilots had participated in the bombing of Damascus. On October 15, *Pravda* cited the *Wall Street Journal,* which said that the participation of American volunteers in the Middle East fighting was part of the U.S. effort to assist Israel. These reports were accompanied by the first public Soviet accusations of American involvement in the war.

Meanwhile, the issue of Soviet propaganda concerning the war was dealt with on October 13 at the Politburo Ad Hoc Commission on the Middle East. This commission had been set up on October 10 and chaired by Mikhail Suslov, the main ideologist of the Communist Party. Suslov acknowledged that the Soviet media were giving too little attention to the Middle East war and not glorifying the military achievements of the Egyptians and the "heroic resistance" of the Syrians. He was supported by Ponomarev and Katushev, who suggested that the Soviet media, especially broadcasts to the Arab states, stress that the Arabs had been trained and armed by the Soviet Union.

The call for Arab unity and solidarity of all "progressive forces" with the Arab peoples continued to be a main thesis of the huge Soviet propaganda machine. In the "October Revolution Slogans of the CC of the CPSU," a guiding document for all Soviet Communists and usually proclaimed on the eve of the anniversary of the revolution, published in 1973 on October 14, this thesis was formulated in the following way: "May solidarity with the Arab peoples in their just struggle broaden and grow stronger." In the weekly review of international events, *Pravda*'s commentator emphasized that the strengthening of Arab unity and the solidarity of all progressive forces with the Arab struggle was playing an increasing role.[14] From time to time, reports from different countries about broadening solidarity with the Arabs emerged in the Soviet press.

An attempt to hail Arab military gains was made in the Defense Ministry's newspaper, *Krasnaya Zvezda*. On October 13 the paper published a commentary by a Captain N. Pustov under the headline "The Aggressor Receives a Rebuff." The general tone of the commentary was optimistic and confident about the Arab military performance, and it praised the Egyptian army especially as "well trained and equipped with modern arms."[15] The article received broad coverage in the Western press mainly because it predicted "a long, tiresome war" in which the Arabs and the Soviet Union both would presumably be embroiled. When Brezhnev was informed by his aide, Alexandrov, of the Western interpretation of Pustov's article, he was furious. "Perhaps, we shall send the captain to the Sinai?" the General Secretary roared. This conversation took place after the Israelis had started their successful counteroffensive on the western bank of the Canal.

## THE DIPLOMATIC GAME OVER A CEASE-FIRE CONTINUES

Although Kremlin leaders dropped the idea of a Soviet initiative in the Security Council for an early cease-fire after a number of fruitless talks between Sadat and Vinogradov in the first days of the war, the cessation of fighting in the Middle East remained a priority task of Soviet policy. This, of course, was not consistent with continued military aid to the Arabs, but the reasons for an early end to the war were becoming clear. On the one hand, the Israelis had turned the tide on the Golan Heights, and the military situation in the Middle East was deteriorating in general, leading to the prospect of a protracted war that could threaten Soviet security interests. On the other hand, tension was rising between Washington and Moscow as each continued to blame the other for the extension of hostilities. In light of these developments, Kremlin leaders concluded that every effort had to be made to end the war.

This had been discussed at a meeting in Brezhnev's office on the morning of October 10. At that meeting, Soviet Foreign Minister Gromyko summed up the latest diplomatic moves on the cease-fire issue in Damascus, Cairo, Washington, and New York, and also noted that Moscow had not yet answered Nixon's proposal of October 6, concerning a cease-fire. Furthermore, the only instruction the Soviet representative in the Security Council had in case a cease-fire resolution unacceptable to the Arabs came to a vote was to veto it. Gromyko suggested that the Americans be told that Moscow was having difficult and protracted consultations with the Syrians and Egyptians aimed at getting them to agree to a cessation of the fighting. Although those consultations were to continue, Washington should be informed that the Soviet Union was at present prepared for the Security Council action on this matter. If a resolution were offered, Gromyko recommended that the Soviet Union abstain on a cease-fire-in-place and veto a call for status quo ante, the return of Arab troops to the prewar lines. He did not, however, suggest that the Soviet Union table a resolution or encourage other members of the Security Council to do so. He rejected a suggestion to inform the Americans about the differences between Sadat and Assad on the cease-fire issue.

First Deputy Kuznetsov, who was invited to participate in the discussion, favored Soviet sponsorship of a Security Council resolution and was persistent in showing the advantages of such a Soviet initiative. According to him, a short resolution containing a call for an immediate cease-fire, as a first step toward a comprehensive, just, and stable settlement in the Middle East, would comply fully with the strategic goals of Assad and Sadat and with the overall policy of the Soviet Union. At the same time, as Kuznetsov saw it, neither the Americans nor the Chinese would dare to veto the resolution. But the opinion of this experienced diplomat was not shared by other participants. Brezhnev believed that such a unilateral step could motivate criticism among the Arabs and be interpreted by the Americans as a challenge to the Soviet-U.S. coordinated line in the conflict. This was another example of a futile attempt to combine two incompatible courses of action.

The result was that our task force drafted instructions to Dobrynin and Malik along the lines of Gromyko's suggestions. In talks with Kissinger, Dobrynin was to stress the Kremlin's readiness to cooperate with Washington on the cease-fire issue, but also Soviet determination to guarantee the liberation of all lands occupied by Israel. Malik was instructed to abstain on a cease-fire resolution and after the vote to make a statement emphasizing the legitimacy of the Arabs' struggle aimed at the withdrawal of the Israeli occupants. Of course, he would have to veto any resolution that called for a status quo ante.

The next day, October 11, we received answers from Washington and New York. Dobrynin reported that he had talked with Kissinger several times but that the latter was delaying an affirmative response and showing no great interest in taking any Security Council action at that moment. Malik's cable was also dissatisfying: No meeting of the Security Council was scheduled yet, and to his knowledge no delegation intended to offer a cease-fire resolution. Malik reported on his meeting with John Scali, at which he had explained the new Soviet position to the American representative. Scali had understood Malik to mean that "Moscow was now *proposing* an immediate end to the fighting," and he had communicated as much to the U.S. State Department.[16] Thus there were no substantial moves on the cease-fire issue at the diplomatic scene on October 11.

Brezhnev was becoming impatient. The stalemate in the diplomatic negotiations, and the American delaying tactic, made him angry. In addition, the arrogant Israeli action, highlighted by the sinking of the Soviet merchant ship, had to be responded to one way or another. On October 12, Gromyko asked our group to come up with some additional steps to get the cease-fire issue moving. After a discussion chaired by Kuznetsov, we came to the conclusion that the Soviet Union should act immediately and, if necessary, unilaterally.

The same day, we and colleagues from the Foreign Ministry's Department of International Organizations drafted instructions for Malik to press for an urgent meeting of the Security Council. We told him that if neither the Americans nor any other delegation had approached the president of the Security Council yet, Malik himself was to ask for a meeting. He was instructed to stipulate that the format should be a short discussion that must end with adoption of a resolution that should read along the following lines:

> The Security Council,
>     deeply concerned with the renewal of hostilities and the threatening situation in the Middle East,
>     taking note of the statements made in the Council,
>     1. urges all governments concerned, as a first step to undertake all measures for an immediate cease-fire and end of all military activity in the region;
>     2. asks the United Nations Secretary General to immediately inform the Security Council of any developments in the situation.

Our draft did not contain a reference to Security Council Resolution 242 because Syria strongly opposed it. The task force was of the opinion that the draft resolution would be tabled by friendly nonaligned members of the Security Council (Yugoslavia, Guinea, India, Peru), so as a last resort Malik was to offer the draft on behalf of the Soviet delegation. After the resolution was adopted, Malik was to state that the warring parties should stay in place.

The next morning, October 13, we showed our draft to Gromyko. Although he did not like it much, he said he was ready to discuss it at the meeting of Suslov's commission later the same morning. The discussion at that meeting was, however, disappointing. Gromyko briefly told the commission what the draft said, and once again we had to listen to empty-headed statements about the need to strengthen cooperation with our "Arab friends" while at the same time avoiding a confrontation with the United States by our unilateral actions. Suslov, Ponomarev, and Katushev were against instructing Malik to offer a draft resolution at the Security Council, as we had suggested, without consulting the Arabs first, and Gromyko did not argue with that. The only idea that got general support was a proposal to urge the nonaligned states to action in the Security Council in cooperation with the Soviet Union.

As a result of this discussion, Vinogradov was advised by cable the same day to meet with Sadat and ask his opinion of a possible Soviet move in the Security Council in the new circumstances because the United States had apparently lost interest in a cease-fire. Vinogradov was also to find out what Sadat thought of an initiative by Yugoslavia or another friendly nonaligned state.

In the early afternoon of October 13, after the cable had been sent to Vinogradov, a report from Dobrynin arrived with news of a Kissinger proposal that Great Britain introduce a cease-fire-in-place resolution at the Security Council meeting on October 13. Pleased that instructions for unilateral action had not yet been sent to Malik, Gromyko asked me to call Malik and ask him about the latest developments at the United Nations. I got the line to New York at approximately 5:00 P.M. Moscow time (10:00 A.M. New York time) and was surprised to learn that no meeting of the Security Council was scheduled for Saturday, October 13, or Sunday, October 14. (Actually, the next Security Council meeting was not called to order until October 21.)

Here was another puzzle in the cease-fire resolution superpower game. Not until Sunday, October 14, did we learn from our ambassadors in Washington, New York, and Cairo that Kissinger's idea had failed. The British, who at first agreed to act as authors of a draft resolution, having been rebuffed by Sadat and being fearful of establishing a relationship with any of the countries participating in the war, finally backed off.

Cheerless and gloomy was our temper when we, the members of the task force, got together at the Foreign Ministry the morning of October 14. Vinogradov's report was waiting for us. The ambassador said the Egyptian president was unimpressed when he heard that the Americans had lost interest in a speedy end to the hostilities in the Middle East and was against a Soviet initiative in the Security Council for a cease-fire-in-place resolution. Because a cease-fire-in-place would be politically detrimental to the Arabs at present, Sadat said, the Soviet Union should not promote a solution that was unacceptable to Egypt and Syria. As far as a proposal by Yugoslavia was concerned, it would be acceptable to Sadat as long as it contained a provision for withdrawal of Israeli troops to the 1967 borders—alas, another taboo broken by the Egyptian president. With regard to Syria, I do not remember Assad being consulted on the eventual new Soviet initiative in the Security Council.

The situation was going from bad to worse. A full week had elapsed since the Soviet Union had tried to bring the hostilities to a favorable end. All efforts had been in vain. We had numerous chats in the task force—sometimes with Gromyko participating, sometimes among ourselves—about the reasons for our failures. Kissinger's last scheme, to ask the British to introduce a cease-fire resolution, had been a move to gain time badly needed by the Israelis—that was obvious. We evaluated it as a typical "Anglo-American imperialist plot" against the foreign policy of the Soviet Union and its friends in the Middle East.

But what was wrong with Sadat? Why did he adamantly reject all Soviet proposals? Was he playing up to the Americans? Some explanation is needed here. The Soviet leaders had been aware of several secret contacts between Sadat and Kissinger via Hafiz Ismail, Sadat's national security adviser. Once, on October 9, Brezhnev even instructed Vinogradov to ask Sadat "in a delicate way" about the secret connections the Egyptians had with the Americans. In carrying out Brezhnev's directive—perhaps with insufficient "delicacy"—Vinogradov provoked Sadat's rage. "We do not have any secrets from our Soviet friends. I will punish anybody who maintains such a connection!" the Egyptian president shouted, according to Vinogradov. The next day, October 10, Ismail had informed Vinogradov of his latest message to Kissinger. Although the KGB resident in Cairo claimed that he and his colleagues had been well informed of American-Egyptian secret links, it seems to me that they were not. At least we diplomats, members of the task force, did not know about the extensive correspondence between Cairo and Washington concerning a settlement in the Middle East. Unfortunately, neither did Vinogradov, as he later admitted.[17]

The main reason for the failure to secure a cease-fire, however, was Moscow's doctrinaire, authoritarian judgment of the position of the United States and the warring parties, and the unwillingness of the Kremlin leaders to understand the specific interests and perceptions of the participants in a perplexing military and diplomatic conflict.

The entire performance on the cease-fire issue was disappointing, but we continued it anyway. Following Gromyko's directive, a message to Yugoslav President Tito in Brezhnev's name was prepared and sent to the Soviet ambassador in Belgrade, Vladimir Stepakov, on October 14 with instructions to deliver it immediately. The Soviet message claimed that Sadat had approved of a cease-fire resolution calling for withdrawal of Israeli troops, maybe in stages but within a strictly limited period of time. Brezhnev asked whether Yugoslavia would be willing to introduce such a draft resolution in the Security Council. Late in the afternoon of the same day, Moscow received a reply from Stepakov asserting that Tito shared Brezhnev's opinion and that Yugoslavia would be ready to introduce a draft resolution on behalf of the eight nonaligned states, the nonpermanent members of the Security Council. We were very much surprised by the speed of Tito's response but had to wait for further developments.

Then we received another surprise, this time from Washington. Dobrynin informed Moscow that as of October 13 Washington's position on a Security Council resolution was based on the following two points: (1) a cease-fire-in-place and (2) subsequent withdrawal of troops (maybe in stages) in accordance with Security Council Resolution 242. At first glance, the American position, the "Basic Principles of an Eventual Resolution of the Security Council," seemed attractive—but only at first glance. Being aware of the loose interpretations of Resolution 242 and of the strong opposition to the resolution by some Arab and nonaligned states, we realized that a resolution with the wording proposed by the Americans would not go through at the present time. Nevertheless, we members of the task force were happy, and so were our bosses. At last Washington was showing a readiness to get down to business on the cease-fire issue. For several days, starting October 10, Dobrynin had been bombarded with instructions from Moscow to urge the Americans to respond to the Soviet ideas concerning the cease-fire. Dobrynin tried with all his diplomatic skill to carry out the instructions during his numerous encounters with Kissinger, thus manifesting Moscow's ardent desire to stop the fighting in the Middle East. Therefore, it was odd for me to read later in Kissinger's memoirs that, to Kissinger, the behavior of the Soviet Union in those days was puzzling: "Had they [the Soviet Union] been stringing us along, never intending to have a cease-fire? Did they maneuver to prolong the war?"[18] How could the grand master of diplomacy have failed to see that the Soviet Union's quest for a speedy cease-fire was guided by a desire to assist its clients in their deteriorating military situation, the same way the American policy aimed at delaying a cease-fire was in the interests of its client, whose military situation was improving very quickly. The motivations of the two superpowers were the same.

Unfortunately, Tito's consent to initiate a move in the Security Council by the nonaligned states manacled any further Soviet action on the cease-fire issue, at least on October 14. Gromyko told us members of the task force to wait for the results of Tito's mission. Furthermore, we learned that in the evening of October 14 Algerian President Boumedienne was expected in the Kremlin for negotiation with Brezhnev. What kind of ideas would he submit to our leaders? How would the forthcoming talks affect the attitude of the Kremlin?

## BOUMEDIENNE'S VISIT TO MOSCOW

Boumedienne's visit to Moscow was not planned ahead of time and took place at the initiative of the Algerian president, who arrived in the Soviet capital with a large delegation on Sunday afternoon, October 14. At 7:00 P.M., he and his colleagues were already in the Kremlin and negotiations had started. The Soviet participants were Brezhnev, Podgorny, Kosygin, Gromyko, and Grechko. Algeria was represented by President Boumedienne, State Minister Sharif Belqasem, Minister of Higher Education and Research Mohammed Ben Yahya, Colonel Hadj Mohammed Zergini, and Algerian Ambassador to Moscow Reda Malek. Our four-man task force was also invited to the Kremlin, but we and the large team of Algerian aides did not participate in the talks directly. Only Kuznetsov was called in several times, and he was able to inform us briefly on the course and content of the negotiations. Incredibly, the negotiations lasted all night, adjourning at 5:30 A.M. All this time we were sitting in the "Round Room" of the Kremlin lobby, briefing our bosses on the latest news from the Middle East and elsewhere.

After greeting the Algerian guests, Brezhnev expressed his hope that the negotiations would be conducted in a friendly atmosphere and that the contents of the talks would be kept confidential, referring pointedly to the recent publication of his personal messages in the Algerian press. In response, the Algerian president thanked Brezhnev and said that between friends there was nothing to conceal. A debatable point.

The main subject of the negotiations was Boumedienne's appeal to the Soviet leaders to intensify and increase the supplies to Egypt and Syria. He spoke at length about the Arab victories and their impact on the world situation, about the great losses that had to be recouped, about the importance of the Soviet Union's effective and timely support, and so on. One time when Kuznetsov returned from the conference hall he said with a smile, "He [Boumedienne] continues to lecture." For almost as long, Brezhnev explained Soviet policy in the Middle East, underlined the crucial role of Soviet weaponry and training in the Arab victories, and complained that the Egyptians and Syrians were disunited and uncoordinated and that their political and military leaders were not following friendly Soviet advice. Brezhnev referred to notes containing data on Soviet supplies sent to Egypt and Syria and drew Boumedienne's attention to the growing Soviet airlift and sealift to the Arabs. He expressed his disappointment with the modest assistance the other Arab states had given to Egypt and Syria.

When Boumedienne said that Algeria would be ready to pay for urgent additional supplies of weapons and equipment for Egypt and Syria, the Soviet participants agreed. An agreement was also reached on the Algerian request to purchase some Soviet weaponry and to replace old equipment.

Much time was devoted to a comprehensive analysis of the prospects for a Middle East settlement, a discussion that revealed different, almost opposite, approaches to the problem. Boumedienne was unequivocally in favor of continuing the war against Israel. He believed that only a military defeat of Israel could guarantee security and peace in the region, as well as restoration of Palestinian rights. Brezhnev, on the other hand, focused on the need to revive the process of coming to political settlement. He referred to the extremely difficult military situation of Syria and to the negative impact of the Egyptian "operational pause" on the conduct of the war.

At this time, first words of the failure of the new Egyptian offensive were beginning to reach Moscow, and they were immediately reported to Brezhnev, who made full use of them in his argument. The Soviet leader pointed out that the Soviet Union was strongly against expanding the conflict, and he firmly emphasized that the Soviet Union did not intend to become involved in the war. Boumedienne stated that he did not want the war to expand either and that he would not oppose any political settlement that was acceptable and favorable to Egypt and Syria, but he was doubtful that at present this could be achieved.

Finally, Boumedienne, in his capacity as a chairman of the Non-Aligned Movement (NAM), informed his Soviet partners of the position of the nonaligned states at the conference on the Middle East held in Algeria in September, and expressed his confidence in NAM's crucial role in international affairs and in particular in a Middle East settlement. Brezhnev, while agreeing with Boumedienne's high appraisal of the Non-Aligned Movement, asked him to support any peaceful initiative advanced by its members that pertained to the Middle East conflict. Boumedienne promised to do his best to ensure NAM's widest backing of any political initiative acceptable to Syria and Egypt.

The participants in the talks agreed to issue a brief communiqué regarding Boumedienne's visit to Moscow that would emphasize the firm determination of both sides to help in every way the liberation of all Arab territories occupied by Israel.

After ten and a half hours of almost uninterrupted negotiations, Brezhnev adjourned the meeting and the Algerian guests left the Kremlin. The Soviet interpreter joined our group in the "Round Room," saying that he had never attended such dull and boring performances. To our great surprise, Brezhnev, Podgorny, Kosygin, Gromyko, and Grechko stayed in the conference room for another hour. It was almost 7:00 A.M., October 15, when Brezhnev's secretary told us that the five had retired for the rest of the day. We followed suit immediately. What was the subject of the last hour's discussion in the aftermath of the protracted negotiations? One could only guess, but some developments of the next day, it seemed to me, provided at least a partial answer.

# CHAPTER 4

# KOSYGIN'S VISIT TO CAIRO

## "THE SOVIET UNION DOES NOT SEEK ANYTHING FOR ITSELF IN THE REGION"

Unable to sleep that morning, I went to my office in the early afternoon of Monday, October 15. At Gromyko's behest, my colleagues from the Department of International Organizations had prepared two versions of a Security Council draft resolution on the cease-fire, in response to the latest American proposal concerning the "Basic Principles of an Eventual Resolution of the Security Council" received in Moscow on Sunday, October 14.

Each was very brief, consisting of two paragraphs. Paragraph one of the first version called on parties in the fighting to agree to a cease-fire and end all military activities immediately; paragraph two urged "a staged withdrawal of Israeli troops from the occupied Arab territories in accordance with Security Council Resolution 242, completing the withdrawal within an agreed upon period of time." The reference to Resolution 242 was included because the American document contained it.

The second version differed little from the first. It defined the terms of the cease-fire more specifically, calling on the parties to remain in the positions they occupied at the moment of the cease-fire, and indicating the duration of the period for the withdrawal of Israeli troops. The authors of the draft left it to Gromyko to fix the precise length of that period. When we discussed the drafts with Gromyko, he preferred the second version, but he made some changes that, from my point of view, were not likely to be accepted by the Americans. He suggested linking the cease-fire to the withdrawal and limiting the length of the withdrawal to three weeks. I tried to point out that this was unrealistic but failed to convince him. Gromyko ordered us to flesh out the final version for discussion at the next Politburo meeting, scheduled for Monday evening, October 15.

I was disappointed with Gromyko's position. Usually he was reasonable, would listen to the arguments of subordinates, and could be persuaded. This time, it was obvious to me that even he did not believe his version of the resolution would carry in the Security Council, but he stubbornly stuck to his position. Throughout my decades of diplomatic service I had occasionally faced such strange behavior of my bosses. Once, in a one-on-one situation when he was in a good mood and I continued to ask the reason for what I thought was a rather odd opinion, he smiled and said: "Look, I'm afraid the answer to your question is too complicated and lies beyond your comprehension." Eventually I came to understand that sometimes Gromyko's positions had nothing to do with international politics, but instead fell in the category of "domestic diplomacy," aimed at gaining points in the competitive struggle among the Kremlin leaders themselves. Perhaps in this instance Gromyko did not want to be accused of being too mild in dealing with the Americans—the greatest crime a Soviet politician could commit—so he decided to demonstrate his Marxist-Leninist orthodoxy and toughness by suggesting a resolution he knew would be totally unacceptable to the Americans. Who knows? The two versions of the draft submitted to Gromyko had linked the cease-fire to troop withdrawal and hence had little chance of being accepted by the United States anyway.

The Politburo meeting scheduled for Monday, October 15, was preceded by some important diplomatic events, in the course of which the war in the Middle East was discussed. On that day, negotiations between the prime minister of Denmark, Anker Jorgensen, and Soviet Prime Minister Kosygin began in Moscow. In addition to stating the Soviet Union's great interest in such vital issues as the relaxation of tension in Europe and elsewhere, Kosygin emphasized in the talks the utmost importance of finding ways to settle the conflict in the Middle East. He also expressed indignation regarding insinuations that the Soviet Union's solidarity with the Arabs was the source of tension in the region. Nothing could be further from the truth, he said. This was a response to those in the West, mainly in the United States, who had accused the Nixon administration of allowing the Soviet Union to use the policy of East-West conciliation to the detriment of Israel. According to Kosygin, the Soviet Union would do everything to promote improved relations with the West, "but of course not at the price of sacrificing its principles," including "the principle of resolute rebuff of imperialist aggression."[1]

Although Kosygin did not touch on the issue of an immediate cease-fire, he several times voiced the Soviet Union's desire to find a long-lasting settlement in the Middle East. "All our actions are aimed at helping the peoples of the Arab countries liberate their lands seized by Israel, achieve a just political settlement, strengthen their independence, create a flourishing national economy, and develop along the road of progress," Kosygin said at the state luncheon. "The Soviet Union does not seek anything for itself in the region," he declared emphatically.[2]

Brezhnev spoke along the same general lines when he met with Jorgensen the next day, October 16. The Soviet-Danish talks did not play a significant role in the settlement of the Middle East crisis, but the Kremlin used them as an opportunity to reject any suggestions by the West that the Soviet Union's solidarity with the Arabs cast doubt on Moscow's sincere commitment to détente. The West liked the tune of Kosygin's and Brezhnev's speeches. "The Soviet leaders were reported today," wrote the *New York Times* correspondent from Moscow on October 16, "to have emphasized in private talks with Premier Anker Jorgensen of Denmark their keen interest in finding a permanent settlement of the Arab-Israeli conflict."[3]

## ANOTHER NIGHT MEETING IN THE KREMLIN

The meeting of the Politburo on October 15 was an important one. The discussion went far beyond the cease-fire issue. Almost all the members of the Politburo and the secretaries of the Central Committee attended that meeting, which went from about nine o'clock in the evening until 4:00 A.M. the next day, October 16. The meeting was conducted in a rather disorderly, almost chaotic, manner. Participants switched from one subject to another, sometimes interrupting one another, now and then repeating themselves. The discussion focused primarily on the following subjects: the military situation in the Middle East, Soviet-Arab cooperation, the United States' increasing support to Israel, Soviet-American relations, and the prospects for a cease-fire. Some other topics, including China's position and the Arab oil embargo, were also touched on. The principal participants in the discussion—apart from Brezhnev, who chaired the meeting—were Kosygin, Podgorny, Gromyko, Grechko, and Andropov.

Brezhnev briefly informed the Politburo members about the negotiations with Algerian President Boumedienne, which he characterized as an Arab attempt to entangle the Soviet Union deeper in the Middle East conflict, and stated that the time had come for effective and decisive measures in the Middle East. The Soviet participants in the talks with Boumedienne, he pointed out, had concluded that an urgent visit of Prime Minister Kosygin to Cairo for talks with President Sadat, which could start as soon as October 16, would serve that purpose. Brezhnev invited the members of the Politburo to express their views on this decision.

No opposition to Kosygin's visit to Cairo was voiced, and no one asked why Kosygin, not Foreign Minister Gromyko, was chosen for the mission. One thing, however, seemed to be obvious: Kosygin himself was not happy with the decision. Throughout the meeting, time and again, he asked the Politburo to formulate clear-cut, distinct instructions for his mission, but none was forthcoming. One could interpret the choice of Kosygin for the mission as recognition of his international prestige and his knowledge of Middle East politics. Perhaps this decision—which was initiated by Brezhnev himself, as Kosygin's aide, Boris Bazanov, told me—was also an issue of "domestic diplomacy"?

Kulikov, in his assessment of the military situation, noted that the early Egyptian offensive had been repulsed, although the Egyptians claimed that their forces were consolidating their position. He expressed disappointment with the military stalemate. I do not remember Kulikov saying anything about the Israeli move to cross the Canal or to outflank the Egyptian Third Army. But he considered an Israeli counteraction reversing Egyptian gains from the first days of the war likely. Whether his anticipation was based on military intelligence reports or was a habitual Soviet assessment of the prospects of the war was not clear.

The military situation in the Middle East was appraised as critical.

Brezhnev recommended that Kosygin draw Sadat's attention to the irreparable consequences of a possible Israeli breakthrough at the Suez Canal. "Remind him [Sadat]," he advised, "that Cairo is not far away from the Canal." Andropov seconded Brezhnev and, referring to the gradually worsening military situation of the Arabs, recommended explaining to Sadat that the Soviet leadership did not intend to stop the struggle in the military or political sphere either. "But now," he said, "for tactical reasons it would be better to consolidate the present situation." Many participants in the discussion, impressed by the initial victories of the Arabs, believed that because Sadat's limited war aims had been achieved the war had to be ended. Podgorny said that although the Egyptians had succeeded in crossing the Canal the liberation of the Sinai Peninsula could not be accomplished. Grechko supported this view, saying that the Egyptians and the Syrians had made good use of their surprise attack against Israel: "It was a great victory, and it was achieved without serious losses."

I was struck by an apparent change in Grechko's view of the Egyptian and Syrian conduct of the war. In the first days of the war he had been skeptical about it, but now he emphasized the extreme difficulties the Arabs were facing in the war, and their high fighting spirit. When Brezhnev interrupted Grechko and declared that the Egyptians were incompetent pilots shooting down their own aircraft, Grechko disagreed and praised the pilots, though mainly the Syrians and the Iraqis.

Grechko pointed out that the Middle East conflict was a coalition war in which other countries besides Egypt and Syria were involved on the Arab side, including Iraq, Jordan, Saudi Arabia, and the Sudan. According to him, this complicated the conduct of military operations, especially on the Syrian front. Grechko thought it would be advisable to take this into consideration when determining Soviet policy, and not jeopardize the Arab coalition by consulting only the Egyptian president. Thus he proposed to limit Kosygin's mission to an exploratory one.

Grechko's position was not shared by others. Many underlined the fact that actually two states were waging the war against Israel——Egypt and Syria—and that other Arab states were only supporting them. Iraq was singled out as the most active and Algeria was a "torpedo," as Brezhnev put it. The proposal that Kosygin's mission to Cairo be exploratory was turned down firmly by several participants in the meeting, who stated that such a mission would only prolong the war. Grechko did not insist on his position, but he shared the general view that the time had come to end the war.

Almost everyone at the meeting believed that, no matter what the military outcome of the war, relations between the Soviet Union and the Arab states should be strengthened and broadened. Naturally, therefore, Moscow's relationship with Cairo was in the foreground of the discussion, with everyone fully aware of the difficulties Kosygin would face in his talks with Sadat. Podgorny, for example, believed that Kosygin's mission would be fruitless, claiming that it would be almost impossible to convince Sadat to end the war. "Sadat can tell [Kosygin] that he would be killed for his agreement to give up the fight [against Israel]," he said.

Brezhnev too devoted much of his concluding remarks to the Kremlin's attitude toward the Arab states, Egypt, and the Egyptian president in particular. All his references concerning the Arabs were much milder than some of his remarks during the discussion. Such phrases as "our Arab friends" and "our common goals with the Arabs" occurred several times. He advised Kosygin to remind Sadat that the Soviet leaders had always warned him of the grave consequences of a war and that, although the friendly advice of Moscow was sometimes ignored, the Soviet Union still supported the Arabs and would continue that support. "You have to conduct the negotiations in a calm, comradely way," Brezhnev continued. "Give him our regards and best wishes, our congratulations on the military victories. Tell him that a friend in need is a friend indeed. Dissuade him from thinking that Moscow does not trust him." His most interesting expression, however, was the following: "Sadat made a number of mistakes—the expulsion of Soviet military personnel to start with. I know he is sorry for that. Unfortunately ambition and prestige do not allow him to say it publicly."

What a totally wrong perception of Sadat! Alas, at the time this was the prevailing Kremlin assessment of the Egyptian president and his policy, and the Soviet Union's overall policy toward Egypt was based on this false perception. "Be flexible, maneuver, do anything required so as not to quarrel with the Arab world. We must not provoke Sadat to declare that we are undermining friendship with the Arabs," Brezhnev instructed Kosygin.

The issue of Soviet military supplies to Egypt and Syria came up again, in connection with the general problem of Soviet-Arab relations. Podgorny strongly favored expanding Soviet aid and assistance to the Arab states, in order to keep up with the increasing amount of military supplies the United States was sending to Israel. Kosygin, however, suggested telling Sadat that if he "continues to lose a thousand tanks a week we will not be able to replace such losses." Brezhnev agreed with Kosygin. He advised reminding Sadat that the Soviet Union had responded positively to many Egyptian requests, and explaining how difficult it was for the Soviet Union to assemble and transport large amounts of weaponry and ammunition. Brezhnev instructed Kosygin to assure Sadat that the Soviet Union could continue sending the supplies but that the Soviets could not endlessly send replacements for huge Arab losses.

In the midst of the discussion, Gromyko asked unpretentiously: "Perhaps we and the Americans should stop military supplies [to the Arabs and to Israel] entirely?" There were no comments on this remark, but, summing up the discussion, Brezhnev turned Gromyko's idea down. He believed that even if the Americans raised this possibility the Soviet Union could not "officially" go along with such an idea. "This would be a violation of our signed agreements to supply the Arabs with defensive weapons," he noted. Instead, Brezhnev suggested urging the Americans to stop their military supplies to Israel unilaterally. Nobody, of course, argued with the General Secretary. His idea reminded me of the typical Soviet formula for international negotiations: "What is mine is mine, what is yours should be negotiated."

The policy of the United States was another subject of discussion. Gromyko noted that there had been a certain increase in American support of Israel, resulting from the activity of Zionists in the United States. American military and financial assistance would gradually increase, he said, and complicate a Middle East settlement. Kuznetsov shared Gromyko's assessment and referred to Dobrynin's cabled reports of conversations with Secretary of State Henry Kissinger. Kosygin complained that Moscow did not have a clear picture of the U.S. position. "In conversations with Dobrynin, the secretary of state time and time again repeats, 'This is my personal opinion, but not the President's.' Is it not a ploy? Kissinger is a tricky person," the prime minister remarked with annoyance.

I would like to note that Kissinger's tactic of expressing his "personal opinion" or "thinking aloud," which he resorted to frequently in diplomatic talks, caused anger in West European states as well as in Moscow. Some of my colleagues told me that this style was not well received in their capitals. "We are not interested in Mr. Kissinger's personal opinion," a French diplomat once told me. "What we want to know is the position of the U.S. government."

Some in the Kremlin understood this practice of Kissinger's to be a reflection of the complicated situation in Washington caused by the Watergate scandal. At the same time, though, I have to admit that the consequences of the Watergate scandal were grossly underestimated and misunderstood in the Soviet Union. There were few comments on Watergate in the Soviet press. For example, the first story relating to Watergate appeared on October 22 in *Pravda* as a brief report on the "Saturday Night Massacre"—the day, October 20, when President Nixon fired Special Watergate Prosecutor Archibald Cox and when Attorney General Elliot Richardson and Former Deputy Attorney General William D. Ruckelshaus submitted their resignations. The Soviet media, following the recommendation of the Central Committee, downgraded the importance of the political developments in Washington. Perhaps this was consistent with Brezhnev's statement at a press conference in the summer of 1973 that he had never given any thought to whether the Watergate scandal might have weakened President Nixon's foreign-policy position and that he did not intend to exploit the issue. It would be "quite indecent and quite unsuitable," he said, for a Soviet leader to intervene in any way in a purely domestic American affair.[4] Did he continue to adhere to this noble philosophy, or was it merely a political miscalculation and shortsightedness?

Very common were such primitive comments on Watergate as: The "reactionary, anti-soviet forces" in the United States want to punish Nixon for his policy of détente with the Soviet Union, but the "progressive forces" are much stronger and won't permit it to happen. I heard such "analysis" even in the Kremlin's corridors. Unfortunately, we professional diplomats did not pay serious attention to the Watergate developments in Washington and to the latter's significant impact on the American attitude toward the war in the Middle East.

Brezhnev also talked about the growing role of Zionism in the United States and stated that the Zionists wanted the broadest military assistance to Israel to become a priority of American foreign policy. At one point he even admitted that there might be direct military intervention by the United States into the war in the Middle East. "In a state of frenzied activity," Brezhnev declared, the United States was helping Israel. Quoting from a document, he informed the Politburo that in the last few days the Americans had sent to Israel 8 large cargo planes, 39 planes of other types, 42 Phantoms, and 29 helicopters, as well as 10 cargo ships; that American military equipment was being delivered regularly to Naples, to be forwarded to Israel; and that $300 million in additional supplies to Israel from the American government had recently been allocated.

At this Politburo meeting, Soviet-American détente was not mentioned at all, and general displeasure with American policy prevailed. The only trace of détente was in the decision to inform the White House about Kosygin's forthcoming visit. We immediately drafted a cable to Dobrynin.

## THE MAIN TASK OF KOSYGIN'S VISIT

The central issue of the October 15 meeting, however, was a discussion of a cease-fire. The Foreign Ministry's draft resolution, cleared by Gromyko, was distributed to the participants. Introducing the draft, Kuznetsov stressed that its main purpose was to secure implementation of Resolution 242, which was supported by the United Nations, most of the Arabs, and the United States. He believed that if the draft emphasized that resolution, a new resolution on the Middle East ending the war could be accepted by all members of the Security Council. Nobody opposed the idea of a cease-fire, although some expressed reservations. Podgorny believed that the Soviet suggestion of an immediate cease-fire differed fundamentally from Sadat's position and from the Soviet position, which was based on the principles of Leninist foreign policy. The very fact, he claimed, that Kosygin in his talks with Sadat would use the argument that the United States would never let Israel lose "was a recognition of our weakness," of the weakness of socialism vis-à-vis capitalism.

The majority of the Politburo members, however, could not see any favorable alternative to a cease-fire. Gromyko predicted that if Sadat turned down the Soviet proposal to have an immediate cease-fire a very difficult situation would result: "The Arabs would be defeated, Sadat himself would be dismissed, and the Soviet Union's relations with the United States, as well as with the Arabs, would deteriorate."

The call for a staged withdrawal of Israeli armed forces to the 1967 boundaries raised some doubts. Andropov was sure that defining the stages would provoke lengthy arguments, and Podgorny believed that a general reference would be sufficient. Three options concerning sponsorship of the resolution were suggested: It should be the Soviet Union's alone, or co-sponsored with the United States, or presented by a group of nonaligned states.

Finally, there was discussion over whether to show the Soviet draft to Sadat or merely to acquaint him with its contents. Podgorny recommended showing it to Sadat, but Gromyko preferred a restrained position. Foreign Minister Gromyko advised informing the Egyptian president about the American "Basic Principles of an Eventual Resolution of the Security Council" and asking for his comments. He was against giving Sadat any commitment regarding the Soviet position in the Security Council.

Brezhnev summed up the discussion by stating that the draft resolution, which contained, as an important element, a reference to Resolution 242, was fully consistent with the security interests of the Soviet Union, but that to move it would require "trading with the Americans." Brezhnev believed that the United States would accept paragraph one of the draft (an immediate cease-fire-in-place), but he expected that there might be great difficulties with paragraph two (withdrawal of Israeli troops). In case the Americans objected to paragraph two, he continued, it could be reformulated—for instance, by limiting it to the part of paragraph two that referred to the necessity of adhering fully to the provisions of Resolution 242.

Brezhnev advised Kosygin to draw Sadat's attention to the growing American reluctance to take concrete measures to stop the war. Early in the war the Americans had asked for a Security Council meeting, he remarked, but now they were wasting time—and in the meantime increasing support to Israel. Kosygin had to convince Sadat that it was necessary to consolidate the position the Arabs had reached during the war and to postpone the goal of liberating other Arab territories. "Tell Sadat," Brezhnev said, "that if the firing is stopped and the Israelis do not withdraw from the Arab territories, we shall help the Egyptians build a powerful, broad, and deep defense system that will be a jumping-off place to finally expel the Israelis. The Americans must understand that one should have respect for the Arabs, who are supported by the Soviet Union."

Brezhnev also asked Kosygin to tell Sadat that President Tito of Yugoslavia had agreed to consult with the nonpermanent members of the Security Council from nonaligned states and to discuss with them a draft resolution consisting of two paragraphs: an appeal to both sides to cease fire immediately and the requirement that Israeli troops withdraw, perhaps gradually, to the positions of June 4, 1967. Brezhnev preferred that such an initiative be taken by the nonaligned states—in that case, he concluded, the Soviets would have more freedom.

The Soviet leader repeated several times that the main task of Kosygin's visit was to ensure Sadat's consent to a cease-fire. His determination to achieve a cease-fire was so strong that he referred to the possibility of a cease-fire *de facto* if Kosygin were to fail in his mission. What he meant by "cease-fire *de facto*" was not clear, but nobody asked him to elaborate. He noted only that such an action could be carried out in cooperation with the Americans.

Perhaps one of the most important instructions Kosygin received at the meeting was to let Sadat know that the Soviet Union would not become a party to the war. "You must declare it officially. There should be no misunderstanding," Brezhnev told him. The Kremlin leaders believed that direct Soviet military involvement in the conflict would lead to a world war.

China's position regarding a cease-fire resolution in the Security Council came up at the meeting several times. Brezhnev, Podgorny, and Grechko were concerned about a possible Chinese veto of any Soviet-American draft that did not fully reflect the Arab position. The champions of "proletarian internationalism" and "brotherly friendship" with the Arabs were very sensitive to being accused of involvement in a "superpower plot." I have to acknowledge that the "China factor" was present at almost all Middle East discussions in the Kremlin. In fact, dread of China's potential influence in the region sometimes overshadowed other concerns of the Soviet leaders. Washington did not have this problem in planning and carrying out its policy in the Middle East.

Another issue that came to the Politburo's attention was the oil embargo, which was becoming extremely important in world politics as the Yom Kippur War went on. When Ponomarev mentioned that the Arabs were planning to use oil to exert pressure on the United States, Kosygin promptly responded that he was not sure whether the Soviet Union should encourage the Arabs to go ahead with the oil embargo. The moment the Arabs start to use oil as a political weapon, he stated, a NATO military force would "descend on the Middle East." He believed he should express that opinion during his visit with Sadat in Cairo. Gromyko strongly supported Kosygin on this issue, noting that the oil embargo is not "our instrument" and that the Soviet Union should not encourage the Arabs to use it.

Others did not comment on the remarks of Kosygin and Gromyko, and I do not recall that the oil embargo ever came up again at Politburo meetings, at least in October 1973. At one encounter Gromyko had with our group, he elaborated on his position, saying that the oil embargo was initiated by Saudi Arabia, Kuwait, Bahrain, and other pro-American Arab states. "They will never dare to challenge America's interests," the foreign minister said, emphasizing, "We should not collaborate with them."

Therefore, to claim, as many Western newspapers and authors have done, that Moscow urged the Arabs to use the oil weapon against the West, promising them instant success from it and even instructing the Arabs in the most effective ways of using it, is in conflict with the views expressed in the Politburo on October 15. It is true that the Soviet media commented with sympathy and understanding on the Arab oil boycott declared on October 17, emphasizing that it was the sovereign right of the Arab states to utilize their own natural resources as they saw fit. In this context the Soviet press stated that whereas in the past, in times of colonialism, it was the Western powers who had used oil as a means for oppressing and exploiting the Arab peoples, "today it is the Arab countries." A Soviet expert on oil problems, Ruben Andreasyan, wrote that the Arab countries were "eager to turn this double-edged weapon against the oil monopolies and aggressive imperialist quarters."[5]

When the NATO powers did not descend on the Middle East in response to the Arab oil embargo, as Kosygin had feared, a certain change occurred in the Soviet attitude toward the Arab oil embargo in the post–Yom Kippur War period, but the Kremlin did not play a backstage role in arranging the embargo. On the contrary, a concern that the Arab oil embargo would complicate and broaden the Middle East conflict prevailed in the Kremlin during the Yom Kippur War.

The Politburo meeting ended with forty minutes of closing remarks from Brezhnev, the contents of which have already been described above. In addition, Brezhnev advised Kosygin to stay in Cairo for several days, and also to keep his visit secret, informing only Washington about the prime minister's mission.

Kosygin's departure was scheduled for 11:00 A.M., October 16, actually several hours after the meeting was adjourned at 4:00 A.M. the same day. Our task force was almost in a panic. On the basis of the notes we had made at the meeting, we had to draft instructions for Kosygin's talks in Cairo that afterward were to be cleared by the Politburo. The problem was not only the time constraints but also and primarily the character of the meeting, in the course of which many diverging views had been expressed. Even in Brezhnev's closing statement the cardinal task of the mission had been defined differently. Brezhnev had said that everything must be done to maintain friendship with the Arabs, with Egypt, but then he had emphasized the priority of ending the war and arranging a cease-fire in the Middle East. It was not quite clear whether Kosygin should discuss the Soviet draft resolution on the cease-fire with Sadat or limit himself to informing Sadat about the American position on that issue. And what did Brezhnev's formula "cease-fire *de facto*" mean? And so on. We had to come up with answers to these and other questions quickly.

To our great relief and surprise, however, Brezhnev said in closing that the instructions for Kosygin would not be formally confirmed. He proposed that his summation of the discussion, transcribed by the stenographer, should be considered as the instructions for the negotiation in Cairo. Everybody readily agreed and rapidly left the Kremlin. Only Brezhnev himself, Gromyko, and our group stayed behind for a while. Brezhnev was in a cheerful mood. He liked the "frank, comradely exchange of views among Communists" at the Politburo. He told stories and anecdotes, and asked us whether his summation had encompassed the relevant points in a conciliatory manner. Of course, our comments were in the most laudatory terms. In reality, Brezhnev's summation demonstrated, at least, his indisputable skill in smoothing over critical situations and making statements that all his colleagues would accept.

## "THE PROPAGANDA INSURANCE"

In Soviet diplomatic practice, every important foreign-policy step the Soviet Union took was accompanied by a number of propaganda actions—including publication of articles, statements by "independent" organizations and public figures supporting the Soviet position, invitations to prominent scientists, writers, and artists to participate in a Soviet V.I.P.'s visit, praising the latter and his position, and so on. Brezhnev's entourage usually consisted of several hundred people. When I was among the crowd of about 400 (!) Soviet diplomats and their families in Washington and New York welcoming Brezhnev on his arrival at Andrews Air Force Base in June 1973, I was astonished by the number of these "advisers" and "experts," most of whom were absolutely useless during the visit. In the Soviet Union, these expensive operations were called "propaganda insurance" or "propaganda backing" for the V.I.P.'s visit.

Prime Minister Kosygin's visit to Cairo on October 16 was different. It was a working visit and also a secret one. There was no entourage, apart from a small group of aides, and no announcement of the visit. However, several steps aimed at "propaganda insurance" for the visit had been carried out. The main goal was to demonstrate how friendly, loyal, and faithful the Soviet people were toward the Arabs and their war against Israel. To that end, the Central Committee initiated a campaign of meetings all over the Soviet Union in support of the Arabs. During Kosygin's visit, reports about such meetings were published in all the Soviet newspapers and broadcast by Soviet radio and television. To demonstrate the alleged unanimity of the Soviet people and their widespread support of the Arabs, meetings were held in factories, universities, collective farms, and offices, among other places. Workers, peasants, students, writers, actors, teachers—all of them sided with the Arabs, without exception, and resolutely condemned the barbaric bombing and shooting of civilians by Israel.

Slogans at a gathering at one of the largest factories in Gorki on October 18 proclaimed: "Arab land should belong to the Arabs!" "The Israeli aggression against the Arab states must be stopped!" "Long live the Leninist foreign policy of the USSR—policy of peace!" The sinking of the merchant ship *Ilya Mechnikov* had caused expressions of indignation and sometimes direct threats to Israel, and the return of the ship's crew to Odessa was hailed as a big public event, with the crew members being welcomed as heroes. The captain's first aide, V. Ivanov, made a lengthy statement emphasizing the Soviet Union's friendship with Syria and the peaceful character of the cargo on the sunken ship.

All these meetings and gatherings ended with adoption—unanimously, of course—of a resolution, addressed to the Central Committee or to Brezhnev personally, that expressed solidarity with the Arabs and support for Soviet foreign policy. The contents of these resolutions were familiar to the Central Committee because the *apparatchiks* of the Central Committee had actually drafted them themselves.

In addition to mounting a public campaign in support of the Arabs, Soviet leaders used every opportunity to encourage the Egyptian and Syrian leaders. For example, on October 19 Grechko congratulated Ahmed Ismail Ali, the Egyptian minister of war and commander-in-chief of Egypt's armed forces, and all forces of the "friendly Arab Republic of Egypt," on the occasion of Army Day. He wished the minister and all Egyptian army personnel "further success in defending the revolutionary gains and in the struggle against imperialist Israeli aggression, for freedom and national independence of the Egyptian people."[6]

In general, however, the public protest campaign orchestrated by the Kremlin in October 1973 was not as spectacular and stunning as many similar campaigns had been in the past. Détente was putting a brake on it. Since Khrushchev's time, the door to the West had remained ajar, and more and more Soviet people had a chance to see the "dying" capitalist world with their own eyes. The successful Soviet-American summits of 1972 and 1973 had broadened contacts between the two states in many fields. Besides, I believe, the attitude toward Israel had changed slightly. Israel did not become popular, of course, but victories over the Arabs created a certain respect for Israel. Meanwhile, Arab defeats and the occasional unfriendly action by an Arab state (for example, the expulsion of Soviet advisers from Egypt) certainly did not contribute to warm sentiments for Arabs among the Soviet people.

The experts on ideology in the Central Committee believed that another method of "propaganda insurance" for Kosygin's visit should be to create broad public recognition of the Soviet Union's aid to the Arabs and of the Arabs' attitude to the Kremlin for that assistance. Organizing such a campaign, however, was much more difficult than arranging public meetings within the Soviet Union. The Egyptian and Syrian leaders did not make any statements of that kind. Ambassador Vinogradov recalled that Sadat had on many occasions stated that the Egyptian army was armed with weapons of high quality, even better than those used by the enemy, and asked the ambassador to convey his gratitude to the Soviet leadership. In return, Vinogradov had asked Sadat to say this to the Egyptian people and soldiers—but he never did so.[7] And neither did the media in the Arab states disseminate any information regarding Soviet aid. Therefore the Central Committee could rely only on Communist and pro-Communist parties in the Arab states.

On October 17, following the "friendly advice" of the Central Committee, the Iraqi, Syrian, and Lebanese Communist parties issued statements praising Soviet support of the Arab states. The leader of the Moroccan party "Istiqlal" visited the Soviet embassy in Rabat and expressed his gratitude to the Soviet government and people for their "resolute support of the just Arab cause," and he stressed that the Arabs had always been grateful for Soviet assistance.[8] The Soviet media, in communications to Arab audiences, broadcast Algerian comments on Boumedienne's visit to Moscow, which supposedly proved that the Soviet Union had a growing interest and commitment to help the Egyptians and the Syrians. Even the Israeli Communists followed suit when they urged the withdrawal of Israeli troops to the 1967 lines. In addition, an article by Meir Wilner, general secretary of the Israeli Communist Party, was published on October 17 in the central Soviet press.

The lack of public recognition by Arab leaders of the Soviet Union's help forced the Central Committee to take an unusual step. On October 19, *Pravda* published documents from the conference of Communist and Workers' Parties representatives that had taken place a month earlier, in September, in Lebanon. The dominant and recurring theme of all the documents, published under the heading "Against Israeli Aggression, for the Anti-imperialist Unity of the Arab Peoples," was the Soviet Union's decisive role in developments in the Arab world. A special statement praised Brezhnev's personal contribution to world peace and international cooperation. Another document claimed: "Arab-Soviet friendship and cooperation is the most important achievement of the national-liberation struggle of the Arab people and the guarantee of its further progress. Not a single social force in the Arab states can abandon or retreat from this alliance without making a step to the right, towards reaction."[9] This belated publication of the conference documents proved that the Kremlin continued to attach great importance to maintaining its special relationship with the Arab world.

During Kosygin's visit, the Soviet Union publicly admitted, for the first time during the war, that it was supplying arms to Egypt and Syria. In a commentary, the Tass news agency included a brief "acknowledgment of continuing Soviet military aid to the Arab combatants"[10] and linked "the growth of the fighting efficiency of both the Syrian and Egyptian armies with the military aid which has been rendered by the Soviet Union." This public admission that the Soviet Union was rearming the Arabs, cleared by the Central Committee, was also in response to the lack of public recognition by Arab leaders of the efficiency of the Soviet Union's assistance.

The attitude of the Arabs disturbed and angered the Kremlin leaders. "These people are ungrateful," noted Brezhnev during a chat with Gromyko when he learned the contents of Sadat's speech in the Egyptian parliament on the day Kosygin arrived in Cairo. And Aleksandrov, talking to our task force, noted that even Golda Meir had referred to

Soviet arms and training as the reasons for Israeli losses to the Arabs, thus acknowledging the Soviet Union's role in the Arab victories. The airlift to Egypt peaked during Kosygin's visit, and on the eve of his departure Kosygin himself gave orders to supply Egypt with as much equipment and weaponry as they needed. The Politburo assumed that this would help the prime minister in his talks in Cairo.

Finally, the Soviet media gave a picture of mounting U.S. military assistance to Israel and broad opposition to the pro-Israeli policy both inside and outside the United States. On October 19, *Pravda* published a story by its Washington correspondent, Nikolai Kurdyumov, titled "Pentagon Supplies Weapons to the Aggressor," which referred to the U.S. Senate's approval of military supplies to Israel as well as to the critique of this decision by the *Christian Science Monitor*.[11] At the same time, citing official and semi-official American statements against U.S. intervention in the Middle East, the Kremlin leaders and the Soviet media withheld direct anti-American statements. Even the rather tough speech given by the Soviet Trade Union leader, Alexandr Shelepin, to the World Federation of Trade Unions in Varna on October 16 (the significance of which was grossly exaggerated in the West) contained only a general reference to reactionary imperialistic circles and to international Zionism.[12]

In sum, the Soviet propaganda machine did its best to create favorable conditions for the success of Kosygin's mission.

## THE "SECRET" MISSION STARTS

Kosygin arrived in Cairo in the evening of October 16 and was met at Cairo International Airport (which had become a military airport during the war) by Egyptian National Security Adviser Hafiz Ismail, Soviet ambassador Vladimir Vinogradov, and other Egyptian and Soviet officials. Although the visit was supposed to be a secret, a large number of officials present had been provided with passes "On the occasion of the visit of the Prime Minister of the USSR." The car that drove Kosygin to Cairo was decorated with two flags—one Soviet, the other Egyptian. The next day the media all over the world heralded the news, with one exception: the Soviet newspapers and broadcasts, which kept the "secret." I could never understand the reason for declaring Kosygin's visit secret, and, to be frank, did not try to find out why. It was our Soviet style.

On the way to his residence, Kosygin was briefed by Vinogradov on the latest developments in Egypt. The main news was that Sadat had addressed the National Assembly earlier that day, declaring his readiness to accept a cease-fire on condition that Israel withdraw from all occupied territories to the 1967 lines. Kosygin thought this was reasonable but not realistic. He asked Vinogradov whether in his speech Sadat had acknowledged or praised the Soviet Union's support. He was disappointed with the ambassador's evasive answer. Probably Kosygin had expected that, on the eve of his arrival in Cairo, the Egyptian president would have to say at least a few words of appreciation about Soviet-Egyptian cooperation.

Kosygin stayed at the Kubba Palace. Before meeting Sadat, he asked the Soviet military attaché in Cairo, Ievlev, who had just returned from the front, to bring him up-to-date on the Israeli breakthrough at the Canal. With this information in hand, Kosygin went to see Sadat.

There were three meetings between Kosygin and Sadat. The first, in the evening of October 16, was a tête-à-tête meeting; the other two (on October 17 and 18) were attended also by Vinogradov and Hafiz Ismail. The negotiations started cordially with welcomes, embraces, and even kisses. Following instructions, Kosygin brought greetings and kind wishes from General Secretary Brezhnev and the Soviet leadership and congratulated Sadat on the successes of the Egyptian armed forces. He said that the goal of his visit was a joint search for the most effective termination of the war, one that would be in the interests of Egypt and Syria, as well as a just settlement for the Middle East in general. He was instructed, Kosygin continued, to find out what Sadat thought about a cease-fire as a first step on the road to a peace settlement, taking into account Egypt's goals in the war and the military situation on the Egyptian-Israeli and Syrian-Israeli fronts.

Sadat emphasized that Egypt's goals—namely, to get a Middle East settlement off the ground and to demonstrate the fighting efficiency of the Egyptian armed forces—were limited. The ultimate goal, however, was to regain the land that Israel had seized and to restore to the Palestinians their legitimate rights. At the same time, Sadat noted, he recognized that the United States would never allow a total military and political defeat of Israel—the constantly increasing military help provided to Israel by the United States was proof of that.

Kosygin agreed with Sadat's evaluation of the American position with respect to Israel, but at the same time called Sadat's attention to the fact that the Americans were calling for a cease-fire-in-place. He acquainted the Egyptian president with the contents of the latest American proposals regarding an eventual Security Council resolution and asked Sadat for his comments.

As Sadat saw it, a cease-fire with troops remaining in place, as proposed by the Americans, would mean that Israeli aggression would result only in some minor border changes. Egypt demanded guarantees that all Arab territories occupied by Israel would be liberated. Without such guarantees, the Egyptian president emphasized, there would be no talk about an eventual cease-fire. Let the Soviet Union and the United States guarantee Israel's compliance with the eventual agreements, he suggested.

Kosygin said that any war ends with peace—or with a peace conference that endorses the results of the war. The difficulty is choosing the right moment for converting military victories into political gains. The Soviet leadership, he pointed out, believed the moment had come. The liberation of all Arab land occupied by Israel must be the final result of the combined political efforts of the Arab states and the Soviet Union.

War is war, the Soviet prime minister went on, and Egypt's military situation might worsen. The Israelis had recovered from their initial defeats and had successfully carried out a number of counteroffensives on the Syrian front. Referring to the latest reports, Kosygin expressed concern about the Israeli penetration of the western bank of the Canal.

Finally, Kosygin stated that the Soviet Union was a firm and vigorous opponent of widening the war and thereby complicating the conflict. A protracted war would also be counterproductive, he stressed. This was the reason the Soviet leadership strongly favored an immediate cease-fire.

Sadat agreed that any war, including the present one, sooner or later had to end with peace, but he felt that the time for a cease-fire had not yet come. He described the military situation of Egypt as stable, and persistently denied that there had been any unfavorable changes on the Egyptian-Israeli front. The penetration of Israeli troops to the western bank of the Canal he called an insignificant event or a "political maneuver" of the Israelis.

The first round of talks, which was outwardly conducted on a friendly basis, did not yield any tangible results. Kosygin was unhappy with it and reported the contents to Brezhnev later that night. The next day, Kosygin went to the Soviet embassy and talked with Soviet diplomats, asking about life in Cairo, their contacts with the Egyptians, and Egypt's attitude toward the Soviet Union. He was very much surprised to see Cairo streets full of young people enjoying themselves and others relaxing in restaurants and cafés. Many stores in the center of the city were open even during the evening hours, and although lights were dimmed here and there, Cairo was not completely blacked out at night. This surprised Kosygin, who remembered well the hard times Soviet cities experienced during the last world war. His image of war differed greatly from what he was seeing in Cairo.

## WHO IS GOING TO GUARANTEE THE CEASE-FIRE?

The second meeting between Kosygin and Sadat, on October 17, focused on the cease-fire issue. Kosygin stated that the problem of guarantees raised by Sadat at the previous meeting deserved special attention. He shared the Egyptian president's view that a mechanism to ensure Israel's compliance with the Security Council's decisions had to be set up, and such a guarantee could be provided by the Soviet Union and the United States jointly. As far as the duration of the Israeli withdrawal was concerned, Kosygin believed that two or three months would be fair. The prime minister noted, though, that some thought had to be given to how all these questions would tie in with getting the earliest possible cease-fire.

Kosygin informed Sadat that a draft cease-fire resolution of the nonaligned members of the Security Council that had been cleared by the Egyptian president in his talks with Ambassador Vinogradov had been delivered to Tito on October 14 along with Brezhnev's personal message. He expressed the hope that the Yugoslavs would succeed in obtaining support for the draft. However, the "Yugoslav draft" would not contain a reference to Resolution 242, which had been unacceptable to the Palestinians and to some Arab states, so Kosygin did not believe that the draft had much chance for success—it would probably be vetoed by the Americans, and possibly by the Chinese as well. Besides, the draft did not contain any provision for guarantees. The whole business could turn out to be a waste of time, he believed.

Meanwhile, according to the latest information from the Egyptian-Israeli front, time was working against the Arabs. Kosygin continued to argue that an immediate cease-fire was of vital interest to the Arab states and to the whole process of political settlement in the Middle East. Any delay would benefit Israel and its supporters.

Sadat said that for him the most important issue was the guarantee. Egypt could go through with the cease-fire only if a clear-cut and unequivocal agreement were reached between the Soviet Union and the United States to guarantee implementation of a Security Council resolution, which called for the liberation of all Arab lands. As for the current military situation, Sadat was confident. Egyptian armed forces had won great victories, and what had happened on a limited piece of land in the region of the Bitter Lakes—well, that was just a small episode, nonsense, Sadat assured Kosygin. The Egyptians had prevented any split in their front in the Sinai and had driven the Israelis back. They had also, according to Sadat, destroyed the greater part of the infiltrating tank force of the Israelis. Ironically, at the same time Sadat was speaking the Israeli armored forces were continuing their second major offensive against the center of the Egyptian front on the western bank of the Canal. The new Israeli infiltration force was a success, and Ievlev predicted a speedy encirclement of the Egyptian Third Army.

At the meeting with Kosygin, Sadat turned to the issue of Soviet supplies. He expressed his gratitude to the Soviet Union for the excellent modern weaponry that had helped Egypt defeat the Israelis, but he was upset about the delayed delivery of tanks, Volga (SA-5) missiles, some spare parts, and other weapons he had asked for on the eve of and throughout the war. Some of the equipment—bridges for crossing the Canal, for example—he considered to be out-of-date.

In response to Sadat's complaints, Kosygin pointed out that the airlift had started and was continuing strictly in accordance with the Soviet Union's promises and commitments. In the last few days alone, he asserted, the Soviet Union had airlifted almost 1,600 tons of supplies to Egypt. We are supplying the Arab states with a huge amount of weaponry, equipment, and ammunition, and replacing the Egyptian and Syrian losses, so there cannot be any complaints, the Soviet premier stated. Besides, he added, the Soviet Union had concentrated its supplies on Syria because of the Israeli breakthrough on the Golan Heights, but if the Arabs were going to lose as many as a thousand tanks a week, the Soviet Union would not be in a position to replace such losses. Kosygin also drew Sadat's attention to the fact that the Egyptians themselves had lost as many as 600 tanks. The Soviet Union will continue to help the Arab states in their just struggle, he stated, but our resources are not unlimited, so it is necessary to think about how to end the war, begin negotiations, and convene a peace conference. That is the approach Moscow favors, Kosygin said.

Once again Sadat agreed with Kosygin that the war had to be terminated by negotiations at a peace conference, but he repeated that the time for a cease-fire had not come.

Afterward Kosygin reported the results of his second session with Sadat to Brezhnev. The KGB representative in Cairo, Kirpichenko, who was present while Kosygin spoke to the Kremlin, described the conversation as a dialogue of the deaf and dumb. The special line from the embassy to Moscow was very poor, and all kinds of technical impediments hindered the conversation. Besides, Kosygin had some hearing problems—he constantly asked Brezhnev to repeat what he was saying, and he restated his own remarks.

I was on the other end of the line, in the Kremlin, watching Brezhnev's reaction to what Kosygin said. Brezhnev was noticeably irritated. He thought the negotiations had been unnecessarily complicated and asked Kosygin several times whether the immediate-cease-fire idea was acceptable to Sadat or not. He did not get a clear answer from Kosygin. "I stated our position so persuasively and convincingly at the Politburo," Brezhnev complained after the telephone conversation, "but he [Kosygin] failed to explain it to Sadat."

The third and last round of Kosygin-Sadat talks took place in the evening of October 18. The Egyptian press had already recognized that a "ferocious" tank battle was under way in the central sector of the Sinai front.[13] Many analysts believed that the Israeli breakthrough could widen the wedge on the western side of the Canal. Kosygin was briefed by Ievlev before he went to the meeting with Sadat. Ievlev drew a cheerless picture of the military situation, claiming that the best Egyptian troops, including the most experienced officers, were on the eastern bank of the Canal, that the rear echelons of the Second and Third Egyptian Armies were exposed, and that there were no defensive fortifications around Cairo. All this meant that it would not be very difficult, the attaché believed, from a military point of view, for Israel to seize the Egyptian capital.

At the last meeting with Kosygin, Sadat reiterated the importance of guarantees in the whole process of a Middle East settlement. He was in favor of signing a special Soviet-American binding agreement that would commit the Soviet Union and the United States to guarantee the borders of the warring sides and to carry out any measures, including military if necessary, aimed at implementing all aspects of an eventual cease-fire.

In addition, he suggested setting up a buffer zone, to disengage Egyptian and Israeli troops. Soviet and American troops would be deployed in that zone.

Sadat stated that without a resolution of the cardinal issues—the withdrawal of Israeli troops to 1967 boundaries, and the Soviet-American guarantees—no cease-fire would be acceptable to Egypt. Egypt's position, the president declared, was that if the key conditions were met the fighting could be stopped and a peace conference could be convened. Sadat did not think it would be a big problem to convene a peace conference under the auspices of the United Nations that members of the Security Council and all interested parties could attend.

Kosygin had no new arguments to get Sadat to agree to a cease-fire. The issue of bilateral Soviet-American guarantees, he said, could be settled only in negotiations with the Americans. Besides, the Americans might not like the idea. Subsequent developments bore this out—the Americans turned down the idea of Soviet-American guarantees when it came up at diplomatic negotiations. But for the present, Kosygin repeated, the time factor was decisive. The Israeli crossing of the Canal had to be taken seriously. He expressed some of the concerns Ievlev had shared with him on the eve of his meeting with Sadat regarding the threat posed to Cairo by the Israeli breakthrough. As far as the peace conference and other follow-up issues were concerned, Kosygin believed they could be settled only when the hostilities had ceased, not in conditions of war and an Israeli offensive.

Sadat disagreed with Kosygin's assessment of the eventual consequences of the "tactical" military operation in the Bitter Lakes region and assured him it would have no impact on the course of the war in general.

The third session was not a long one. Both statesmen felt they had exhausted their arguments, and the meeting was adjourned in the traditional way of Soviet-Egyptian "brotherly" relations. Sadat and Kosygin embraced, expressed friendly feelings, and the former wished the latter bon voyage. At the embassy, Kosygin called Brezhnev to report on the last encounter with Sadat.

That evening, October 18, Brezhnev summoned members of the Politburo and acquainted them with the course of Kosygin's talks in Cairo. Suslov read the notes on the Brezhnev-Kosygin telephone talks. The poor quality of the notes and the misunderstandings between the two caused a messy discussion in the Politburo. It was not quite clear whether Sadat had accepted the immediate cease-fire proposal or not, who had suggested the guarantees, whether Sadat's position was supported by Assad or by other Arab leaders, and so on. In general, the Kremlin leaders liked the idea of joint Soviet-American guarantees, which Brezhnev had favored since the outbreak of the war. "We have to get in touch with the Americans on this point," Brezhnev said. But he could not answer many questions others at the meeting raised. He limited himself to informing the Politburo that Israeli forces had crossed the Canal and might encircle the Egyptian positions, and acquainted his colleagues with the contents of Hafiz Ismail's latest contacts with Henry Kissinger.

The Politburo decided to take up consideration of Kosygin's visit to Cairo at a meeting when Kosygin could be present. The only outcome of the present, October 18, meeting was the decision to instruct Dobrynin to link the cease-fire to a political settlement in the Middle East in his encounters with Kissinger.

## THE INGLORIOUS RETURN TO MOSCOW

Kosygin's visit to Cairo was far from a success. The prime minister could not win Sadat's agreement to an immediate cease-fire, in spite of the Israeli crossing of the Canal and Egypt's obviously worsening military situation. Sadat's assertion in an interview with *Al-Hawadith* on April 26, 1974, that at 1:00 A.M. on October 19 he had conveyed to Kosygin his consent to a cease-fire-in-place before Kosygin left Cairo is not confirmed by Vinogradov, Boris Bazanov (Kosygin's aide), or Pogos Akopov, minister-consular of the Soviet embassy in Egypt—the officials who accompanied the prime minister almost the entire time he stayed in Cairo. Nor can I remember any message from Kosygin on October 19 reporting Sadat's acceptance of a cease-fire-in-place. At the follow-up meetings of the Politburo, Kosygin himself never mentioned the alleged agreement of the Egyptian president to a cease-fire. Moreover, in Sadat's memoirs, which were published after the above-mentioned interview, Sadat conceded: "I told him [Kosygin] on departure: 'I won't have a cease-fire until the final stage of my War Plan has been carried out. I hope this is clear enough for you.' "[14]

I share the view of Vinogradov, who believes the dates had merely been muddled in the *Al-Hawadith* interview. The Egyptian president did inform the Kremlin of his explicit acceptance of a cease-fire-in-place two days later, on October 21. Two days earlier, during Kosygin's visit, he had turned it down.

There was also no truth to the rumors that Kosygin had brought with him a Soviet, or even a Soviet-American, peace plan that was accepted by Sadat. The rumors were initiated by the usually well-informed Yugoslav press agency, Tanjug. The presence of Yugoslav Foreign Minister Miloš Minić in Cairo at the time of Kosygin-Sadat talks (October 16 and 17) lent credibility to Tanjug's story.

In reality, Kosygin did not bring any Soviet peace plan, let alone any Soviet-American plan, and Sadat did not join any peace plan. Some have claimed that as a result of the talks in Cairo an "Egyptian agreement" on a cease-fire formula had apparently been reached.[15] That also was not the case. The alleged "Soviet peace plan," "Soviet-American peace plan," or "Egyptian agreement" supposedly contained the following main provisions: The Soviet Union and the United States would help arrange a cease-fire and a withdrawal of Israel to the 1967 boundaries; the "physical presence either separately or with the others" of the two superpowers would guarantee the borders; the cease-fire agreement would be verified mainly by the Soviet Union and the United States; and so on.

Kosygin and Sadat had discussed or touched on all these issues. On some points their views coincided, and sometimes they differed, but there was no final agreement and neither side had committed itself on any of the issues. At the same time, the Tanjug document included some problems that to my knowledge had not been discussed at all ("small corrections of the 1967 borders") and that omitted some other important ones, such as the future peace conference that heralded Egypt's readiness for direct negotiations with Israel. Heikal, for example, claims that "Kosygin left the next day [October 19], convinced that Egypt was ready for a peace conference, provided it included all fourteen members of the Security Council, the Secretary General of the United Nations, and all interested parties including the Palestinians."[16] Perhaps so, but I wonder whom Egypt, or rather Heikal, excluded from the list of peace conference participants, because there were fifteen members of the Security Council. Clearly the Tanjug document was a "free impromptu" about the results of Kosygin-Sadat talks. Unfortunately, there was no fixed agreement on any of the substantive issues related to the Middle East conflict. The participants limited themselves to an exchange of views.

It is common practice in world diplomacy to describe even fruitless negotiations as useful because they aid understanding the participants' positions, but I am afraid that does not apply to the Cairo talks. I do not think they improved the Kremlin's understanding of Sadat's vision of the world in general or his goals in the Yom Kippur War in particular. The Kremlin leaders were certainly not aware of the full content and character of Cairo's contacts with Washington, although some information about them, including information from Sadat himself, reached Moscow. Nonetheless, the Kremlin continued its fruitless and counterproductive attempts to "educate" Sadat, to explain the American policy to him, or to speak with the Americans on behalf of Cairo.

This only provoked Sadat's anger. Sometimes Sadat received information about the American position from Soviet representatives—after he had already been informed more accurately by the Americans themselves. In the course of Kosygin's talks in Cairo, for example, the Soviet premier tried to acquaint Sadat with the American attitude to the cease-fire, even though the Egyptian president already knew about it from Secretary of State Kissinger.

The root of the Kremlin's failure to understand Sadat and many other leaders of the nonaligned, developing countries was not, however, lack of information, but rather the orthodox, doctrinaire Soviet approach to world developments. The main impression Kosygin brought back with him to Moscow was that Sadat was stubborn, persistent, adamant, and irresponsible. Like Brezhnev, Kosygin was convinced that Sadat did not understand Egypt's real national interests, that Egypt could settle its domestic and foreign affairs only by following the Soviet line. The Kosygin-Sadat talks in Cairo did not subvert Soviet-Egyptian relations, but they did not strengthen them either.

Vinogradov later attested that Kosygin did his best to conduct the negotiations in a calm and amicable way, as Brezhnev had advised. "The talks were held in a very friendly atmosphere," the ambassador recalled. "I remember that President Sadat spoke to the Soviet premier about the Mig-17 that had shot down two Phantoms in one engagement, saying that the Mig-17 had proved its superiority to the Phantom. Comrade Kosygin replied: 'No, Mr. President, the Phantom is technically more advanced than the Mig-17; it was the courage of the Egyptian pilot who was flying it that made the Mig-17 superior to the Phantom.' "[17]

At the same time, Kosygin did not feel friendly toward Sadat. According to his aide, Bazanov, the prime minister frequently compared Sadat with his predecessor Nasser, always emphasizing Nasser's greatness and Sadat's pettiness. Sadat did not like Kosygin either. He considered him to be an aggressive bureaucrat, and he claimed that Kosygin was noted in the Soviet Union for having served for thirteen years in government posts under Stalin without being liquidated or sent to Siberia, as was the fate of all who worked under Stalin. "Not one of them except Kosygin was spared—as Khrushchev told us when he visited Egypt in 1964," Sadat wrote in his memoirs.[18] I wonder whether Sadat asked about Khrushchev himself, who worked under Stalin much longer than Kosygin.

The heated, emotional character of the talks was evident in at least one episode. When Kosygin referred to the threat the Israelis posed to Cairo, Sadat replied: "I am sorry to disappoint you, but no threat will ever be posed to Cairo."[19] Why should Kosygin be "disappointed"?

The mutual unfriendly feelings of the negotiators certainly had some effect on the outcome of the Cairo talks. Sadat was not happy with the results of the negotiations with Kosygin either. The Kremlin wanted to impose its own strategy on Sadat, but that did not correspond to Sadat's own plans. Besides, regarding Soviet-Egyptian relations he had reason to complain. At no time, including during the talks with Kosygin, did he receive any information from the Soviet satellites, which had been following the battle from the beginning of the war. He asked for copies of the photographs but received no reply.[20] Heikal's assertion that at a meeting in Kubba Palace "he [Kosygin] gave the pictorial evidence of the extent of the Israeli crossing to the west bank of the Suez Canal"[21] is correct, but the pictures Kosygin showed Sadat during their last meeting were not from the Soviet satellite but from Mig-25 reconnaissance flights, which proved that the Israeli thrust west of the Canal could unlock the Egyptian position. Vinogradov later confirmed that the Soviet prime minister did not provide Sadat with any aerial photography from the Soviet satellites. Likewise, Sadat was less than successful in his appeal for Soviet military supplies. The quantity of supplies delivered by air began to drop, starting on October 20. I do not think it was politically motivated, but the decrease in supplies was obvious.

One more point needs to be made. Although Brezhnev had instructed Kosygin to declare officially during his talks with Sadat that the Soviet Union would not participate in the war in the Middle East, neither Sadat's memoirs and statements nor the Soviet documents I am familiar with contain references to any such declaration. Vinogradov assured me later that at the meetings he attended Kosygin made no such statement—in the ambassador's view because as an experienced statesman Kosygin believed it would only worsen the already tense relations between Moscow and Cairo. At the Politburo meeting on October 25, however, Kosygin claimed he had stated in Cairo that the Soviet Union would not become involved in the war. It is also quite unlikely that Kosygin could at that time assure Sadat that the Soviet Union was prepared to act on its own, as Chaim Herzog claimed.[22] So whether Kosygin carried out Brezhnev's instruction is not entirely clear.

On October 19, Tass ended the news blackout on Kosygin's visit to Egypt by reporting in one terse sentence that he was in Cairo from October 16 to October 19 and had held meetings with President Anwar Sadat of Egypt. It gave no details whatsoever. The absence of a joint Soviet-Egyptian communiqué or a more positive-sounding statement from the Soviet press agency was correctly interpreted in the West as an indication that no breakthrough toward a settlement of the war had been achieved in Cairo.[23]

Kosygin was gloomy and disappointed on his return to Moscow. The KGB resident in Cairo, Kirpichenko, who had spent many hours with the prime minister, recalled that at times Kosygin seemed very sad and lonely, dwelt on his deceased wife, and complained about his age. Kosygin could see that his mission would not contribute much to settling the Middle East crisis or strengthening Soviet-Egyptian relations, and he was probably concerned about how his visit would affect his political career and standing in the Kremlin. His opponents, first and foremost Brezhnev himself, might use the poor results of the mission as a reason to downgrade him—something which did, in fact, happen.

At the same time, Kosygin could not imagine that his visit to Cairo would be the last visit of a top-level Soviet official to the Egyptian capital in the entire history of the relations between the Soviet Union and Egypt. Nor could he envision that two days after the completion of his mission other negotiations, this time in Moscow, would open the door for a Middle East settlement, thus emphasizing the failure of his mission even more. He would not be invited to take part in the negotiations that followed.

The author with Arab diplomats at the United Nations in New York in early 1973. From 1968 until mid-1973, Israelyan was the Soviet First Deputy Permanent Representative to the U.N. In July, he returned to the Foreign Ministry in Moscow, where he was director of the Department of International Organizations when the October war began.

The author talks with Abdel Meguid during the summer of 1972 regarding the prospects of a political settlement in the Middle East. Meguid was Egypt's permanent representative to the United Nations at the time.

Vladimir Vinogradov, the Soviet Ambassador to Egypt. His extensive contacts in Cairo proved invaluable to Moscow during the war.

Vinogradov claimed to have had thirty-five encounters with Egyptian President Anwar al-Sadat on the eve of and during the war. Here the two meet on October 3, 1973—three days before the war. That day Sadat warned the Soviet ambassador of an impending attack on Israel, but he did not specify a date.

Syrian President Hafiz al-Assad. Unlike Sadat, Assad favored a quick military strike against Israel and an early peace settlement to ensure Arab gains.

Nuritdin Mukhitdinov, the Soviet Ambassador to Syria. After the war began, he conveyed to Moscow Assad's plea for an early cease-fire, but nothing came of it.

The Soviet Union's chief diplomatic officials. From left to right, Foreign Minister Andrei Gromyko; Permanent Representative to the United Nations Yakov Malik; and Ambassador to the United States Anatolii Dobrynin. Behind Malik is the author. United Nations Photo

Cold Warrior Yakov Malik (seated). According to George Bush, Malik was one of the Russian diplomats who "made the word *'nyet'* known to the English-speaking world." This 1968 photo shows Malik, in typical fashion, arguing with Arthur Goldberg, the U.S. Permanent Representative to the U.N. at the time. United Nations Photo

Vasilii Kuznetsov (left) was one of the Soviet Union's star diplomats and the senior member of the four-man task force. After the war he was promoted to the post of Deputy Head of the Soviet Union. This 1975 photo shows Kuznetsov awarding the author for his service.

As the Soviet ambassador to the United States, Anatolii Dobrynin (right) met regularly with American officials and kept Moscow well-informed of developments. Here he is shown in conversation with Cyrus Vance. Photo by Albert

Leonid Brezhnev with leading Soviet officials. In the bottom row, from left to right, are Yuri Andropov (Chairman of the KGB), Andrei Gromyko, and Nikolai Podgorny (Chairman of the Presidium of the Supreme Soviet). Author is in top row. This photo shows the signing of an arms-control treaty in Moscow in July 1974.

Inside the Kremlin during Brezhnev's first meeting with Kissinger, late in the evening on October 20, Brezhnev is informally dressed (no tie) but replete with decorations. Note that Brezhnev signed the photo twice, perhaps to stress the significance of the meeting. Courtesy, Joseph Sisco

Kissinger and his close adviser Joseph Sisco walking in the garden outside their residence before Kissinger's second meeting with Brezhnev. The Americans felt they must talk outside for fear that the residence was bugged. Courtesy, Joseph Sisco

UNDERSTANDING

It is understood that the phrase "under appropriate auspices" in point 3 of the Security Council Resolution shall mean that the negotiations between the parties concerned will take place with the active participation of the United States and the Soviet Union at the beginning and thereafter in the course of negotiations when key issues of a settlement are dealt with. Throughout the entire process of negotiation the United States and the Soviet Union will in any case maintain the closest contact with each other and the negotiating parties.

*K*
*A.G.*

During Brezhnev's second meeting with Kissinger on October 21, the two parties agreed on wording for a Security Council cease-fire resolution. They also prepared this "Understanding" to highlight the role of the Soviet Union and the United States in the peace process. Russian and English versions were prepared and initialed by Gromyko and Kissinger.

Перевод с английского

ВЗАИМОПОНИМАНИЕ

Понимается, что выражение "под соответствующей эгидой" в пункте 3 резолюции Совета Безопасности означает, что переговоры между заинтересованными сторонами будут иметь место при активном участии Соединенных Штатов и Советского Союза в начале. и затем в ходе переговоров при рассмотрении ключевых вопросов урегулирования. На протяжении всего процесса переговоров Соединенные Штаты и Советский Союз будут в любом случае поддерживать теснейший контакт друг с другом и со сторонами, ведущими переговоры.

The Geneva Conference on the Middle East was held in December 1973 to settle the war. At top are the Israeli and Soviet delegations. At bottom are the Egyptian, American, and Jordanian delegations. Syria boycotted the meetings, so their table on the right is empty.

The author and his wife, Alla, with George and Barbara Bush. George Bush was the U.S. Permanent Representative to the U.N. just before the October war.

# CHAPTER 5

# KISSINGER IN MOSCOW

## BREZHNEV'S MESSAGE TO NIXON

The first word of the Israeli counteroffensive in the Sinai began to reach Moscow on Tuesday, October 16, the day Kosygin left for Cairo. According to the military intelligence (GRU) reports and the pictures made by the Soviet satellites, which were submitted to Brezhnev and some other members of the Politburo, large concentrations of tanks, other mechanized forces, and aircraft had been forming on the Israeli side of the line over the last few days. The spearhead of the Israeli force had driven across the Canal and was attacking Egyptian positions and surface-to-air missile sites on the western bank.

Military experts warned the Kremlin that a successful Israeli offensive could cut off the retreat of the large Egyptian force dug into the eastern side of the Canal and lead to the military and political collapse of Egypt. In addition, intelligence showed that significant American arms shipments were reaching Israel. Another source of information in the Egyptian capital reported to the Kremlin that the Israeli crossing of the Canal had created a situation of near panic among many Egyptian political and military leaders. Some of them, the informant claimed, were considering withdrawing the government to Asyut and organizing popular resistance against the Israeli invaders.

The Soviet media, however, portrayed the situation on the Sinai front and in Egypt differently, referring to or simply repeating the Arab version of the story. Only on October 18 did the Soviet newspapers mention that a small group of seven Israeli tanks had "desperately tried" to cross the Canal and lost three of them. On October 19, *Izvestia* announced that "an Israeli regiment penetrated into the western bank of the Suez Canal and was liquidated."[1] These lies were for the Soviet public, but the Soviet leaders knew the bitter truth. Sadat's bravado could not mislead them. Nevertheless, Kosygin's talks in Cairo had proved that an immediate cease-fire with the cooperation of Sadat was hopeless. That was one reason the Kremlin's contacts with Washington became more active in those days.

Foreign Minister Gromyko informed our task force that Brezhnev had decided to address President Nixon and express to him the Soviet leadership's comprehensive assessment of the situation in the Middle East. Brezhnev did not want the message to be confrontational, though he wanted it to be convincing. A draft was drawn up with the help of Brezhnev's aides, edited by Gromyko, reviewed, and finally cleared by Brezhnev himself, who attached great importance to it.

Although Kissinger characterized the message as "conventional rhetoric,"[2] it seems to me that it precisely and accurately reflected the way the Soviet leadership perceived the Yom Kippur War and the Middle East situation, and its eventual settlement. Many of the assertions in that message proved to be correct in the years after the war. This is why the full text of the message (my own translation from the Russian text) deserves to be quoted. General Secretary Brezhnev wrote to President Nixon on October 16:

> The current developments in the Middle East are to some extent a test of both our powers to strictly comply with the course we have accepted in our [bilateral] relations and in international affairs.
>
> The situation is undoubtedly complicated. This is clear to us, as well as to you. Let us be straightforward: The United States and the Soviet Union are strongly engaged with Israel and the Arab states, respectively.
>
> The trouble is, however, not only and perhaps not insomuch that we maintain different positions on the Middle East issue.

The main problem here is that we assess the situation in the Middle East differently. The Soviet leadership continuously, including quite recently, has drawn the President's attention to the dangerous situation, which threatened a new explosion at any moment. Unfortunately, however, the American side has been rather indifferent to these our warnings.

We do not want to think that the United States wanted such a development. This would not correspond to the apparent interests of the United States as we understand them and as we have been told by the American side.

One could, certainly, regret the divergences in our evaluation of the danger of the absence of a settlement of the Arab-Israeli conflict. But at present this is not the issue, and we should not talk about that. Now we must search for ways to reduce the tension.

After this introduction, Brezhnev expressed the Kremlin's views on the prospects of a Middle East settlement:

Thinking about the present situation and about ways to solve it, one inevitably comes to a conclusion that is probably not new but that strikes at the core of the problem. No matter what the outcome of the present military operations—which is difficult to predict—it is clear that unless Israel withdraws from the Arab lands it seized, there will not be peace in the Middle East. This is the essence. We are convinced that without liberating the Arab lands one cannot design and establish a durable peace in the region.

Well, is it not high time to embark on a realistic road? Is it not better to deal with the matter on the most reliable basis instead of searching for palliative measures?

The next paragraph contained several concrete steps that, in Brezhnev's view, could be taken to end the confrontation in the Middle East:

An unambiguous statement by Israel that it is ready to withdraw its troops from all the Arab territories it occupied in 1967 would help the matter. Certainly, concurrently with that step the security of all states in the region, Israel included, and their borders, could be guaranteed either by a decision of the Security

Council or by the great powers. And with the withdrawal of Israeli troops the war would end, and freedom of navigation through the Suez Canal and the straits, including for Israeli ships, would be secured. Other issues in which Israel has an interest could be settled as well, but certainly there is no room for gratification of Israel's territorial ambitions.

Brezhnev was asking Nixon what in such an approach could possibly be unacceptable to Israel or to Israel's supporters. From his point of view, all these measures would only strengthen the security and the very existence of Israel as a sovereign state.

Those were the outlines of a future durable peace in the Middle East—as the Kremlin leaders saw them in the midst of the Yom Kippur War—but it would take decades for the states of the Middle East and for the world community to establish new peaceful relationships in the region along lines similar to those sketched in Brezhnev's message. The few lines Henry Kissinger devoted to the message in his memoirs were not entirely accurate. Brezhnev did not suggest that Israel's security could be guaranteed by the superpowers, as Kissinger claimed.[3] Although Brezhnev was a strong proponent of the special role and responsibility of the Soviet Union and the United States in a Middle East settlement, in this message Brezhnev was referring to guarantees of the Security Council or *of the great powers*—meaning the permanent members of the Security Council.

The next part of the message was more emotional. Brezhnev reminded Nixon that in the late 1940s the Soviet Union and the United States had contributed to the creation of Israel:

> And the Soviet Union never favored and does not favor the liquidation of Israel as a state, although in Israel, and not only there, one can now find people who make slanderous statements about the Soviet Union, having forgotten these facts and the gratefulness they have expressed for the rescue of millions of Jews from the bloody retribution of the Hitler butchers. There was a time when those in the United States, and in other countries who anathematize us now, prayed in honor of the Soviet weapons that saved many nations—the Jewish people included—from annihilation in the years of the joint struggle of the Soviet Union and the United States against the fascist plague.

Brezhnev explained the Soviet position at the United Nations and commented on the American position regarding a Security Council cease-fire resolution:

> If somebody got the impression that by taking such a stand we simply want to put the United States in an awkward position and force it to exercise its veto power in the Security Council, that impression is totally groundless. Such an idea must be tossed out.
>
> We are deeply convinced, however, that it is unrealistic for the Security Council resolution, in addition to the provision concerning the cease-fire, to make a foggy reference to Security Council Resolution 242 instead of stating a clear requirement that Israeli troops withdraw to the June 4, 1967, lines. Simply referring to a resolution that for six years has been interpreted differently by each party is useless. However, the American side does not put forward other suggestions of how to solve the problem.

This was, unfortunately, a hasty statement, for less than a week later the Soviet Union co-sponsored a Security Council resolution that contained the "foggy reference" to Resolution 242.

The final passage of the message was very important. Brezhnev wrote:

> In conclusion, I would like to emphasize the main idea: No matter how far current events have gone, they have not passed the point of no return. Hence, neither the leaders of the Soviet Union nor those of the United States should forsake restraint.
>
> We know there are influential circles in the United States that want to destroy what we have already built at quite a large cost. It should not be permitted. For our part, we have done and will continue to do everything to prevent such a trend. We would like to hope that the American side will follow suit.
>
> If both sides strictly adhere to such a restrained approach, despite the difficulties each side is facing, future developments will undoubtedly bring only positive results. And we will continue to build the edifice that we have started.

That concluding passage was optimistic and contained many personal elements. Brezhnev was quite an emotional person, and, having formulated some parts of the message himself, he was expecting President

Nixon to respond in the same friendly and frank way. How could the general secretary know that he was actually corresponding mainly with the secretary of state because President Nixon was preoccupied with entirely different problems?

As a follow-up to Brezhnev's message, a draft of the Security Council resolution that the Soviet Union was ready to support was sent to Washington. The draft was based on the text discussed by the Politburo on October 15, with slight modifications. In addition to a call for an immediate cease-fire (paragraph one), it contained a demand for a staged withdrawal of Israeli troops from the occupied Arab territories to the lines designated in Resolution 242 of the Security Council. It did not define how long the withdrawal would take, but said only that it must be completed in the "shortest time possible" (paragraph two). The third paragraph was new. It reflected Brezhnev's image of Soviet-American cooperation in the Middle East settlement and was worded as a call for "appropriate consultations" aimed at attaining a just peace in the Middle East.

The reply in Nixon's name to Brezhnev's general message came in three days later, on October 19. Very formal, it avoided responding to many of the key issues the Soviet leader had raised. There were no comments on the Soviet draft resolution either. Brezhnev was very disappointed and unhappy.

### WHO INITIATED KISSINGER'S INVITATION TO MOSCOW?

The news from Belgrade was not promising either. From Ambassador Stepakov's cables it was evident that the Yugoslavs were facing some difficulty getting approval for a Security Council cease-fire resolution from the nonaligned states. For many of us the situation seemed hopeless. We believed we had done everything we could to ensure an end to the fighting that would be beneficial to the Arabs, and that now whatever would be, would be. I think many in the Kremlin's highest echelon felt the same way.

However, the tide of world diplomacy turned again, as it had several times in the recent weeks. In one cable to Moscow, Ambassador Dobrynin referred to his confidential relations with Secretary of State Kissinger and suggested that it would be worthwhile to invite Kissinger to Moscow to review the situation. It was a timely and courageous step by the ambassador, who was convinced that Kissinger would accept the invitation.

The cable from Dobrynin initiated a lengthy discussion in Gromyko's office. The question that troubled many of us, especially Gromyko, was: What if the secretary of state turned down the invitation? To be consistent, the Soviet side would then be forced to suggest that a Soviet V.I.P. visit Washington—and who should be chosen for such a mission? An alternative to a Kissinger visit to Moscow could have been, of course, a visit by Gromyko to Washington. Kissinger recalled that he had once asked Dobrynin whether Gromyko could come to Washington and that the ambassador supposedly answered that Soviet decisions would require the participation of Brezhnev and Kosygin.[4]

I do not remember Dobrynin reporting this conversation to Moscow. If he did, it certainly would not have pleased his boss—Foreign Minister Gromyko—who according to Kissinger's interpretation of Dobrynin's view could not make any decisions without the head of state participating in the process—unlike his American counterpart.

When the alternative of a Gromyko visit to Washington was mentioned at our meeting in the foreign minister's office, Gromyko turned the idea down flat. I believe he did not want to show up on the Politburo stage too much, preferring that Brezhnev be the star, even at diplomatic negotiations. Having been promoted to Politburo membership only a short time ago, Gromyko did not feel very confident. Besides, to suggest that the Soviet foreign minister meet with the American President after the prime minister had been sent to Cairo for negotiations with the Egyptian president would downgrade the importance of Soviet-American relations. Furthermore, everybody understood that Brezhnev would not like the idea of a Nixon-Kosygin meeting and would not support it.

All these questions and thoughts came up during the discussion, but the more we talked the more we became convinced that Dobrynin must have had some assurance that an invitation to Kissinger would be accepted. Indeed, how could such an experienced diplomat as Dobrynin advise Moscow to take an important political action in the midst of a war without such an assurance? Some of us who knew Dobrynin fairly well, Kornienko and myself included, had totally excluded such a possibility. The devastating effect on Dobrynin's personal career if Kissinger refused to come to Moscow was certain, so the possibility that this was merely frivolous impromptu on the part of the ambassador had to be fully discounted.

I even believed that it was Kissinger himself who had sold the idea to

Dobrynin. "*He* might be fishing for an invitation," I said. Gromyko and Kuznetsov shared my belief. "This man is a self-promoter," Kuznetsov noted, and when Gromyko reported on Dobrynin's cable to Brezhnev, he indicated his belief that Kissinger might have engineered the invitation in order to be able to present the American position to the Soviet leadership personally, thus upgrading his political standing in Washington. "The visit to Moscow would be Kissinger's first visit abroad since he became secretary of state [in September 1973]," Gromyko noted with satisfaction.

In his memoirs, Kissinger said that Brezhnev's invitation was a surprise to him. "When I read the invitation," he recalled, "I felt it solved most of our problems. It would keep the issue out of the United Nations until we had shaped an acceptable outcome. It would discourage Soviet bluster while I was in transit and negotiating. It would gain at least another seventy-two hours for military pressure to build."[5] Joseph Sisco, Kissinger's main adviser on the Middle East, later confirmed that the secretary of state was well disposed toward going to Moscow and had instructed him to start preparatory work for the visit immediately.

No matter how Kissinger felt about direct negotiations with the Soviet leaders at that time, Dobrynin's message was welcomed in the Kremlin. But even apart from Kissinger's personal interests, a high-level Soviet-American encounter was needed at that moment—and even more, inevitable—if, of course, both sides were concerned with maintaining détente. And they were.

The Kremlin leaders and the Soviet diplomats viewed Kissinger differently. I do not think Brezhnev and the other leaders knew anything about Kissinger before he became Nixon's national security adviser, but many diplomats were familiar with him as a political scientist. Sometimes they quoted critical remarks he had made about U.S. foreign policy, and referred to him as the "well-known American bourgeois historian" who had admitted in his writings the miscalculations and blunders of American imperialism. As a professor at the Diplomatic Academy at the time, I suppose I was among those who quoted Kissinger that way. His appointment to the post of Assistant to President for National Security Affairs in 1969 was considered by Gromyko and many of his colleagues as President Nixon's attempt to follow President Kennedy's pattern of having somebody from the intellectual community in his entourage. The appointment had not been viewed as significant, but that changed quickly. The growing role of the "Kissinger-Dobrynin channel" in the Soviet-American dialogue set up in 1969, especially in arms-control negotiations, resulted in recognition of Kissinger's businesslike character and pragmatism. Kissinger's contacts with Dobrynin were very close. He had a direct telephone line to the Soviet ambassador and had established an informal, friendly relationship with him.

Kissinger exerted much effort into depicting himself as a creator and originator of American foreign policy, thereby downgrading Nixon's role and prestige in that area. He tried to convince Dobrynin and Yuli Vorontsov, minister-consular of the Soviet embassy, who frequently acted as chargé d'affaires, that he, not Nixon, was the man in Washington to deal with on crucial issues of international politics and bilateral relations. Kissinger's secret visit to Moscow in the spring of 1972 (before he became secretary of state) contributed greatly to the Kremlin's reevaluation of him as a political figure. Vorontsov recalled how Kissinger's attempts to conceal that mission from the U.S. State Department had amazed Soviet diplomats. He did his best to keep the U.S. embassy in Moscow unaware of his stay in Moscow—and, with the assistance of his Soviet hosts, he succeeded.

One episode was both typical of the balance of political forces in Washington and at the same time unprecedented in diplomatic practice. In the fall of 1972, I attended a meeting between Secretary of State William Rogers and Foreign Minister Gromyko in New York. During the discussion, Gromyko touched on an important arms-control matter that was on the agenda of several meetings between Dobrynin and Kissinger and asked Rogers's opinion. To the surprise of all, Rogers was totally unaware of the matter, and it became clear that President Nixon and then National Security Adviser Kissinger had not shared some vital information with the secretary of state. Gromyko himself was even a little taken aback by the confusion that his question caused.

Kissinger's previous visits to Moscow in 1972 and 1973 as national security adviser had been effective—they had contributed to the success of the Brezhnev-Nixon summits. Kissinger had been impressed by General Secretary Brezhnev, who, he later wrote, "was a mixture of crudeness and warmth, that was at the same time brutal and engaging, cunning and disarming."[6] My colleagues at the Soviet embassy in Washington recalled that, after his secret visit to Moscow in 1972 Kissinger spoke with pride about "the lengthy, fascinating one-on-one discussions" with Brezhnev. They admitted later, however, that he changed the tone of his remarks about Brezhnev—but that was after the Yom Kippur War. For his part, Brezhnev respected Kissinger as a partner, liked to negotiate with him, and even invited him to the

Politburo hunting preserve in Zavidovo near Moscow. When Brezhnev read Dobrynin's cable he said that Kissinger should be invited. "We can make a deal with him," Brezhnev stated.

The other Kremlin leader who had met Kissinger several times was Gromyko. Of the generations of American secretaries of state he had known, Gromyko singled out Kissinger as a highly capable statesman and diplomat. But he always emphasized caution in dealing with Kissinger. "Don't give him a finger—he will bite off your hand," he warned.

Both the covert and the outspoken anti-Semites, of course, speculated and joked about Kissinger's Jewish identity. "How can a Jew be an anti-Communist if he was born in Germany and became a political scientist when he settled down abroad, following the pattern of Karl Marx?" "Why should the Soviet Jews emigrate to Israel and not to the United States, where Zionists are dominant in business, the media, and the arts; where now a Jew has become the foreign minister; and where most probably the next American President is going to be a Jew as well." And so on.

In connection with Kissinger's visit to Moscow, one detail was peculiar. Brezhnev pronounced Kissinger's name incorrectly, stressing the second syllable, Kiss*in*ger. Although many people who were close to Brezhnev—Kosygin, Gromyko, Kuznetsov—knew how to pronounce the name correctly, everybody played up to the Soviet leader by using his pronunciation (at meetings of the Foreign Ministry, Gromyko pronounced it correctly). The name that came up most often during this thirty-six hours in the Kremlin was "Kiss*in*ger," or "Kisa."[7]

In response to Dobrynin's cable, in the afternoon of October 19, Brezhnev sent a message to Nixon with the invitation to his "closest associate" Kissinger to come to Moscow in "an urgent manner." He was expected in Moscow the next day. Dobrynin cabled a positive reply from Washington very soon that evening, informing us that the secretary of state would arrive in Moscow the next day, October 20. According to Dobrynin, Kissinger wanted to start the negotiations on Sunday, October 21, and had asked that the announcement of his visit state that he was coming to Moscow at the invitation of the Soviet government. When Brezhnev read the cable he laughed—Aleksandrov recalled—and ordered Aleksandrov to get ready for negotiations to begin Saturday evening. As for Kissinger's request that the Kremlin announce he was coming by invitation, Brezhnev joked that otherwise it would look as if he had invited himself or that he was expecting to be invited. The Soviet announcement of the visit said nothing about an invitation. At any rate, the speed with which Kissinger did all the things he had to do in preparation for the visit was additional proof that the visit was very important for him personally as well as for the settlement of the crisis.

In the evening of October 20, Kissinger and a group of his assistants arrived in Moscow. From then on, for almost thirty-six hours, all attention at the Kremlin was devoted to the negotiations with the Americans. The results of Kosygin's talks in Cairo got moved to the background.

An important message from President Nixon to Brezhnev arrived on October 20, before Kissinger arrived in Moscow. The gist of the message was Nixon's appeal to Brezhnev for "a firm commitment from both of us to devote our personal efforts to achieve that goal [a final peace] and to provide the strong leadership which our respective friends in the area will find persuasive." In the course of further discussions on the Middle East issue, Brezhnev referred to this appeal several times. "I am sending a message to Dr. Kissinger," Nixon continued, "which he will convey orally to you, of my strong personal commitment in this regard."

In his message, President Nixon informed the Soviet leader that he was granting Kissinger "full authority" and that "the commitments that he [Kissinger] may make in the course of your discussions have my complete support."[8] Kissinger interpreted this part of the message as being "its essence," but in Moscow its substance was considered to be Nixon's appeal for a joint commitment to achieve a final peace settlement. It was taken for granted that the secretary of state had the "complete support" of the President. How could it be otherwise? Nobody in the Kremlin even dreamed that there were serious differences—or even "a sharp split," as Stephen Ambrose put it[9]—between Nixon and Kissinger.

Nixon's handwritten postscript to the message—"Mrs. Nixon joins me in sending our best personal regards to Mrs. Brezhnev and to you"—touched the Soviet leader deeply. But again, how could the Kremlin know that the handwritten postscript was partly aimed at making it impossible for Kissinger to rewrite Nixon's message before delivering it to Brezhnev, and was therefore an indication that President Nixon did not quite trust his secretary of state?[10]

Gromyko's comments about Nixon's message were very positive. We shared his assessment. Indeed, Nixon's appeal for a firm and mutual commitment from both states to achieve peace was encouraging and forecasted successful negotiations in Moscow.

Unaware of the complicated relationships within the White House, Brezhnev replied to Nixon's message promptly:

> I understand it exactly the way you stated, that Dr. Kissinger, being your closest associate who enjoys your full confidence, will this time as well speak on your behalf, and that the commitments he may make in the course of our discussions with him will have your complete support.

And in an act unprecedented in Soviet diplomatic practice, he added a handwritten postscript of his own: "Mrs. Brezhnev is grateful for the regards and in turn joins me in sending our best personal regards to Mrs. Nixon and to you."

Although Kissinger did not intend to start the talks on the day of his arrival, Brezhnev invited him to the Kremlin and initiated an exchange of views on Soviet-American relations in general and on joint efforts for ending the war in the Middle East in particular. "Kissinger did not want to start negotiations immediately upon his arrival, but I insisted on it," Brezhnev stated the next morning at the Politburo meeting. In the first round of negotiations, the Soviet side was represented, apart from Brezhnev, by Gromyko, Dobrynin, Aleksandrov, and Kornienko. Kissinger was accompanied by Joseph Sisco, assistant secretary of state for Near Eastern and South Asian affairs; Helmut Sonnenfeldt, senior staff member of the National Security Council; Alfred Atherton, Sisco's deputy; and Winston Lord, director of the Policy Planning Staff of the State Department.

Brezhnev welcomed the secretary of state and expressed his hope that, because of the urgency of the situation, a mutually acceptable way to end the fighting in the Middle East would be found during his visit to Moscow. He stated that the Arab countries would never reconcile themselves to the Israeli aggression, and he was very critical of Israel's policy, which he believed would have serious consequences for world peace and international security. The increasingly dangerous situation in the Middle East might harm Soviet-American relations as well, Brezhnev emphasized. Kissinger responded by thanking Brezhnev for the invitation. He joked about how disappointed the Chinese ambassador in Washington was when Kissinger, at the party hosted by the ambassador on the eve of his departure, informed the Chinese that in a few hours he was leaving not for Beijing but for Moscow. Brezhnev liked the joke.

Then Brezhnev gave his assessment of the Soviet-American détente in light of the Middle East crisis and appealed for restraint along the lines of his October 19 message to Nixon. He also mentioned Kosygin's visit to Cairo as being a part of the Soviet Union's efforts to bring the war to an end, and justified the sending of Soviet supplies to Egypt and Syria by characterizing them as fulfillment of obligations, fixed in a number of Soviet-Egyptian and Soviet-Syrian agreements. But the main idea of Brezhnev's statement was that it was urgent that the Soviet Union and the United States enter into an agreement that would force Israel to withdraw to the 1967 borders in return for an end to the hostilities. The peace settlement would be guaranteed by the Soviet Union and the United States. Brezhnev also expressed his satisfaction with Nixon's latest message, in which the President favored joint action toward achieving peace in the Middle East.

The Soviet leader suggested that the Moscow negotiations be based on the following principles: (1) Neither side should seek unilateral advantages; (2) the Soviet document of October 19 should be used as the basis for a Security Council resolution; and (3) the direction of the discussion should not be shaped by the changing situation at the war fronts.

Kissinger did not oppose these principles, but at the same time he emphasized that he had come to Moscow to discuss a cease-fire, not a peace settlement, and noted that he would have to report back to Washington any plan for a comprehensive settlement in the Middle East. He pointed out that the latter would require complicated and lengthy consultations, while the cease-fire was the more pressing matter at the moment. "Come on, you have all the power you need to make decisions," Brezhnev noted, having in mind the credentials given to Kissinger by Nixon. Brezhnev had a favorite tactic for when he felt Kissinger was getting tough—he would threaten to contact Nixon directly and complain that his secretary of state was not complying with the instructions the President had given him.

According to Brezhnev's report to the Politburo, Kissinger characterized the Soviet draft resolution as constructive. He accepted paragraph one, which called for an immediate cease-fire, and at the same time rejected paragraph two, on the withdrawal of Israeli troops to the 1967 borders, referring to the Israeli position and saying that a suitable formula could be found in the course of further negotiations. He was ready to accept paragraph three, concerning the consultations, if certain alternatives were given.

After Kissinger's first meeting with Brezhnev was adjourned late Saturday night, he was given an impressive dinner by the Kremlin host. It was midnight, the Americans were tired after the flight from Washington, and the dinner was shorter than usual, featuring only an abbreviated version of the normal cascade of Brezhnev anecdotes. After the dinner, Kissinger proposed continuing the negotiations the next morning, the sooner the better, but Brezhnev wanted to start the talks at noon, at which suggestion Kissinger joked that the late hour was undoubtedly designed to enable Dobrynin to attend church services. "Both of us knew, in fact, that we would need time to assess military reports to determine our bargaining positions," Kissinger guessed.[11] But he was mistaken. Brezhnev wanted the time to discuss the matter with his colleagues and get clearance for a deal with the United States from the Politburo.

## "NIXON FEELS DEEP RESPECT FOR ALL SOVIET LEADERS AND FOR ME PERSONALLY"

The next morning, Sunday, October 21, another session of the full Politburo was held, from 9:00 A.M. until 11:30 A.M. The topic was the negotiations with Kissinger. Brezhnev started by emphasizing the utmost importance of the Soviet-American negotiations, for world peace and international security as well as for bilateral relations. He said he was pleased Kissinger had come to Moscow, and took that as evidence that Washington was willing to continue Soviet-American cooperation. He characterized Nixon's message of October 20 as showing a recognition that the Soviet Union and the United States should jointly create a comprehensive peace plan for the Middle East, an idea he had shared with President Nixon in San Clemente in the summer of 1973. Brezhnev liked Nixon's message, although Nixon in his memoirs called it a "stern letter."[12] Brezhnev was convinced that if the two leaders continued to cooperate and to exert their influence with friends and allies a stable peace could be achieved, and he spoke warmly about the President. At the same time, without unnecessary modesty, he said: "Nixon feels a deep respect for all Soviet leaders and for me personally." I believe Brezhnev based this remark on Nixon's handwritten postscript.

Brezhnev informed his colleagues that the meeting with Kissinger had been "quiet, businesslike, and proceeded in a constructive manner," and that Kissinger's attitude to the Soviet draft resolution was positive "on the whole."

Then Brezhnev turned to another subject, which was a great surprise to all participants in the meeting. He told them about his telephone talks with Vinogradov on the night of October 21. I give an almost word-for-word transcript of Brezhnev's account:

> I had hardly fallen asleep after I returned from the Kremlin when, at 4:00 A.M., I was awakened by Vinogradov's call. He said: "I have just been invited by Sadat, who after saying he was sorry to call at such a late hour informed me that he had returned from the command post, where his commanders reported on the situation at the front. Sadat asked me to tell Leonid Ilyich [Brezhnev] that while at the front he had decided to ask the Soviet comrades to take all possible measures to arrange an immediate cease-fire." "What are the conditions?" Vinogradov asked. Sadat replied that the troops should stay in the positions they occupied at that time; he did not mind the Israeli troops staying on the western bank of the Canal. Sadat also wanted the Soviet Union to make efforts to arrange disengagement of the troops. He expressed his desire that the Soviet Union sponsor a cease-fire motion at the Security Council. After the cease-fire, a peace conference could be held, in which the Soviet Union, the United States, and perhaps some other great power would participate.

Brezhnev said that in response he had instructed Vinogradov to determine how Sadat felt about the link between the cease-fire and the withdrawal of Israeli troops and to ask Sadat about the Syrian president's position on the Egyptian proposal, the position of other Arab leaders, and clearing the Strait of Bab al-Mandab of mines.

Vinogradov's own recollection of his first evening meeting with Sadat on October 21 added some details to Brezhnev's account. According to the ambassador, Sadat was accompanied by Minister of War Industry A. al-Fattah and Hafiz Ismail, Sadat's national security adviser. One argument Sadat used for a cease-fire was the impact of the United States. Sadat said: "I can fight the Israelis but not the United States. I cannot cope with the huge flow of American tanks and aircraft. We destroy them, but the flow goes on." Sadat repeated several times that Egypt could not match the military might of the United States. "Make use of all Soviet contacts with Washington and New York to bring about a cease-fire in the Middle East," he concluded. For his part, Hafiz

Ismail described the situation of the Egyptian forces after the Israeli breakthrough on the western bank of the Canal as extremely dangerous. For the first time in Sadat's presence, Hafiz Ismail acknowledged a serious threat to Cairo.

Following Brezhnev's instruction, Vinogradov called on Sadat around five o'clock in the morning. The Egyptian president had retired, but Vinogradov insisted on waking him up. At their second meeting that night, Sadat, clad in pajamas and refreshed after a short sleep, was in a good mood—as if for him the war already had ended. He answered Brezhnev's questions briefly and wanted the ambassador to rush his report back to Moscow.

Sadat's description of the night talks with Vinogradov in his memoirs was unfortunately very brief. He told Vinogradov he had accepted a cease-fire on the existing lines, and he said: "The two superpowers should guarantee the cease-fire and immediate implementation of Security Council Resolution 242."[13] He said nothing about a second encounter with Vinogradov or what Brezhnev's questions and comments were.

Continuing his story of the sleepless night, Brezhnev described his second night talk with Vinogradov this way:

> I finished my talk with Vinogradov, drank a cup of tea, and went to bed. Shortly afterward, I was awakened by a second call from Vinogradov. It was almost six o'clock in the morning. The ambassador had had another meeting with Sadat, and, according to Vinogradov, Sadat agreed with everything. "Of course, the Arabs will continue their struggle against Israel, but the sooner the agreement to cease fire is reached, the better for our common goal," he said. Sadat also noted that he had informed Assad about his appeal to Moscow, but he reminded me that Assad himself asked the Soviet Union to propose a cease-fire, and he recommended ignoring the position of King Hussein of Jordan and the positions of Boumedienne and other Arab leaders as well.

At the same time, Sadat asked Brezhnev to draw the Palestinians into participating in plans for a peaceful settlement in the Middle East. And finally, he said there was no problem with the Strait of Bab al-Mandab—there were no mines there.

Concluding his report on his talk with Vinogradov, Brezhnev pointed out that Sadat's "desperate appeal" had changed the situation. "He got what was coming to him," Brezhnev rejoiced, referring to Sadat's unfortunate situation. According to him, the situation was now even more urgent than it had been on the eve of Kissinger's arrival, because an agreement with the Americans on a cease-fire had to be reached within hours. Brezhnev's assessment was seconded by Gromyko and Andropov. Brezhnev thought the Americans did not know about Sadat's changed position, so he warned all participants against mentioning Vinogradov's evening calls. "If Kissinger learns of Sadat's appeal to me, his position will be much tougher," he added.

What inexcusable naiveté on the part of the General Secretary of the CPSU! At the time he was telling Politburo members the story of his sleepless night, Kissinger, not far from the Kremlin in his residence at the Lenin Hills, was reading a message from Cairo that reached Moscow via Washington. "Hafiz Ismail for the first time," recalled Kissinger, "indicated that Sadat might be willing to separate a cease-fire from an overall settlement. Cairo would content itself, he wrote, with the convening of a peace conference and a 'guarantee' by the United States and the Soviet Union of the cease-fire and the speedy subsequent withdrawal of Israeli forces."[14] So Kissinger knew about the change in Sadat's position and his acceptance of a cease-fire-in-place resolution separate from the peace settlement—before the second and final round of Soviet-American talks started. On a sunny Sunday morning, walking in the residence garden with his closest associate, Sisco, Kissinger apparently discussed the American tactics for the forthcoming meeting in the Kremlin. To do this inside the residence would be risky—the Americans were sure the conversation would be bugged.

And yet there was a slight difference between Sadat's appeals to Brezhnev and his appeals to Kissinger. In the first case, he asked that the Soviet Union introduce a cease-fire resolution; in the second case, he did not touch on that at all. In addition, Sadat informed neither man about his communication with the other. That was *his* game. For their part, both founders and giants of détente—Brezhnev and Kissinger—concealed from each other their latest contacts with Sadat, trying to make use of them to the prejudice of their counterparts. That was *their* game.

At the Politburo meeting, Kosygin, disappointed by his own failure to elicit the kind of flexibility Sadat had now shown to Vinogradov, insisted that Vinogradov require a written appeal from Sadat to Brezhnev. "Let him make a straightforward statement that he accepts a cease-fire without any preconditions," Kosygin demanded. "Otherwise he might change his mind and misinterpret our actions." He was also concerned that Sadat might make a direct appeal to the Americans. His concern was shared by Andropov, who believed that any delay in Soviet action would result in an Egyptian appeal to the Americans. In light of this remark by Andropov, I am quite certain the KGB was not aware of Sadat's latest communication with Kissinger. Andropov was rather critical of United Nations Secretary General Kurt Waldheim, who, as he put it, had become conceited, calling Kissinger three times a day and then pretending he could make a decision.

Once again Brezhnev revealed himself to be too simplistic. "Sadat has asked us to introduce a resolution in the Security Council, and this proves that he relies on and trusts us," he remarked. I had the impression that Brezhnev did not believe in an American-Egyptian deal that could jeopardize détente and the international standing of the United States in general. Once, during the meeting, he referred to the "domestic complications" in the United States—the Watergate scandal, which, as he saw it, would keep the Nixon administration from a confrontation with the Soviet Union.

In this connection it is worth noting that, almost at the same time Brezhnev was mentioning the "domestic complications" in America at the Politburo meeting, President Nixon in Washington was warning that "Brezhnev would never understand such upheavals inside the U.S. Administration and would only interpret them as *signs of weakness to be exploited*" (emphasis added).[15] Nothing of the kind. In fact, neither Brezhnev nor any of his colleagues had suggested "exploiting" the problems that had arisen from Watergate. Was this a manifestation of political decency, or just unfamiliarity with the nature of the American system and democratic society? I think the latter. Nixon's unnecessary concern only proved again what a poor perception he had of his Soviet counterpart.

Kosygin's suggestion to have Sadat send his appeal in writing was rejected by Brezhnev, Andropov, and Gromyko. Gromyko believed that in response to such a request Sadat might suggest a number of conditions that would deadlock any agreement. Podgorny noted that such a demand could humiliate Sadat.

The military situation was reviewed briefly by Grechko and Kulikov. The information did not make them happy. The military claimed that if the Israeli breakthrough in the area of the Canal continued, the Egyptian army would be completely surrounded and the war would be lost. Syrian plans to mount a major counterattack would not change the course of the war, they believed. Brezhnev and Podgorny referred to the statement made by Israeli Defense Minister Moshe Dayan on October 18—that the decisive moment in the Sinai battle was several days, not weeks or months, away. "He might be right," Podgorny noted. "Then the Egyptians would be forced to accept a cease-fire under any conditions." Kulikov then explained that during their retreat the Syrians and the Egyptians were leaving behind repairable and sometimes even undamaged tanks and much weaponry. Dayan would later write in his memoirs: "It seemed to me that the replacements we would obtain this way from the Russians would be much greater than the number of tanks we received from the United States."[16] Dobrynin, who was invited to participate in the meeting, made an interesting comparison. He said that Kissinger, while aboard the Air Force jet on the way to Moscow, had shown him a report of the American military in which the position of the Arabs did not seem to be as desperate as it seemed when the information was presented at the Politburo meeting by the Soviet military.

The main issue at the meeting, however, was formulation of the Soviet position for Brezhnev's forthcoming meeting with Kissinger. All participants agreed that, in light of Sadat's appeal, the drafting of proposals for a comprehensive peace settlement would delay the cease-fire. Kosygin believed that the fighting should be stopped immediately, lest the Arabs surrender. Brezhnev stated that he wanted to negotiate the outlines of the peace settlement, including the format of the conference and the treaty, with Kissinger. That was also what Nixon wanted, as Brezhnev understood his message, but because Sadat was urging the cease-fire and separating that issue out from the overall peace settlement, the Soviet Union should take that into account. While agreeing in principle with the need for a cease-fire, Andropov said: "We should maintain our position and dignity and not beg Kissinger to grant us a cease-fire." He did not exclude a Soviet unilateral proposal in the Security Council, and he suggested that the Americans might not always be able to keep the Israelis under control. Therefore, Andropov believed, Sadat had to be advised to continue Egyptian resistance.

The idea of a unilateral action in the Security Council by the Soviet Union was not supported by others, but a joint Soviet-American initiative was favored. Dobrynin noted that Kissinger had said he would not leave Moscow until he reached an agreement with Brezhnev. Brezhnev's aide, Alexandrov, then read a paragraph from the record of Brezhnev's first meeting with Kissinger, according to which Kissinger had said "The primary task is to stop military operations, end the fighting, and after that to think about the future." Kissinger's words evoked such remarks as "How true!" and "How clever!"

Having reached a consensus to confine the negotiations to the task of drafting a cease-fire resolution, some participants at the same time anticipated an eventual negative international response. Kosygin and Podgorny, for example, were concerned that the Soviet Union could be criticized for making a deal with the Americans, for bypassing the Arabs and ignoring some of their demands. To avoid this, Kosygin suggested encouraging the Arab states to set up a special group with the task of maintaining Arab unity and working out a common policy toward a peace settlement. Brezhnev responded to this concern in the following way: "Of course we should not ignore Arab interests. Today we will have a cease-fire agreement; tomorrow we will reach an agreement on other issues. This is the only right course. Later we will have time to announce that we have done it in accordance with Sadat's request [his appeal to us the night of October 21], not now." Then he defined the role of the Soviet Union and the United States in the process, saying that the leaders of the two states had agreed to cooperate actively and to "command" their respective clients.

Brezhnev was so eager to reach an agreement and end the war that he was ready to take an extreme position. He suggested drafting with Kissinger a simple resolution that would contain only one paragraph—a call for an immediate cease-fire—leaving other related issues for subsequent negotiations. Here we have to act independently of Sadat and Assad, he noted. Brezhnev was strongly supported by Grechko. Gromyko, however, was in favor of continuing negotiations with Kissinger on the basis of the Soviet draft resolution. The foreign minister shared the opinion that the most important part of the resolution was the call for a cease-fire, but Gromyko also believed that the idea of conducting appropriate consultations on the peace process could be accepted at the same time. "The Americans would agree to that," he said. As for paragraph two, which dealt with the withdrawal of Israeli troops, the foreign minister's opinion was that "whatever positive remains from that paragraph after negotiations with Kissinger should also be accepted." The sooner the cease-fire took effect, the better, Gromyko believed. In his opinion, China would not veto such a resolution. Gromyko was against meeting Sadat's appeal concerning the disengagement of troops. Andropov agreed with Gromyko's approach.

The meeting ended at 11:30 A.M. on an optimistic note. In his concluding remarks, Brezhnev emphasized the extreme urgency of reaching an agreement with the Americans aimed at ending the fighting, and he assured the Politburo that in negotiations with Kissinger he would be guided by the views expressed at the meeting. Perhaps to remind the Politburo members of his mastery in Middle East affairs, he referred to his chat with Kissinger in which the secretary of state recognized that Brezhnev was right when he warned President Nixon that the situation in the Middle East was an explosive one.

## BREZHNEV'S SECOND MEETING WITH KISSINGER

At noon on October 21, Brezhnev resumed his talks with Kissinger. The Soviet team was joined by Kuznetsov, and the American team was joined by William G. Hyland, a National Security Council specialist on Soviet affairs. Brezhnev did not touch on the problem of an overall peace settlement in his opening statement, instead inviting Kissinger to continue his comments on the Soviet draft resolution for a cease-fire, which, as he saw it, the parties had accepted as a basis for the negotiations. Kissinger repeated what he had said about the Soviet draft at the first meeting, and stated that he had prepared his own version of the draft. After reading Kissinger's version and consulting Gromyko and Kuznetsov, Brezhnev stated that Kissinger's draft went in the same direction as the Soviet draft and could therefore be considered as a next step in the elaboration of a final joint text.

After the meeting, Kuznetsov said that Kissinger's draft was a pleasant surprise for Brezhnev. The Soviet leader had been prepared, as he stated at the Politburo meeting, to go along with a "simple" cease-fire resolution, but Kissinger was instead proposing a draft that contained the two main provisions the Kremlin was most interested in: an immediate cease-fire, and recognition of the special role of the Soviet Union and the United States in the peace settlement (paragraphs one and three).

The biggest differences between the Soviet draft and Kissinger's version were in paragraph two. While the Soviet draft contained a demand for a staged withdrawal of Israeli troops from the occupied Arab territories to the lines, in accordance with Resolution 242, Kissinger's called on the parties to begin implementation of Resolution 242 in all its parts. Kissinger reiterated his position, saying that it was meaningless to demand an immediate Israeli withdrawal to lines that had not yet been agreed on by the parties.[17] The Soviet proposal, reflecting the Arab stance and favoring a fixed date for the withdrawal, had been rejected by Kissinger. The agreed general reference to Resolution 242 was certainly weaker and could be criticized by the Arabs, but Brezhnev believed that if necessary the blame for a weak paragraph two could be put publicly on the United States.

After Brezhnev accepted Kissinger's draft, there were no serious difficulties. Brezhnev wanted the cease-fire to take effect the moment the resolution was passed by the Security Council. Kissinger, eager to buy more time for Israel to continue its offensive, objected to that. Brezhnev wanted the implementation of Resolution 242, including the convocation of the peace conference, to be timely defined, but Kissinger could not agree with that because he did not want to commit himself to any issues other than the cease-fire. Manipulating the adverb "immediately," the parties came to a compromise. It was also agreed that the reference to "appropriate consultations" aimed at attaining a just and durable peace in the Soviet draft, and to "appropriate auspices" under which negotiations between the parties had to start in the Kissinger version, had to be clarified in a special document. Within a couple of hours the parties were involved in a joint drafting of the text, translating, checking the texts, and so on. A significant contribution to this process was made by the professionals, members of both delegations. "Mr. Sisco, I am ready to hire you in the Soviet Ministry of Foreign Affairs," said Gromyko, impressed by the efficiency of the American diplomat. This joke sounded like the highest praise.

The final text of the agreed-on resolution, Resolution 338, read as follows:

> The Security Council
> 1. calls upon all parties to the present fighting to cease all firing and to terminate all military activity immediately, no later than twelve hours after the moment of the adoption of this resolution, in the positions they now occupy;
> 2. calls upon the parties concerned to start immediately after the cease-fire the implementation of Security Council Resolution 242 in all its parts;
> 3. decides that immediately and concurrently with the cease-fire, negotiations start between the parties concerned under ap-

propriate auspices aimed at establishing a just and durable peace settlement in the Middle East.[18]

The text was the result of a compromise, and like any compromise it contained ambiguities and contradictions. First of all, the adverb "immediately," which appeared in every paragraph, had been applied to three different actions: a cease-fire, implementation of Resolution 242, and the start of negotiations. Such ambiguous wording left room for different interpretations. For instance, paragraph one of the resolution calls on the parties to cease fire "immediately, no later than twelve hours" after its adoption. Kissinger claimed that this meant "the cease-fire should not go into effect until twelve hours *after* the resolution had been adopted."[19] In subsequent discussions in the Security Council, however, some Council members interpreted the wording to mean that the fighting should stop immediately—that is, as soon as the resolution was adopted and certainly no later than twelve hours afterward. Furthermore, the reference to positions the parties "now occupy" was very puzzling. Did that mean the positions they occupied at the moment the resolution was passed, or twelve hours later?

The most dubious and obscure part of the resolution was its paragraph three, which from my point of view deserves to be quoted in textbooks on diplomacy as an example of how ambiguous wording can cause international misunderstanding, arguments, and even conflicts. The formula "under appropriate auspices" provoked a variety of explanations and elucidations on the part of members of the Security Council and the parties to the conflict.

Because the authors of the resolution wanted paragraph three to single out the role of the Soviet Union and the United States in the peace settlement process, Gromyko and Kissinger initialed a document under the title "Understanding" worked out during the negotiations. The document, which was not published, read:

> It is understood that the phrase "under appropriate auspices" in point 3 of the Security Council Resolution shall mean that the negotiations between the parties concerned will take place with the active participation of the United States and the Soviet Union at the beginning and thereafter in the course of negotiations when key issues of a settlement are dealt with. Throughout the entire process of negotiation the United States and the Soviet Union

will in any case maintain the closest contact with each other and the negotiating parties.

The "Understanding" did not prevent different interpretations of this document by Washington and Moscow, however. As time passed, each side acted only according to its own perception. This was one reason for the serious conflict between the superpowers that occurred a couple of days after the Moscow meeting.

With the initialing of the "Understanding" by Gromyko and Kissinger, the substantial part of the Soviet-American negotiations came to an end. The foreign ministers agreed to send instructions of analogous content to their respective permanent representatives to the United Nations. Kissinger kindly handed over to Gromyko a draft of his cable to Scali, and the instructions to Malik were prepared on the basis of the American draft. In accordance with the instructions, Malik was to do the following: (1) At 6:00 P.M. New York time, October 21 (1:00 A.M., October 22, Moscow time) he was to ask, together with Ambassador Scali, that an urgent meeting of the Security Council be convened at 9:00 P.M. the same day. (2) He was to introduce, together with Scali, the Security Council resolution agreed on by the two governments (the text of the resolution followed). (3) He was to forward jointly the resolution to the United Nations Secretariat at 8:30 P.M. so it could be circulated at 9:00 P.M. before the meeting was to be called to order. (4) He was to act in close contact with Ambassador Scali to ensure the support of the other Security Council members. (5) He was to exert efforts to get the resolution adopted by midnight if possible. (6) And finally, he was to make only a short explanatory statement while introducing the resolution. The hope was expressed that joint Soviet-American efforts would prevent any attempts to amend or change the resolution. Malik was informed that it had been agreed in Moscow that neither side would accept any changes in the resolution without mutual approval.

Kissinger's and Gromyko's instructions to Scali and Malik were remarkable documents. I do not remember such harmony in words and deeds of the two superpowers at the United Nations throughout the entire period of the Cold War. Malik joked later: "The instruction was excellent, but there was one omission. It did not say whether I should clear with Scali my going out to the restroom during the meeting of the Security Council."

## "LEONID ILYICH IS TOO TIRED"

By 4:00 P.M., Kissinger left the Kremlin and returned to his residence. The task force went to the Foreign Ministry, where we met with Gromyko in the evening. The foreign minister was relaxed and in a good mood. Brezhnev, he said, was pleased with the talks, but he expressed regret that Brezhnev had refused to have another dinner with Kissinger. "Leonid Ilyich is too tired after the sleepless night, and besides, Vinogradov bothers him too often," the foreign minister grumbled.

During our chat, a cable from Washington with the startling news about the "Saturday night massacre" was shown to Gromyko. He read it, briefly informed us of its contents, and said that one could expect tough measures from Nixon, who, as he noted, had to put an end to the mess. I think he had welcomed Nixon's line. Afterward he called Brezhnev to report the news—in a very short conversation. It seemed to me that Brezhnev did not care much about the event and did not disagree with Gromyko's assessment.

The main subject of our meeting, however, was how to inform other states about the results of the Moscow negotiations. First, Sadat and Assad had to get the news. Vinogradov would see Sadat and convey Brezhnev's message "that the Soviet leaders considered his urgent appeal very seriously" and accordingly had succeeded in working out in negotiations with Kissinger a desirable text for a Security Council resolution. Vinogradov was briefed on the contents of the negotiations, and in particular on the superpowers' differences concerning the withdrawal of Israeli troops.

The next day, October 22, Vinogradov talked with Sadat several times. The Egyptian president expressed his satisfaction with the success of Soviet-American negotiations and stated that Egypt would comply with the Security Council's decision. He understood that the formula "under appropriate auspices" in the resolution reflected his idea of Soviet-American guarantees. The United States and the Soviet Union would not only participate throughout the entire process of the negotiations, but would also guarantee the implementation of the Security Council's decision—that is how Sadat interpreted paragraph three of the resolution. Vinogradov shared Sadat's interpretation and said that the resolution in general was very close to Sadat's vision of the cease-fire. Sadat agreed with the ambassador. At the same time, he was unhappy that no decision on the issue of troop disengagement had been made in Moscow.

Informing Assad of the Soviet-American accord was much more difficult. The Syrian leader realized that the decision made in Moscow was a response to Sadat's appeal, while Assad's own plea for a cease-fire a fortnight earlier had been, as he saw it, ignored. Since then, Syria's relations with the Soviet Union had become much cooler, with Assad limiting himself mainly to issues concerning military supplies. Ambassador Mukhitdinov had reported this negative trend to Moscow. After completion of the Kissinger talks, Mukhitdinov was instructed to explain to Assad that the situation was of the utmost complexity and to emphasize how the agreement reached in Moscow would benefit Syria. The hope was expressed that Syria would support the cease-fire resolution.

The arguments did not seem to convince Assad, and he did not agree to comply with the proposal of the superpowers. Mukhitdinov reported that Assad had informed him about his telephone conversations with Sadat in which the Egyptian leader had assured him that Israel was going to withdraw from the territories it had occupied in 1967 and that, by virtue of the Moscow accord, the Soviet Union and the United States would guarantee the withdrawal. The reaction of Damascus to the Soviet-American decision was skeptical, to say the least, and the Kremlin leaders realized that.

Another important cable was drafted that evening. Gromyko instructed Ambassador Stepakov in Belgrade to see Tito or Foreign Minister Minić immediately and inform the Yugoslavs of Sadat's urgent appeal for a cease-fire-in-place and of Kissinger's visit to Moscow.

> The Soviet Union and the United States [the instructions continued], in the course of complicated negotiations, have worked out a joint Security Council draft resolution. Having in mind Yugoslavia's relations to the Arab states and to Egypt in particular, the Soviet Union requests the government of Yugoslavia to support the resolution.

Stepakov replied on Monday, October 22, reporting that he had met with Minić, who promised to convey the very important message to Tito at once. The minister stated that Yugoslavia did not want to initiate a cease-fire resolution on its own but would be ready to support a Soviet-American resolution acceptable to the Arab states.

A number of messages, in which the Soviet-American accord was described as an important step toward a peace settlement in the Middle East and as a manifestation of the Soviet Union's peaceful foreign policy, were sent to the heads of socialist and nonaligned states. The Kremlin expressed its hope that all states would support the Security Council resolution co-sponsored by the Soviet Union and the United States.

## WHAT DOES "UNDER APPROPRIATE AUSPICES" MEAN?

As directed by Gromyko and Kissinger, the two permanent representatives to the United Nations succeeded in having the Security Council meeting convened at 9:00 P.M. New York time on Sunday, October 21. Scali was the first to introduce the draft resolution circulated by the United Nations Secretariat just before the meeting. Malik, in what was perhaps his shortest speech ever in the Security Council, seconded the draft. Afterward a discussion that lasted until 1:30 A.M., October 22, began. No one opposed the Soviet-American draft.

Two observations are, from my point of view, worth mentioning. The first concerns the interpretation of paragraph three. As one can easily imagine, almost every participant tried to submit its own view of the phrase "under appropriate auspices":

De Guiringaud (France): "My delegation wishes to stress that the phrase 'under appropriate auspices' can mean nothing other than under the aegis of the Security Council."[20]

Maitland (United Kingdom): "My government believes that efforts aimed at establishing a just and durable peace in the Middle East would best be pursued under the aegis of the United Nations. This is how my delegation would interpret the reference to 'appropriate auspices' in p. 3 of the draft resolution before us."[21]

Perez de Cuellar (Peru): "We trust that the 'appropriate auspices' mentioned in the draft will directly involve the United Nations through the Secretary General and the Security Council."[22]

Sen (India): "We are prepared to support the joint draft resolution, with many hesitations and several reservations, not the least of which is with regard to the reference to 'appropriate auspices' under which the negotiations are to be held."[23]

Now, what did the co-sponsors of the resolution have to say about paragraph three? Both permanent representatives to the United Nations, Scali and Malik, did not give any specific interpretation of the formula at the Security Council. Kissinger, in a conversation with the chargé d'affaires of the Soviet embassy in Washington, Yuli Vorontsov, claimed that the agreed-upon joint "auspices" presupposed the rapid fulfillment of Brezhnev's promise to bring about the release of Israeli prisoners of war.[24] (However, neither during the Moscow talks nor later did I hear from any Soviet participant in the talks that such an understanding existed.) Later in his memoirs, Kissinger explained his attitude toward the "Understanding" as follows: "The vaguely defined U.S.-Soviet 'auspices' had the advantage . . . of preventing the intrusion into the negotiating process of other parties liable to bring pressure on us—I fear I meant some of our European allies."[25]

The Kremlin leaders' understanding of the Soviet-American agreement reached in Moscow was crystal-clear: The formula meant that the Soviet Union and the United States had a special role throughout the entire process of coming up with a settlement in the Middle East; it meant guarantees of Israel's compliance with Resolution 242 concerning the withdrawal from the Occupied Territories in particular; and it meant a commitment to exert pressure on their friends, if necessary, in order to ensure their compliance with the agreements of the superpowers and the United Nations.

My second comment relates to the Security Council proceedings, very typical for the activity of that body, especially in the years of the Cold War. To stop the fighting in the Middle East was a priority of the Security Council. After protracted consultations between the most interested parties, a basis for a cease-fire agreement was finally achieved, but instead of taking immediate action the Security Council embarked on a buffoonish discussion that lasted four and a half hours. The members of the Security Council, responding to the appeal of the council president and the co-sponsors of the resolution, made short statements expressing their readiness to support the resolution. But an argument about Zionism—its roots, historical role, and so on—initiated by the representative of Saudi Arabia, Jamil Baroody, and responded to by the Israeli representative, Yosef Tekoah, delayed the action. At the meeting, Baroody had the floor fourteen times, and Tekoah had the floor four times. Some of the speeches lasted thirty to thirty-five minutes. In a time of continuing bloodshed in the Middle East, it was sheer bombast.

At 12:52 A.M., October 22, the draft resolution was finally adopted 14 to 0. China did not participate in the voting. Baroody's tirades and Tekoah's rebuffs went on for another hour and a half. When we received the report of the meeting, Gromyko noted: "Well, Tekoah's interest in delaying adoption of the cease-fire resolution one could understand, but what was wrong with Baroody? Doesn't he understand that he was playing into the hands of the Zionists?"

## "GO THE HELL AHEAD AND FIRE IT!"

A few minutes before the cease-fire went into effect, a whirlwind of fire rushed over Cairo, horrifying some and eliciting feelings of satisfaction and pride in others. Soviet surface-to-surface SCUD missiles were being fired at Israeli targets. This event was extraordinary because of the special status of the SCUD missiles. In accordance with the Soviet-Egyptian agreement, the SCUDs were guarded by a Soviet military unit. The use restrictions and certain consultation procedures before the SCUDs were employed put the missiles practically under full Soviet control. Sadat had complained about this to the Kremlin several times, but in vain. The Soviet military leaders were disposed to agree with the Egyptian request to employ the SCUDs but did not get the support of the Politburo. According to the deputy director of the Middle East Department, Evgenii Pyrlin, Gromyko on one occasion refused to clear a cable from the chief of staff ordering Soviet military personnel in Cairo to permit the use of SCUD missiles for an attack against Al'Arish, a small port city in the northern Sinai near which an Israeli military base was located and where the Americans had unloaded their supplies.

The firing of the SCUD missiles on October 22 was an unusual and curious story. On that day it was expected that the war was drawing to a close—and yet the most dangerous and sophisticated weapon deployed on Egyptian soil had not been in action. The Egyptian leadership as well as the Soviet military advisers in Cairo did not hide their disappointment. Vinogradov decided to contact Moscow and draw the Kremlin's attention to this extraordinary situation. According to Vinogradov, in the late afternoon of October 22 he called the Foreign Ministry, but Gromyko was not available. Because of the urgency of the matter, he decided to contact Grechko, the minister of defense. When Vinogradov asked him what should be done with the "quiet" SCUDs, Grechko did not hesitate to yell, "Go the hell ahead and fire it!" Vinogradov then passed the order on to Ievlev, and the "hell" was fired.

A few minutes later there was a call to Vinogradov from Moscow—

Gromyko was on the line. "What did you talk about with Grechko?" he asked. When he learned of Grechko's order, Gromyko was outraged and strictly prohibited Vinogradov from carrying out the order. "I am sorry, Andrei Andreyevich [Gromyko], I can't help it. The missiles have already been fired," Vinogradov replied.

Here is Sadat's version of the story: "On October 22, just before the cease-fire came into effect, I went to the Operations Room and ordered two ground-to-ground rockets fired at Deversoir. I wanted Israel to learn that such a weapon was indeed in our hands and we could use it at a later stage of the war, even though Israel had in fact realized from the moment the war broke out that we meant and did what we said."[26] Although several times throughout the war—the last time in his speech on October 16—Sadat had threatened to attack Israeli cities with long-range missiles called "Al Zafir," he was probably referring to the SCUD missiles. Vinogradov did not recall that in his communication with Sadat on October 22 the issue of firing the SCUD missiles had been raised, but knowing Sadat's position from many previous encounters, Vinogradov felt he could act on his own on that supposedly last day of the war. Having received Grechko's blessing, the Soviet military personnel cooperated with the Egyptians in executing the launches.

The firing of the SCUD missiles, and offensive military action in which Soviet personnel participated directly, has been seen by some as marking an important escalation in the degree of Soviet involvement in the Middle East war. "Whether this shift to direct offensive participation had been approved by the highest political and military authorities in Moscow remains a moot, though extremely important, point," said Ion Glassman.[27] In response to Glassman I would agree that the firing of the SCUDs was approved by the highest military authority in Moscow, but on the other hand, it contradicted the Kremlin line, which was aimed at de-escalating the degree of Soviet involvement in the Middle East. It seems to me, therefore, that this episode should be seen less as a policy problem and more as simply evidence of a dysfunctional chain of command.

The SCUD missiles fired on October 22 apparently all missed their targets in the Sinai and therefore did not play a significant military role. Nevertheless, Vinogradov and the Soviet military in Egypt believed that the launches had an important political effect and manifested the military potential of Egypt supported by the Soviet Union. On the other hand, twenty years after the SCUD firing, General Chaim Bar-Lev, who became Israel's ambassador to Moscow in the 1990s, claimed in an interview with me that the missiles were very inaccurate and did not damage Israeli targets. "It was a big excitement," he recalled.

## KISSINGER'S VISIT AS MOSCOW SAW IT

The month of October 1973 was saturated with important diplomatic events in the Soviet capital. Moscow had hosted the prime ministers of Japan and Denmark, the president of Algeria, the emperor of Ethiopia, and some other V.I.P.'s. These visits were highlighted by the media—pictures of the Soviet and foreign dignitaries, their speeches at official receptions, and communiqués on the talks were widely published.

But that was not the case with Kissinger's visit, even though the negotiations with the secretary of state were undoubtedly the most important and productive of the many encounters the Kremlin leaders had that month. No pictures, no announcement of the dinner Brezhnev gave in honor of Kissinger, no final communiqué on the visit were published. Only very brief accounts of Brezhnev's and Gromyko's talks with Kissinger disclosed that their subject was "the comprehensive review of the present situation in the Middle East and the consideration of eventual avenues of establishing peace in the region."[28] There was no official Soviet assessment of the talks with Kissinger, and the media followed suit, keeping silent. The only comment, apparently, was made in a very special way. Tass included in its report of Kissinger's departure from Moscow a reference to the secretary of state's view that the "talks in Moscow were fruitful."[29]

Kissinger's visit did not change the character of the Soviet propaganda campaign. On October 20 and 21, *Pravda, Izvestia, Krasnaya Zvezda,* and other Soviet newspapers continued to condemn the Israeli aggressors and those "imperialist circles" supporting them and to urge cessation of hostilities in the region. Generally, the articles cheered the military operations of the Arabs and boasted about Soviet contributions of weaponry and training to the Arabs. At the same time, they expressed some concern about the latest Israeli thrusts, admitting that all kinds of turns of events "are still possible."[30] Whatever the subsequent course of combat, *Pravda* predicted, Israel would suffer a political defeat.[31] "The aggressive policy of Israel," Colonel A. Leontyev wrote in *Krasnaya Zvezda,* "is fraught with serious consequences for the entire international situation. It is dangerous for Israel itself. The chase after an illusory 'victory' can lead it only to catastrophe."[32] *Izvestia*'s commentator, A. Bovin, believed that continuation of the conflict would merely increase the number of casualties and complicate the final settlement.[33] *Pravda*'s V. Ovchinnikov expressed indignation at the charge that the Soviet Union's solidarity with the Arabs was a serious cause of international tension.[34] Reports of U.S. military supplies, as well as information on meetings protesting Israeli aggression and "those imperialist circles" supporting it, had become compulsory for the Soviet propaganda, and Kissinger's visit did not change the tune.

The West viewed the agreement reached in Moscow as a serious Soviet concession on at least two issues: negotiations between the parties, and Soviet-American guarantees. For example, President Nixon commented on the Soviet-American resolution in the following way: "These terms were especially notable because they were the first in which the Soviets had agreed to a resolution that called for direct negotiation between the parties without conditions or qualifications."[35] A State Department report echoed this view by stating that Resolution 338 "marks the first time the Council has endorsed the need for negotiations between the parties, which the U.S. Government had long been urging."[36] Joseph Sisco recalled that the American delegation in Moscow considered Brezhnev's acceptance of the need for negotiations between the Arabs and the Israelis as one of the most important achievements of the talks. At the same time one could find opposite affirmations. For example, Walter Laqueur claimed that "the American representatives [at Moscow talks] were reportedly reluctant to accept Soviet proposals to link the cease-fire with immediate negotiations for a settlement, naming a time and place for the negotiations."[37]

The assertion that the Kremlin opposed in principle any direct negotiation between the Arabs and the Israelis did not correspond to reality. The political settlement strongly supported by the Soviet Union envisioned talks between the parties in the conflict. Having favored convening a peace conference with the participation of the Arab states and Israel, the Soviet Union realized that a final settlement of the Middle East crisis could be achieved in negotiation and cooperation between them as *equal* partners in the peace process. Although the February 1969 Soviet Big Four Plan for the Middle East did not mention direct negotiations among the parties concerned, it presumed contacts between them by signing a multilateral document. In the spring of 1972, on the eve of Nixon's visit, a document that reaffirmed Soviet support for a political settlement in the Middle East on the basis of Resolution 242 was elaborated in the Foreign Ministry. David Kimche wrote: "It was to be a comprehensive agreement which was to be negotiated by the parties concerned on the voluntary basis."[38]

Under conditions of Israel's continuing occupation of Arab land and the nonimplementation of Resolution 242, the Arabs adamantly rejected any negotiations with Israel that could be regarded as a conference between victorious Israel and defeated Arabs. I remember being instructed by the Foreign Ministry in the summer of 1972 to talk in New York with Egypt's permanent representative to the United Nations, Ismat Abdel Meguid, about the prospects of a political settlement in the Middle East. The issue of contacts and talks with the Israelis came up in our chat, especially because New York was the site of several encounters between high-ranking Soviet officials (including Deputy Foreign Minister Vladimir Semyenov) and Israeli representatives. Meguid stated that Egypt would never talk to an unpunished aggressor who had seized its land. This attitude of the Arabs was shared in general by Moscow. In addition, guided by the principle of proletarian internationalism and anti-imperialist struggle, the Kremlin did not encourage the Arabs to establish direct contacts with Israel, the "agent of American imperialism and international Zionism."

But in October 1973 the situation had changed profoundly. The Arabs were in a better bargaining position than at any time since 1948. Therefore, steadfastly asserting the need for a long-term settlement, the Kremlin reasonably favored negotiations between the parties. In any case, I do not recall any opposition to such negotiations being raised at the Politburo throughout the Yom Kippur War.

On the other hand, to claim as Marvin and Bernard Kalb do that "Brezhnev won Sadat's agreement to direct talks with Israel—an approach Egypt had never before accepted—only after sending his additional assurances that Russia would—if necessary, alone—guarantee the observance of the cease-fire,"[39] seems to me inaccurate. The decision to start negotiations "between the parties concerned" under certain conditions had been Sadat's own.

It is true that the Moscow talks about Soviet-American guarantees of any cease-fire or any long-term settlement did not clarify anything. The Security Council resolution said nothing about those things either. But there seemed to be a mutual understanding that the issue should be thoroughly considered both in Moscow and in Washington. That is the way Brezhnev interpreted Nixon's message of October 20 as recognizing the crucial role that guarantees played with respect to the attitudes of both Israel and the Arab states as they pondered this superpower initiative. In his speech on October 26, Brezhnev once again stated that the Soviet Union was ready to "participate in appropriate guarantees." Thus, neither during the talks with Kissinger nor later did the Kremlin give up its favorite idea of joint Soviet-American guarantees of a long-term settlement in the Middle East. However, the incompatible principles of Soviet foreign policy—the desire, as the Russian proverb says, to kill two hares with one shot—buried what was, from my point of view, an effective instrument in the process of peace settlement in the Middle East.

Yet the Kremlin was satisfied with the results of the Soviet-American talks. Brezhnev could meet Sadat's personal appeal for an immediate cease-fire almost within twelve hours. He succeeded in agreeing with Kissinger on a joint Soviet-American resolution that, as he saw it, corresponded to Egyptian views. He believed also that in the long run the resolution was in accord with the desire to stop the fighting that Assad had expressed in the first days of the war. Thus, the Kremlin leaders believed that the Security Council draft resolution worked out in Moscow was in the best interests of the Arabs and complied fully with the Soviet foreign-policy principle of proletarian internationalism.

At the same time, Brezhnev emphasized several times that Nixon's October 20 message and the Moscow talks demonstrated the vitality and power of the cooperation between the Soviet Union and the United States. Once, chatting in our presence with Gromyko, Brezhnev noted: "What Kosygin could not achieve in three days of negotiations in Cairo with our friend Sadat I could achieve in three hours with our adversary Kissinger." The very fact that an agreement with the United States had been reached in the midst of a war in which the interests of the superpowers were so different was considered in the Kremlin as a triumph of the Soviet foreign-policy principle of peaceful coexistence.

Another important reason that the Kremlin was satisfied with the Moscow talks was that the cease-fire canceled direct Soviet military involvement in the war and ensured Soviet disengagement from all further developments related to the fighting. Because the Kremlin had opposed the Arab-initiated war and was not interested in and not ready for participation in the fighting, a protracted war could only challenge Soviet military power. Besides, the cease-fire initiated by the Soviet Union would, as the Kremlin leaders believed, strengthen the image of peace-loving Soviets. Finally, a big Soviet propaganda show to start in Moscow on October 25 was planned: The World Congress of Peace

Forces. Because I saw Brezhnev and other Soviet leaders almost every day at that time, I knew that they were attaching great significance to that event. Unfortunately, neither the Western politicians nor the political scientists fully comprehended the importance of such events for the Soviet system.

All these factors taken together explain why the Kremlin was so satisfied with the results of the talks with Kissinger. According to some commentators, "Kissinger had the impression that Brezhnev was so eager to preserve at least the spirit of détente that he would make a major concession" at the Moscow talks.[40] Such an assessment is certainly a narrow-minded one. Several factors beyond détente, including maintaining special relations with the Arabs, account for Brezhnev's flexibility. The day Kissinger was leaving Moscow, good feelings and satisfaction prevailed, but the dramatic events of the next few days would prevent the Kremlin from expressing its satisfaction publicly, and new developments would force it to revive some of its original apprehensions.

# CHAPTER 6

# THE ESCALATION

## THE TWO-SUPERPOWERS-DOMINATING-THE-WORLD MENTALITY

On Monday, October 22, we were waiting impatiently for word that the military operations had ceased. Throughout the last two weeks we had been entirely preoccupied with the Middle East, putting aside all other issues. Volumes of different papers and letters were waiting for action in our offices. Now that the Security Council had adopted the cease-fire resolution, we felt we could relax a little. We thought the war had stopped and we could go back to business as usual.

However, alarming information from the Middle East interfered with our plans once again. News about fighting on both fronts and about the continuing advance of Israeli troops on the western bank began to come in from Cairo and Damascus. Soon we learned that the Third Egyptian Army and the Egyptian stronghold at Suez were surrounded by Israeli troops. The situation on the Syrian-Israeli front was more stable, but there were no indications that both sides were in the process of ceasing fire.

At noon, Gromyko talked with our task force about steps the Soviet

Union should take in response to violations of the cease-fire. Several views were expressed, including adoption of a new Security Council resolution condemning the violators and issuance of a strong statement by the Soviet government. I argued the necessity of sending a group of United Nations observers to the cease-fire line but was rebuffed by Gromyko. "The idea is inappropriate," he noted, without giving any explanation. Most probably, he did not want to involve the United Nations in ensuring implementation of Resolution 338 because he considered that the superpowers' responsibility. I was glad to learn later that my counterpart in Washington, David Popper, assistant secretary of state in charge of United Nations affairs, also believed that the handiest method of policing the cease-fire was to have a United Nations observer group stationed along the Suez Canal. Anyway, in a couple of days it became obvious that using United Nations personnel to supervise the cease-fire was inevitable.

That evening our task force was called to the Kremlin again. The meeting in Brezhnev's study included only Gromyko, Andropov, and Grechko. Brezhnev, in contrast to his cheerful mood of the previous day, was somber, irritated. The guests for the World Congress of Peace Forces were beginning to arrive in Moscow, and many delegations had asked for an appointment with Brezhnev. The shaky situation in the Middle East, however, constrained him from making any public statements, so instead of making sensational announcements about the successful ending of the war, he had to keep it to himself. He did not like that. Indeed, he believed the crisis had passed. "Brezhnev had an interest not only in presenting the cease-fire as a positive and effective measure but also in ensuring that this was indeed the case," Galia Golan correctly surmised in her book.[1]

Brezhnev invited his closest colleagues to discuss immediate measures to take in response to the Israeli action. Gromyko proposed sending a message to President Nixon urging him to "force" the Israelis to comply with the Security Council decision. He also suggested an urgent meeting of the Security Council aimed at adopting a resolution condemning Israel's violation of the council's decision and demanding the withdrawal of Israeli troops to the positions they occupied when Resolution 338 was passed. We prepared a rough draft of the resolution right on the spot, but when we showed it to the participants it was clear that the Americans would find it unacceptable and veto the draft, which contained a condemnation of Israel. Besides, a unilateral Soviet action in the Security Council would diminish the importance of Resolution

338 and challenge the efficiency of the joint Soviet-American action. Therefore it was decided to act together with the United States and to introduce another joint resolution in the Security Council.

Brezhnev suggested an urgent contact with Kissinger to clear with him the draft we had prepared without the paragraph condemning Israel and with language limiting the resolution to a call to both sides to cease fire immediately and return to positions they occupied at the moment Resolution 338 went into force. We assumed that the cable to Kissinger would be signed by his counterpart, the Soviet foreign minister, but Gromyko proposed sending it in the name of General Secretary Brezhnev. "It would be much more authoritative and weighty," he remarked, and of course nobody argued with him. At the same time, to avoid any insult to Nixon by bypassing him, Brezhnev instructed us to prepare a personal message of a more general character addressed to President Nixon.

I would like to note that direct communication (written or oral) between heads of states is a method in diplomacy as old as diplomacy itself. During World War II, when all important international issues were solved at the meetings of the three leaders—Churchill, Roosevelt, and Stalin—or in their correspondence, the Soviet diplomacy had recognized this method. In the postwar period, contacts on the highest level were maintained. The value of such communications lies mainly in their extraordinary character. It is understood that they deal only with the most important or urgent matters, lest they become routine and quickly devalued. This happened, I believe, during the Yom Kippur War. Brezhnev addressed President Nixon too many times. He sent him more than twice as many messages as he received from him, and from my point of view some of them, such as the one we were ordered to draft on October 23, were not necessary. Again, this was mainly a matter of internal politics. The Soviet leader's personal messages were meant to confirm his importance and unparalleled activity in foreign affairs, so any suggestion that a personal message be sent to world leaders on behalf of Brezhnev was automatically supported in the Politburo. Nobody dared object, knowing that Brezhnev liked it. I remember that Sytenko once joked that if the authors of the proposals were forced to draft them there would be very few personal messages.

The meeting in Brezhnev's study on October 23 was held in the spirit of acknowledgment of the special responsibility of the Soviet Union and the United States for the cease-fire. The blame for the continuation of the fighting was put entirely on Israel. All four participants repeatedly said, referring to the Resolution 338, that "it is the duty" of the two superpowers to ensure that the resolution is carried out, to make Israel obey that resolution, and so on. Although an eventual direct Soviet-American peacekeeping operation in the Middle East was not discussed at that meeting, such a possibility was not excluded. At one point, Grechko suggested that if the Soviet Union and the United States were to use their armed forces, the peace in the Middle East would be restored overnight. In support, he recalled Khrushchev's proposal to Eisenhower to send joint Soviet and American troops to the Middle East during the Suez Crisis in 1956. The two-superpowers-dominating-the-world mentality still prevailed.

Gromyko once again raised the question of possibly limiting arms supplies to the belligerent parties and proposed talking to Washington to find out what the attitude of the United States toward such a joint action would be. Brezhnev said the idea was good but that Soviet and American arms aid could not be equated, because the Soviet Union was helping the victims of aggression, while the United States was the aggressor. In addition, he noted, an agreement on such a delicate issue as balanced limitation of arms shipments to the Arabs and to Israel would take a long time. Perhaps we could stop the airlift for a short time and see how the Americans responded to such a move, he speculated. No decision on this was made at that meeting, although nobody raised any objections to it. Late that night we left the Kremlin with feelings of anxiety and uncertainty.

## NEW PROBLEMS WITH SADAT AND ASSAD

The next morning, October 23, while new joint steps with the Americans were in the works, the situation in the Middle East deteriorated. Vinogradov recalls that on that day he talked with Sadat four times, primarily on the latter's initiative. Sadat complained about the continuing Israeli violations of the cease-fire and the difficult military situation, especially of the Third Army. The main theme of those conversations, however, was Sadat's appeal for a strong Soviet action aimed at implementing Resolution 338. He asked the Kremlin about it, according to Vinogradov, at 3:00 P.M. Cairo time on October 23, and again in the evening of the same day. He emphasized that, as a co-sponsor of the cease-fire resolution and guarantor of its implementation, the Soviet

Union was obliged to take all necessary steps to prevent flagrant violation of the resolution by Israel. Sadat referred to the talks he had with Kosygin regarding the Soviet-American guarantees as a basic precondition of a cease-fire and said that his agreement to end the fighting was based on this understanding. This was, of course, a frivolous interpretation of the Cairo talks, because Kosygin did not and could not make any commitment concerning Soviet-American guarantees. He said only that bilateral guarantees had to be cleared with the Americans.

Vinogradov drew Moscow's attention to the assertion in the Egyptian media that Sadat made his decision to cease fire after taking into account guarantees he received in the message from Brezhnev, even though the message had contained nothing about any unilateral Soviet guarantee. Sadat also urged Moscow to approach Washington and demand that the United States carry out its obligation as the Security Council resolution's co-guarantor. On the same day, Sadat sent a message to Nixon urging the United States to intervene in the Middle East conflict in order to guarantee full implementation of the cease-fire resolution "in accordance with the joint US-USSR agreement," even if that necessitated the use of force.[2] Sadat did not mention to Vinogradov his appeal to Nixon, despite his promise to keep Moscow informed of his contacts with Washington.

Vinogradov's information on Sadat's assessment of the critical military situation was confirmed by the reports from the Defense Ministry in Moscow. Experts from the ministry were of the opinion that the Egyptian armed forces were in deep trouble. They did not see any reliable way out of the deadlock if the Israeli advance on the western bank continued.

The situation on the Syrian front was far from being as desperate for the Arabs. In fact, the Syrians, strongly supported by the Iraqis, were planning a new offensive on the Golan Heights. Syria did not make any statements concerning Resolution 338 and did not commit itself to stop fighting. On October 23, Syrian Foreign Minister Khaddam summoned Soviet Ambassador Mukhitdinov and asked him the Kremlin's opinion about the new situation: Should Syria reject the Security Council resolution and initiate new military operations against Israel, or accept the resolution and cease fire? Mukhitdinov, having no instructions from Moscow, did not comment on Khaddam's alternatives.

The assertion of the *London Sunday Times* Insight Team that Assad called off the attack on the Golan Heights on Monday, October 22, because "under Ambassador Mukhitdinov's pressure, he had little choice," was not accurate.[3] The Insight Team, alas, distorted Mukhitdinov's role in the events, portraying him as a capricious boss in Damascus who could effectively pressure the Syrians, threaten them, order supplies to be cut off, and so on.[4] Assad was never a man to be threatened or ordered successfully by anybody, let alone by an ambassador, even of a superpower. In his chats he stressed that he would not tolerate a superpower "condominium" and that "he was not a Soviet puppet."[5]

Reporting to the Foreign Ministry about his conversation with Khaddam, Mukhitdinov said Khaddam had asked the representatives of Arab states in Damascus the same question about honoring the cease-fire. Referring to reliable sources, Mukhitdinov reported to Moscow that Syria's intention to continue the war was not supported by other Arab states, who agreed that Syria had no other choice but to comply with the decision of the Security Council. The Soviet military advisers were also skeptical about a new Syrian offensive, because they did not believe Syria had much of a chance against Israel by itself.

In its reply to Khaddam's inquiry, the Kremlin stated that the final decision regarding such an important question as whether to continue military operations against Israel or to cease fire was obviously completely within the competence of the leadership of the Syrian state. It was important, however, to take into account all circumstances in the concrete situation, the Soviet reply went on. If the war on the Egyptian front were stopped or were about to be stopped, any action that gave Israel a pretext for resuming military operations against Syria would not be justified.

In brief, the Kremlin's stand on the duration of the fighting on the Syrian front was negative. Having no support for continuation of the war either from the Arab states or from the Soviet Union, Syria announced that it would accept the cease-fire, on the understanding that Resolution 338 was based on "the complete withdrawal of Israeli forces from all Arab territories occupied in June 1967 and subsequently" and "the safeguarding of the legitimate national rights of the Palestinian people in accordance with the resolutions of the United Nations."[6] Moscow was happy with Assad's decision.

## ANOTHER JOINT SOVIET-AMERICAN ACTION IN THE SECURITY COUNCIL

Israeli troops continued their offensive against the encircled Egyptian Third Army. Alarming news was coming from Cairo almost constantly.

## THE ESCALATION    157

Stopping the war was becoming ever more urgent—that was the mood in the Kremlin. By noon, October 23, Brezhnev's messages to Nixon and Kissinger were ready. The messages to Nixon—two of them, sent to Washington within less than three hours—differed from the previous one addressed to Nixon on the eve of Kissinger's visit not only in content but also in tone. They reflected the Kremlin's anger about Israeli violations of the cease-fire and about the indulgent attitude of the Americans toward those violations. They stressed the need to implement Soviet-American commitments to guarantee the cease-fire, while appealing for immediate joint action to end the fighting. The special responsibility of the superpowers was mentioned, and there was reference to the existing understanding to act jointly and effectively. Nixon recalled:

> Although it began "Esteemed Mr. President," the words were hard and cold. Brezhnev ignored the Egyptian provocations and charged the Israelis with rupturing the cease-fire. He urged that the United States move decisively to stop the violations. He curtly implied that we might even have colluded in Israel's action.[7]

The draft of the second message from Brezhnev to Nixon included the same appeal to the President but without any new arguments. We advised Gromyko to refrain from sending it, arguing that such a repetition could unnecessarily dramatize the situation in Israel's favor. The minister disagreed, quoting a Russian saying: "One can't spoil porridge with butter."

The letter to Kissinger dealt mainly with the proposal to convene an urgent meeting of the Security Council to consider the situation and adopt a new resolution to stop the fighting immediately and return the parties to the positions they occupied when Resolution 338 was passed. A draft of a resolution was attached to the letter. Brezhnev proposed asking for an urgent meeting at noon New York time, October 23. Following Brezhnev's instruction, I called Malik in New York and informed him in general terms of our plan, advising him to keep in touch with Scali. Malik said the Egyptians had already asked for a Security Council meeting and that consultations with the member states had begun.

In the meantime, the text of another Soviet-American resolution was agreed on. In addition to confirming the cease-fire, this proposed resolution requested the United Nations Secretary General to take measures for immediate dispatch of United Nations observers to supervise the observance of the cease-fire between the forces of Israel and Egypt, using the United Nations personnel in the Middle East and, first of all, the personnel in Cairo. Gromyko had changed his original negative attitude toward observers, realizing that to use United Nations personnel was the only mechanism ready at that moment to supervise observance of the Security Council decision. The agreed text was sent to Cairo for Sadat's clearance. Vinogradov reported promptly and simply that Sadat agreed with the text.

Heikal's description of the Sadat-Vinogradov encounter was more picturesque. According to him, when Vinogradov showed Sadat the draft resolution the Egyptian president made some critical remarks:

> Vinogradov demurred: making amendments now, he said, would complicate matters. The President [Sadat] said that as it stood the resolution was inadequate. "Mr. President, do you want us to veto it then?" Vinogradov asked. The Ambassador's question annoyed the President. Of course he did not want the resolution vetoed. His only aim was to get the cease-fire to stick and not to give the Israelis any excuses for going on fighting.[8]

Following the request of Egypt, the Security Council was called to order at 4:00 P.M. New York time on Tuesday, October 23, for what was to be one of its most tumultuous sessions. The meeting started with a short statement by Egyptian Foreign Minister Zayyat condemning the Israeli violation of the cease-fire and urging the Security Council to take appropriate measures to stop the fighting. He explained, among other things, the reason Sadat had accepted Resolution 338:

> It was the weight of the two countries proposing the draft resolution, the United States and the USSR, that *guaranteed* to us that whatever we were trying to do by ourselves would indeed be done by the international community and the Permanent Members of the Security Council, mainly responsible for the maintenance of peace and order (emphasis added).[9]

In a far more protracted speech, the Israeli representative, Tekoah, tried to put the blame for the fighting on Egypt.

After that, Scali and Malik introduced the new Soviet-American draft and asked for a vote. The Chinese deputy foreign minister, Chiao Khuan-hua, referring to the instruction he had received from his government to make a statement before the vote, asked for the floor. He had hardly begun to speak when Malik interrupted him on a point of order, demanding that the Security Council take action immediately. Naturally this was opposed by the Chinese, who accused the Soviet Union and the United States of trying to manipulate the Security Council to their own ends: "China firmly opposes that the Council should be used as a tool of the two superpowers."[10] Six or seven times Malik interrupted the Chinese representative, preventing him from speaking. In response the deputy foreign minister of China waved his arms wildly in Malik's direction and shouted, "You should stop and wait!" At one point Tekoah also began to shout, and that immediately led to Saudi Arabia's representative, Baroody, getting into the fray. "You'd better shut up," Baroody threatened the Israeli representative. The whole meeting was a shameful mess. The council president had to suspend the meeting because of all the shouting. "I should like to put on record my delegation's deep regret that our proceedings were interrupted by unfortunate disorder," stated Scali bitterly.[11] In spite of all this, and as a result of the council president's several appeals, Resolution 339 was finally adopted.[12]

When a few days later I described the confrontation in the Security Council at the meeting of the Suslov Commission, I felt that some members liked the confrontational character—especially Malik's performance and the way he had rebuffed the "Chinese hegemonists" and the "Israeli Zionists." Nobody cared that the tumultuous session resulted in a further delay of an end to the fighting.

## THE CLOUDS THICKEN

The new resolution did not change the situation in the Middle East. The fighting continued. Israel's tough stand caused indignation in the Kremlin, and in a sharply worded statement by the Soviet government, drafted on October 23 under Suslov's supervision, Moscow charged that Israel's acceptance of the cease-fire had been "proven in fact a gross lie under cover of which the Israeli military perfidiously attacked the position of Egyptian troops and peaceful populated localities of the Arab Republic of Egypt." In an effort to apply maximum pressure on Israel, the Kremlin used unusually strong language for the first time: "The Soviet government warns the government of Israel of the gravest consequences that continuation of its aggressive actions against the Arab Republic of Egypt and the Syrian Arab Republic will entail."[13]

Criticism of the United States was growing sharper too, and a deal between the United States and Israel was regarded as highly probable. The October 23 statement served notice on Washington that Moscow believed the United States should prod Israel. The Soviet statement marked an abrupt shift from the mood that had prevailed in the Kremlin at the time when Soviet-American efforts to bring about the cease-fire resulted in a joint initiative in the Security Council. Now Brezhnev remarked, "Here, in Moscow, Kissinger behaved in a cunning way. He vowed fidelity to the policy of détente, and then while in Tel-Aviv he made a deal with Golda." That was the assessment of Kissinger's policy expressed by many Kremlin leaders who only a couple of days earlier were impressed by his "businesslike approach" and "practicality." In their judgment, Kissinger had intentionally deceived them by giving the Israelis his blessing to violate the cease-fire. In lobby discussions and at various meetings of the Central Committee, the Foreign Ministry, and other offices, the desire to take "a firm stand" both toward the United States and toward Israel was garnering more and more support: "One cannot trust the imperialists," "The Americans will never give up their support of Israel and international Zionism," "We should demonstrate the might of world socialism's unity and its solidarity with the peoples fighting aggressors," "We should force the Americans to carry out their commitments"—such were the sentiments now turning up here and there.

Gradually, the idea of sending Soviet and American troops to the Middle East was taking form. The formula "under appropriate auspices" began to be interpreted as unequivocally implying joint action by the United States and the Soviet Union—military if necessary—to halt the fighting and to implement Resolution 338. These inclinations became clear at the Politburo sessions and Suslov Commission meetings on October 23 and 24.

To understand how the Kremlin leaders perceived the issue of joint Soviet-American action in the Middle East crisis, one must keep a few things in mind. First, the Kremlin assumed that both President Nixon and General Secretary Brezhnev, in line with the general political agreements between the Soviet Union and the United States in 1972 and 1973, which emphasized détente in their bilateral relations, had since the first days of the war stressed the need to cooperate in order to stop the fighting, despite the obvious differences in their Middle East policy.

Both the Soviet Union and the United States were strongly engaged with the Arab states and with Israel, respectively, Brezhnev wrote to Nixon on October 18, but neither the Soviet Union nor the United States should forsake restraint. Nixon, in his message of October 20, went further. He appealed to Brezhnev for firm commitments "from both of us" to devote personal efforts to ensure the peace settlement and "to provide the strong leadership which our respective friends in the area will find persuasive." This sentence was understood in Moscow as a clear appeal for joint action using any leverage the Israelis and the Arabs would find "persuasive." The effective outcome of Kissinger's negotiation in Moscow and of the "Understanding" had given Moscow every reason to believe that the two superpowers were committed to exerting their influence on their "respective friends" in order to stop the fighting.

Second, the "Understanding" initialed by Gromyko and Kissinger was interpreted by the Kremlin leaders in the context of the two-superpowers-dominating-the-world mentality and Nixon's appeal for strong Soviet-American leadership. In the press of events, few cared to read the document. It was widely assumed that the document, singling out the special role of the Soviet Union and the United States in the process of peace settlement, included statements of their obligations to monitor the cease-fire and guarantee implementation of the Security Council decision. Listening to the discussion, however, I realized that the participants were commenting not on the "Understanding" but on each others' frivolous interpretations of it.

Third, the special responsibility of the Soviet Union and the United States for implementing Resolutions 338 and 339 was widely recognized and expressed to Moscow through many bilateral diplomatic channels, as well as in international organizations. For example, speaking on behalf of the nonaligned members of the Security Council, Kenya's ambassador, Joseph Odeo-Jowi, stated:

> When we voted for Resolutions 338 and 339 we had hoped that the two superpowers which were the sponsors of the two draft resolutions would spare no effort to stop the war; we have hoped that they would *use all their influence, and indeed all their power to vindicate peace and ensure the cease-fire called for by the Council* (emphasis added).[14]

The representative of Yugoslavia, Lazar Moisov, declared at the United Nations:

By undertaking their initiative in the two joint resolutions and having them adopted by this Council, the two permanent members of the Security Council, the United States and the USSR, have assumed a clear responsibility that *they would act to ensure implementation of the resolutions.* We have quoted the statement on their making their joint good offices available. (Emphasis added)[15]

In addition, Sadat's continued appeals to the Soviet Union and the United States to ensure implementation of the cease-fire as the guarantors of the resolutions of the Security Council strengthened the Kremlin's belief that it had not only the right but also the international obligation to interfere in order to prevent further violations of the cease-fire.

These arguments were expressed by the participants in meetings in the Kremlin. For example, on October 23 Kosygin suggested sending a joint Soviet-American team of military officials to observe the cease-fire. The idea was that this group would include 200 to 250 observers from each side. Kosygin was supported by Ustinov, who believed that such a step should be taken with the approval of the Americans, who should be reminded that when Kissinger was in Moscow the agreement had been "to act as guarantors." This view was shared by some other participants. However, Gromyko, while confirming that during the negotiations with Kissinger the readiness of both sides to act in cooperation had been agreed on, confessed that the document he initialed with Kissinger did not contain any specific Soviet or American obligation to guarantee implementation of the cease-fire. For this reason, he had some reservations about sending Soviet and American observers, and explained that that step would require a special decision of the Security Council. Taking into account the Chinese position on any Soviet-American move, Gromyko believed that such a decision would be vetoed by the Chinese. Besides, he noted, there were already United Nations observers in Cairo, which could be used as a pretext for objecting to such a Soviet proposal.

Kosygin replied irritably to Gromyko's remarks: "Those observers are 'dead souls.' The undeniable fact is that both we and the Americans committed ourselves to carry out the Security Council decision, and we should proceed from that assumption." Kosygin insisted on his proposal to send up to 250 Soviet and American observers from each side to the Middle East immediately. Marshal Kulikov raised serious reservations about this proposal, emphasizing that Israeli and Egyptian troops had to be disengaged before Soviet observers were sent to the Middle East. Otherwise, he warned, the Soviet military would be pushed into military operations, with unpredictable consequences.

In a lengthy discussion on the issue of guarantees, Brezhnev noted that the vague language of Resolution 338 and of the "Understanding" was caused by the urgency of the situation and was quite justified. The important thing was not the vague language of the diplomatic documents, he noted, but the mutual desire to cooperate that emerged from his correspondence with Nixon. Listening to Brezhnev's explanation, I had the feeling he was uneasy. He did not sound as confident in his arguments as he usually did. Perhaps he felt deceived by Kissinger, although he did not want to admit it publicly.

Despite certain reservations expressed at the meeting, Brezhnev and some of the other participants were still carried away by the idea of sending Soviet and American observers in order to guarantee implementation of the Security Council resolutions co-authored by the two superpowers. No decision on that issue was made on October 23. It is important to note, however, that at that meeting no participant suggested sending Soviet troops to the region. The idea was to dispatch only a limited number of observers. And none of the participants proposed sending Soviet observers unilaterally. They had to be part of a joint Soviet-American team. The main result of the meeting was the decision to deliver to Washington a new set of messages—an outcome very familiar to us but not always the most effective one.

The two new messages—one from Brezhnev to Nixon, the other from Gromyko to Kissinger—were sent to Washington on October 24. They reflected the Kremlin's disappointment, anger, and suspicion regarding the American position. Referring to Israel's various violations of the resolution worked out together by the Soviet Union and the United States, the Soviet leaders characterized such behavior as a challenge to world security and to the credibility of the Soviet-American cooperation. "What is behind all this?" Brezhnev asked President Nixon. Moscow was convinced that "the provocative behavior of Tel Aviv" was backed by Washington. Both Brezhnev and Gromyko urged their counterparts to exert their influence on Israel to comply with the cease-fire and hoped that Washington would inform Moscow about any American steps aimed at securing Israel's strict and immediate compliance with the resolutions of the Security Council. Although in their tone these messages were much tougher than the previous ones, they did contain conciliatory notes. "We would like to hope that we both will be true to our word and to the understanding we have reached," wrote Brezhnev.

## THE BUSIEST DAY

It is difficult to say which was the main preoccupation of the political leadership of the Soviet Union on October 24—the convocation of the World Congress of Peace Forces, or ending the war in the Middle East. The World Congress, preparations for which had begun in early 1973, was not just another worldwide propaganda campaign orchestrated by the Communist Party of the Soviet Union. The Congress was meant to confirm Brezhnev's role and authority as a world leader, to solidify his image as both a founder of the policy of relaxation of international relations and détente and a consistent defender of the interests of working people all over the world. For Brezhnev, the Congress was also important in his struggle for absolute power in the Politburo. His concealed opponents in the Politburo and the Central Committee would certainly use any failure of the Congress against him.

Brezhnev had to make a lengthy statement at the opening session, a statement designed to be the basis for the discussion and the documents to be adopted at the Congress. The huge apparatus of the Central Committee was embarked on the preparatory work. Speeches, resolutions, declarations, and other documents had been drafted. All these documents had to be cleared with the key delegations well in advance, in order to avoid any confusion at the Congress. The organizers of the Congress envisioned that the decisions made at the World Congress would be adopted in the best Soviet style—unanimously.

Brezhnev's speech was designed to be the main event of the World Congress. A large group of speechwriters was living in a special dacha residence of the Central Committee and drafting the speech. From time to time the draft was circulated among members of the Politburo and the Central Committee and revised several times. All the preparatory work was headed by Suslov and Ponomarev. A number of commissions and working groups, with the participation of representatives of the Foreign Ministry, the Defense Ministry, the KGB, and other Soviet agencies, were involved in the preparation for the Congress.

The opening of the World Congress was scheduled for October 25, and the few days preceding it coincided with growing tension in the Middle East and constant violations of the cease-fire. The threat of further deterioration of the international situation jeopardized the very idea behind the Congress—which was to demonstrate that the forces of peace are stronger than the forces of war. On October 24, Brezhnev was in a difficult position, because it would be almost impossible to cancel or postpone the Congress now. He cleared the opening of the Congress as scheduled but left the date he would make his statement open.

The atmosphere in the Kremlin was tense. Some members of the Politburo were involved more with the work of the Congress, others were mostly involved in settling the Middle East conflict. But many had to deal with both. For example, Suslov chaired the Politburo commission on the Middle East and at the same time, as the main ideologist, was in charge of the convocation of the Congress. The clumsy Soviet bureaucratic machine caused additional difficulties: the complicated decision-making mechanism was lagging behind events. All this created a very conflicted psychological climate in the Kremlin, which became a major factor in the character of the discussion and in the decisions the Soviet leaders made in those days. Unfortunately, neither the political counterparts of the Soviets nor the analysts noticed or acknowledged the importance of this phenomenon—the collision between the goals of the Congress and the Middle East reality—in the actions of the Soviet leaders in those critical days.

October 24 was marked by a new flow of disturbing news from Egypt. The efforts of the 20,000-man Third Army to break out had failed. The Israelis had cut off all supplies, including blood for transfusions, from the encircled Egyptian troops. The Soviet embassy in Cairo informed Moscow that the Egyptian militia was mobilized and that Cairo's authorities had made an appeal for civil resistance. It reported that Israeli forces were preventing the United Nations observers from reaching their destinations. As of October 24 at 9:00 A.M., there was not a single observer in the cease-fire area, and, according to the report, the headquarters of the United Nations observers in Jerusalem "did not show any signs of life."

It was an obvious breakdown of all resolutions on the cease-fire. Ambassador Vinogradov was again summoned by Sadat, who described the situation as a new Israeli aggression and asked for a salvage operation. He insisted that the Soviet Union and the United States intervene to force Israel to comply with the cease-fire. Sadat said he was appealing to General Secretary Brezhnev and President Nixon as heads of state and sponsors of the cease-fire resolution. In addition, Sadat reminded Vinogradov of the Soviet pledges to resupply Egypt with urgently needed weaponry. Finally, he informed the ambassador that he had decided to ask for another urgent meeting of the Security Council and expressed hope that the Soviet representative in New York would support Egypt's position.

In the afternoon of October 24, Sadat's formal appeal to Brezhnev urging the dispatch of Soviet observers or troops to the Egyptian side of the front came in. Vinogradov reported that Sadat was also urging the United States to dispatch observers or troops immediately, that very night. If the United States did not comply, Sadat, according to Vinogradov, *asked that the Soviet Union act separately* (emphasis added).[16] This request caused an extremely delicate situation within the context of Soviet-American détente and played an important role in setting up the next Soviet diplomatic moves.

From Vinogradov's point of view as well as that of the other Soviet representatives, Akopov and Kirpichenko, who worked in Cairo during the Yom Kippur War, Sadat's tactic was not very subtle. The Soviet diplomats were used to that. Whenever Egypt's military position became desperate and the threat to its independence became a reality, Sadat would make an urgent appeal to the Soviet Union for support, sometimes suggesting extreme measures. This happened when the Israelis succeeded in their breakthrough at the west bank, and he repeated the same tactic when it seemed that the encirclement of the Third Army might result in the military collapse of Egypt.

Not that Sadat actually wanted to increase Egypt's dependence on the Soviet Union or to have any unilateral Soviet military action in the area—far from it. From his talks with Kosygin, Sadat understood that the Soviet Union was not interested in jeopardizing détente by intervening. Sadat's extreme appeal for Soviet military action was merely his way of trying to make Washington more cooperative in the implementation of his strategic plan. It was the "Soviet card" in his game with the United States. Thus Heikal's denial—"There was not on this day—nor on any other day, for that matter—any suggestion by us or the Syrians that the Russians should move their forces into the area"—seems at best disingenuous.[17]

The Soviet response to Sadat's first request was prompt and positive. At a Politburo meeting late in the evening of October 24, the decision was made to form a group of fifty Soviet observers and send them to Cairo, accompanied by twenty interpreters. Together with General

Sergei Akhromeyev, at that time chief of one of the departments of the Soviet General Staff, I was involved in setting up the group. It turned out to be a difficult task, because the Soviet military did not have appropriate experience. Malik was instructed to meet with United Nations Secretary General Waldheim immediately and inform him of the Soviet government's decision, made in response to the Egyptian request.

The other alternative suggested by Sadat—to send Soviet troops—became an issue of long and sometimes heated discussion in the Kremlin that evening. A response to Sadat's suggestion was needed, one way or another—that was the general opinion. But should the Soviet Union send troops to the Middle East together with the Americans or unilaterally? Here there were different opinions. Some were proponents of a joint action. Others were very reluctant to send troops, whether jointly or separately. But it was obvious to everyone that carrying out a complicated military operation in the final stage of the war was very risky and almost impossible. I remember Kulikov at one point saying that by the time joint Soviet-American forces, or only Soviet forces, were ready for full-scale action, Cairo would have fallen and the war would be over. Nevertheless, something had to be done to prevent an unconditional surrender by Sadat, especially on the eve of the great political performance, the World Congress of Peace Forces.

President Nixon's message in response to Brezhnev's letter of October 23 had an important impact on the Kremlin's final decision. The message had come in to Moscow the morning of October 24 (time difference between Washington and Moscow), a few hours earlier than Sadat's appeal. Both messages were discussed at the evening meeting in the Kremlin on the 24th. The profound differences between the two assessments of the situation, and the tone of the messages, made the Kremlin leaders indignant. While the Egyptian Third Army was in a desperate situation and Sadat was begging for rescue, Nixon was claiming that it was relatively quiet at the battlefront and advising Brezhnev to press Egypt and Syria to comply with the cease-fire. Although Nixon concluded his message to Brezhnev by saying that both leaders had "achieved a historic settlement over the past weekend and should not permit it to be destroyed,"[18] the message was received bitterly and created the conviction that the Americans were trying to fool Moscow.

"The time for empty words has passed," noted Brezhnev at the meeting, and invited his colleagues to express their views regarding Sadat's request. Kosygin repeated his proposal to dispatch several hundred Soviet and American observers to the region to ensure the cease-fire, but that idea was not realistic. The Americans had already indicated to Dobrynin that they would strongly oppose any call on the United States and the Soviet Union to provide forces for implementing the cease-fire resolutions. To limit a new message to Washington to a suggestion to act jointly in accordance with Sadat's request was a waste of time. "Sadat asks us to take concrete measures to save Egypt this very night," Ustinov pointed out, suggesting that the meeting continue as long as necessary for reaching a consensus and agreeing on a response to Sadat's appeal and on the text of a message to be sent to Washington.

Then the issue of sending Soviet troops unilaterally came up. Nobody liked or supported that idea. "We have already made a principal decision not to be involved in the Middle East war, and there are no reasons to change our decision," noted Brezhnev. Thus any military involvement, unilateral or together with the United States, was ruled out.

Here I want to add some personal observations. In those days I had contacts with many military men. We had to ensure the speedy deployment of Soviet observers at the Egyptian-Israeli front, and even their transportation became an issue. The General Staff had insisted on delivering the observers by airlines of neutral states, not by Soviet planes, so we had to communicate with Finnish authorities to get their clearance. Therefore, although I talked with General Akhromeyev and his aides in the General Staff several times, I never noticed or felt that the General Staff was preoccupied with preparation for any large-scale military operation. The main concern of the General Staff in those days was to implement promptly the Politburo's decision regarding the observers. I did not hear about any plans for unilaterally sending even a small Soviet military force to the Middle East. Maybe I did not notice the preparatory work for a landing, or maybe it was effectively hidden from us diplomats—who were never fully trusted by our military colleagues—but I don't think so. "From the evidence available, it seems unlikely that the Soviets ever contemplated a massive military intervention," William Quandt wrote in 1976—and I agree.[19]

With the situation hopeless for Sadat, and not wanting to become a party in the war, the Kremlin leaders concluded that the only way out of the deadlock was to exert effective pressure on Washington and force the Americans to pressure Israel. Therefore it was decided to hint to the Americans that in case the United States was not ready for joint action the Kremlin would not exclude the possibility of unilateral action in the Middle East. The participants were convinced that even a reference to such an eventuality would frighten Washington and force it to take appropriate measures with Israel. However, no military measures in connection with such a Soviet statement were considered at the meeting.

As Kuznetsov recalled later, Brezhnev's message was drafted cautiously in order "not to frighten the Americans too much" (I was busy with the observers issue so did not participate in the drafting). Therefore, instead of declaring Soviet readiness to send troops unilaterally, the authors used vague language: The Soviet Union would consider taking appropriate steps unilaterally. Besides, in the correspondence with Nixon an understanding was reached that the word "contingents," which could be interpreted as meaning military personnel with limited functions, would be substituted for the word "troops," which had appeared in Sadat's message.

Because of the urgency, the text of Brezhnev's menacing message to Nixon was drafted in Brezhnev's study. After Politburo approval it was signed by Brezhnev and sent to Nixon early in the morning of October 25 (late in the evening of October 24, Washington time). The message began with an assertion that the mutual understanding to act jointly in the interests of peace was of greatest value and that it had to be implemented in the current complicated circumstances. Brezhnev repeated that Israel was continuing to fight despite the Security Council resolution, and he drew attention to Sadat's appeal to the leaders of the Soviet Union and the United States to ensure the cease-fire. In accordance with this appeal, Brezhnev suggested:

> Let us together, the Soviet Union and the United States, urgently dispatch Soviet and American military contingents to Egypt to ensure implementation of the Security Council decision of October 22 and 23 concerning the cessation of fire and all military activities, and also of our understanding with you on the guarantee of the implementation of the Security Council decisions. It is necessary to adhere without delay.

This part of the message almost fully repeated the wording of Sadat's appeal and once again referred to the understanding with Nixon regarding Soviet and American "strong leadership" with their respective friends in the area, which Brezhnev interpreted as a bilateral commitment to guarantee the cease-fire.

Then came the sentences that were to cause panic among some in Washington: *"I will say it straight that if you find it impossible to act jointly with us in this matter, we should be faced with the necessity urgently to consider taking appropriate steps unilaterally. We cannot allow arbitrariness on the part of Israel"* (emphasis added). This part of the message was also consistent with Sadat's appeal to Moscow to carry out unilateral Soviet military action in case Washington rejected his proposal.

The Kremlin leaders were satisfied with the message. They had played their trump card with the Americans: the threat of Soviet military intervention in the Middle East. I doubt that Moscow knew about a conversation in Washington on October 19 between Elliot Richardson and Alexander Haig, in the course of which the former wondered: "Won't Israel hold back, in light of that prospect [possible Soviet military action]?"[20] Moscow, however, was confident that Washington now would do everything possible to stop Israel from defeating the Arabs totally. Thus the Soviet Union would meet Sadat's appeal, save its Arab friends, and demonstrate its solidarity with the "victims of aggression." At the same time, in urging Washington to act jointly in accordance with the ideas shared by the superpower leaders, the Kremlin was fostering détente. Everything looked very nice, certainly from the Kremlin's point of view.

## "THE HONOR AND DIGNITY OF . . . MR. KISSINGER ARE NOW BEING SUBJECTED TO SEARCHING SCRUTINY"

Almost simultaneously with the October 24 meeting in the Kremlin, the Security Council resumed its activity. Egyptian Foreign Minister Zayyat had requested an urgent Security Council meeting to "consider the continuing violations committed by Israel of the cease-fire," and Council President Laurence McIntyre, the Australian ambassador, started consultations, which unfortunately led nowhere. It was known that the Egyptians wanted the Security Council to take strong and effective measures, including dispatching foreign troops to the region, but no concrete proposal or draft resolution was in circulation. The Soviet representative to the United Nations, Malik, had instructions to maintain close contacts with the Egyptians and the Syrians and to support Egypt's request for a Security Council meeting, but that was about the extent of his instructions. Dobrynin, who in the afternoon of October 24 had returned from Moscow, where he had several discussions with Soviet leaders, understood the mood of the Kremlin better than Malik.

When he was leaving Moscow, the two-superpowers-dominating-the-world-mentality prevailed, but soon afterward, in Washington, he understood that the Kremlin was about to begin pressuring Washington. Dobrynin was instructed to inform Kissinger that the Soviet Union supported the Egyptian request, although Malik was not authorized to introduce any resolution regarding the dispatch of Soviet and American troops in the region, as the Kalbs have claimed.[21] Malik, unlike Dobrynin, was not aware of the contents of Brezhnev's "menacing" message. When the question of informing Malik arose in the Kremlin, it was decided to refrain from doing it. "We do not want to frighten the whole world. We have a limited task," joked Brezhnev in response to our inquiry. Malik was ordered to follow our "principal line," condemning Israel and criticizing the American stand, and this time Malik did not have to cooperate with Scali. That gave Malik more than enough latitude to demonstrate the best Cold War diplomatic style.

The Soviet representative spoke of the "troika"—Golda Meir, Moshe Dayan, Abba Eban—who bore "direct responsibility for all these criminal and internationally punished acts," and of the aggressive actions of the Israeli government that demonstrated "brazen disdain for the decision of the [Security] Council and defiance of all the Members of the United Nations and of the world at large" etc., etc.[22] There was nothing new in Malik's anti-Israeli vocabulary, but what was new for those few weeks of Soviet-American relations during the war was the public criticism of the U.S. position. Malik stated that the United States had assumed a great international responsibility and an obligation to guarantee Israel's compliance with the Security Council resolutions. He expressed the hope that the United States would use every means at its disposal and bring its weight "to bear in order to check the adventurers in Tel Aviv." He claimed that "no reasonable man" would believe that the United States was powerless in this matter and declared emphatically: "The honor and dignity of the United States and international trust in it and in the new United States Secretary of State, Mr. Kissinger, are now being subjected to searching scrutiny."[23]

As far as the subject of the Security Council meeting was concerned—the Egyptian appeal to the superpowers for urgent adoption of measures, including even the dispatch of their military contingents—Malik was much more cautious. He limited himself to stating that the appeal and the measure proposed by Egypt were "fully warranted" and "in accord with the charter and the recent decisions of the Security Council." He did not mention, of course, that the Soviet Union might be forced to consider taking appropriate steps unilaterally, and he did not call on the Security Council to adopt a resolution in accordance with the Egyptian request. Instead, he continued his improvisations, suggesting that strict sanctions against Israel be adopted and appealing to all the members of the United Nations to sever diplomatic relations and all other ties with Israel. Suffice it to say that Malik was not empowered to make such proposals, but in accordance with the anti-imperialist mood prevailing in those days in Moscow, nobody cared much about the tone of Malik's contributions to the United Nations discussions.

Meanwhile, Soviet-Egyptian dialogue continued in Cairo. After Brezhnev's message had been sent to Washington, Vinogradov was instructed to inform Sadat of its contents. At 8:00 A.M. on October 25 the ambassador reported that Sadat had expressed "great and sincere gratitude" for everything the Soviet Union had done during the night and that he was impressed by Brezhnev's message to Nixon and by the Soviet decision to send seventy observers to Egypt. Sadat instructed his minister of war to help the observers carry out their important duties.

Sadat also informed Vinogradov that he had received a message from Nixon in which the American president strongly opposed sending outside military forces—including those of the United States and the Soviet Union—to the Middle East to enforce the cease-fire. If such a resolution were introduced in the Security Council, Nixon warned, it would be vetoed by the United States. He could agree only with dispatching United Nations observers to the region. Sadat told Vinogradov that Egypt would insist in the Security Council that military contingents be sent. If the Americans vetoed such a resolution, Egypt would ask for an urgent General Assembly meeting and insist that it adopt a decision to set up United Nations military contingents, as was the case during the 1956 aggression against Egypt. Sadat asked Moscow to instruct the Soviet delegation at the General Assembly to cooperate with the Egyptian representatives. Finally, he stressed that the latest events clearly demonstrated that the Americans were indeed plotting with the Israelis against Egypt. Thus the Egyptian reaction to the Kremlin's diplomatic move was positive. Sadat apparently liked the tough position of the Soviet Union and was happy that there were no signs of any Soviet intention to send troops to Egypt. He enjoyed how he had played his trump card.

Assad too was informed of the content of Brezhnev's message to Nixon and of the decision to send a group of Soviet observers to Cairo, but there was no immediate reaction from the U.S. President.

## WASHINGTON'S OVERREACTION

When Brezhnev's message reached Washington it was the evening of October 24. Soviet Ambassador Dobrynin immediately telephoned Kissinger at 9:35 P.M. and read it to him. By that time, the Politburo members had already left the Kremlin, since it was early in the morning of October 25 in Moscow. The last preparation for the opening of the World Congress of Peace Forces was under way. For many Muscovites participating in the Congress and in other activities around the capital, the day promised to be a pleasant and busy one. Nobody—including, I'm afraid, the Kremlin leaders—imagined that the world was on the verge of a nuclear confrontation because of a letter Brezhnev had just sent to President Nixon.

I was in my office in the Foreign Ministry at 8:30 A.M. Moscow time, October 25 (12:30 A.M. Washington time). I summoned my colleagues from the Department of International Organizations and briefly informed them of the contents of Brezhnev's latest message to Nixon. A lively discussion ensued, in the course of which we considered how the Americans might respond to the message. Some believed that Nixon might strongly oppose any bilateral or unilateral military action of the superpowers and would threaten Brezhnev with the prospect of serious deterioration in Soviet-American relations if the Soviet military should intervene unilaterally. Someone said that the Soviet Union might face joint political remonstrance from NATO orchestrated by Washington. Many of us, myself included, believed that the response might be twofold: that Nixon in an urgent message to Brezhnev would strongly reject Soviet proposals, and that at the same time he would put effective pressure on the Israelis to force them to stop fighting immediately. "I don't think Nixon will make much ado about Brezhnev's message," I said. "It is not in his interest to show how fragile détente really is. He already has several irons in the fire, and they are all red hot."

There was no speculation about the consequences of a unilateral Soviet military action in the Middle East for a very simple reason: Nobody thought there would be one, given current circumstances. It seemed to be out of the question. And here, I believe, we were right. But how wrong was our forecast of the American reaction! Only a few hours passed before we realized we had miscalculated.

As it turned out, Washington had failed to grasp the real meaning and objective of Brezhnev's message. Nixon, Kissinger, and Haig were shocked at the message. Kissinger was frightened not only by Brezhnev's proposal to Washington to act together or face eventual unilateral Soviet "appropriate steps," but also even by the way Dobrynin had delivered the message. This is how Kissinger described it:

> No reassurance; no claim of having been misunderstood; no suggestion that at midnight we all go to bed and resume our discussions in the morning because there was no real threat. Only the laconic comment that he would stand by for our reply. If Dobrynin's pose was designed to heighten our sense of menace, it succeeded admirably.[24]

When I asked Dobrynin to comment on Kissinger's description, Dobrynin stated that when delivering Brezhnev's message to Kissinger he had been guided by the strict instruction to relay the message to the White House and to report back to Moscow that the instructions had been carried out. Because he had not been asked to comment on the message, and because he understood the seriousness and importance of the issue, he did not soften the message, nor did he do anything to create the impression that the crisis was inevitable.

There are different descriptions, by Nixon, Kissinger, and Haig—and other countervailing views—of what happened that night in the White House, but to dwell on the American decision-making process is not my task. Kissinger says he tried to get in touch with Nixon at 9:50 P.M. to inform him of Brezhnev's message but was told by the President's aide, Alexander Haig, that Nixon had retired for the night. Haig refused to comply with Kissinger's request that Nixon be awakened.

As a result, a National Security Council meeting without either the President or the Vice President commenced at 10:40 P.M. At about 11:30 P.M., a decision was reached to put American troops all over the world at a state of enhanced readiness with a nuclear alert known as Defense Condition III, or Defcon III. Secretary of Defense James Schlesinger instructed Admiral Ernest Moorer, chairman of the Joint Chiefs of Staff, to go ahead with the enhanced readiness conditions. In the course of the meeting, a message to Brezhnev in Nixon's name was drafted. The meeting lasted three and a half hours, and between 2:30 and 3:30 A.M., October 25, the participants joined Nixon and the rest of America in going to bed.

At 5:40 A.M., Deputy National Security Adviser Brent Scowcroft called Dobrynin and said he was sending to the Soviet embassy by special messenger the text of the "oral reply" of the President to General

Secretary Brezhnev. Fifteen minutes later the messenger delivered the text to the embassy. It was almost 6:00 A.M. in Washington and 2:00 P.M. in Moscow.

The night had been a hectic one for Kissinger. In addition to chairing the meeting in the White House, he had five important talks with Israeli Ambassador Simcha Dinitz. Kissinger expressed the grave displeasure of the United States at the prospect that Soviet troops would be used to intimidate Israel into implementing the cease-fire. At the same time, however, although Kissinger's memoirs contain only short references to these talks, the Israelis were probably warned of severe consequences if they continued noncompliance with the cease-fire. Early in the morning of October 25, an extraordinary session of the Israeli cabinet was called to order. For four hours the grave situation caused by the Soviet démarche was discussed, and as a result Israel nearly ceased its military activity.

Before leaving the White House, Kissinger called the British ambassador, Lord Cromer, to inform him about the alert status of American forces. The ambassador responded: "Why tell us, Henry? Tell your friends—the Russians."[25] Later I asked Dobrynin whether Kissinger had told him about the alert, and if not how he had learned about it. No, he said, he had not been informed by Kissinger, but learned about the alert from the morning broadcast of the American media. It was perhaps the only time in Dobrynin's long career that the Kremlin learned about an extraordinary event in the United States—a nuclear alert—earlier than its trusted and reliable ambassador in Washington, and even earlier than the President of the United States!

Kissinger and his colleagues, leaving the White House Situation Room, believed they had gained time. "We decided that going to Defcon III would not be noted quickly enough by Soviet decisionmakers," Kissinger wrote in his memoirs.[26] This turned out to be a huge miscalculation. Soon after Admiral Moorer announced the readiness condition—about 11:30 P.M., October 24, Washington time (7:30 A.M., October 25, Moscow time)—Soviet intelligence reported Defcon III.

# CHAPTER 7

## THE DE-ESCALATION

**A QUIET DAY IN MOSCOW**

On October 25 the Soviet media did not mention that American armed forces had been placed on alert. The priority subject on that day, as well as during the next week, was the World Congress of Peace Forces, the opening of which was scheduled for 4:00 P.M. in the prestigious Kremlin Palace of Unions.

*Pravda* published an editorial titled "The Will of the People," written in the Central Committee of the CPSU, which included a quotation from Brezhnev emphasizing the importance of the Congress. It stressed the benefits of détente and of mutually advantageous international cooperation in diverse fields on the basis of the principles of peaceful coexistence, and declared that never before had the forces striving to abolish wars, combat imperialism, and do away with oppression and exploitation been so united and strong. Concerning the Middle East war, it pointed out that the whole world welcomed the Security Council resolution introduced by the Soviet Union and the United States aimed at establishing stable peace in the region.[1] Certainly, *Pravda*'s editors had no idea that one of the superpowers that proclaimed détente had placed its armed forces on alert and that the other one might follow suit in a few hours.

*Izvestia* published a number of articles, and interviews with participants in the World Congress. All glorified the Congress, the leading role of the Soviet Union in the struggle for peace and international security, and of course the extraordinary contributions of Comrade Leonid Ilyich Brezhnev. For example, the general secretary of the Communist Party of the United States, Gus Hall, expressed confidence that "the World Congress of Peace Forces would become one of the most important international gatherings in the entire history of mankind."[2] Gunasena Vithana, from Sri Lanka, praised Brezhnev's visits to the United States, West Germany, and France as extremely important steps toward strengthening world peace.[3] And James Forest, a member of the U.S. National Preparatory Committee, stated: "The Congress should support the just demands of the peoples of the Arab countries and strive for a settlement of the Middle East conflict on the basis of the decisions of the Security Council."[4]

The Soviet media did not indicate that there was any special tension with regard to the Middle East on October 25. The Moscow papers continued to signal concern over the fate of the Egyptian forces encircled by the Israelis, charging Israel with repeated violations of the cease-fire and with attempts to capture the city of Suez. At the same time, Syria's acceptance of the Security Council resolution was hailed as a positive development. No particular anti-American sentiment occurred in the papers. Tass continued to carry reports emphasizing a heavy and continuous flow of American arms to Israel. A television newscast in Moscow highlighted a West German complaint to the U.S. embassy in Bonn about the cargo of American arms for Israel on an Israeli ship leaving Bremerhaven.

The Soviet Foreign Ministry would not comment on the American nuclear alert or on Washington's charges that there had been signs that the Soviet Union was preparing to intervene in the Middle East. There were no reports in the Soviet press of Soviet troop movement. The most important foreign military affairs event reported was the arrival in the Soviet Union of the Finnish military delegation headed by the commander of the Finnish defense forces.

On the surface everything was very quiet in Moscow on October 25.

## ONCE BITTEN, TWICE SHY

That was a Thursday, the day the Politburo held its regular meetings, which usually started at 11:00 A.M. In the middle of the morning discussion in my office at the Foreign Ministry about possible American options in response to Brezhnev's "menacing" message to Nixon, I was asked to come to the Kremlin by 10:00 A.M. When our task force arrived later, the Politburo was already in session, and we found a large group of party bosses, ministers, and other V.I.P.'s sitting in the reception hall, all waiting to be invited to take part in the discussion of some agenda item. Sometimes the Politburo's agenda consisted of dozens of items, and many of the invited V.I.P.'s had to wait for several hours, but because "our" agenda item—the war in the Middle East—was already under consideration, we were shown in immediately.

This meeting turned out to be one of the most important ones held during the Yom Kippur War. Brezhnev presided, and almost all the Soviet leaders took part in the discussion. The meeting lasted for more than four hours and was devoted entirely to the war and the American nuclear alert. Everyone else waiting in the reception hall had to go back to their offices empty-handed.

All participants in the meeting understood that the conflict was heading toward a confrontation between the Soviet Union and the United States. The only question was whether or not the Soviet Union was prepared to engage in a large-scale war. The meeting started with Grechko and Andropov informing the participants about Defcon III. Brezhnev, who had received the report about the alert before the meeting started, said he had been consulting "with comrades" (probably Suslov, Ponomarev, and Katushev) and that they had unanimously concluded that because of the new developments Brezhnev's speech at the World Congress scheduled for that afternoon would have to be postponed. All agreed.

Using strong language and characterizing Nixon's decision as irresponsible, everyone at the meeting expressed indignation at the news that the Americans were preparing their troops for military action. Some saw no reason for such an action and were plainly taken by surprise. Others saw it in orthodox Marxist-Leninist terms as part of the class struggle in the international arena. Some wondered, "The Americans say we threaten them, but how did they get that into their heads?" And several believed that the Soviet Union's decisive role in maintaining peace and strengthening international security was making the American imperialists furious.

Very few indeed guessed that the pretext for Washington's decision was Brezhnev's latest message to Nixon. "What has this to do with the letter I sent to Nixon?" asked Brezhnev, who believed the emphasis in the letter was on joint Soviet-American action in accordance with the understanding reached during Kissinger's visit to Moscow. Brezhnev once again reminded everyone of Nixon's earlier message, in which the American President had suggested that the two leaders exert their influence to bring an end to the hostilities by putting pressure on their respective clients. "The Americans had no right to put their troops on alert all over the world, including their nuclear forces. It is a gross violation of the Soviet-American treaty on the prevention of nuclear war signed in 1972," stated Grechko. "Who could have imagined that the Americans would be so easily frightened?" asked Podgorny, astonished. "The possibility of a unilateral Soviet action only caused a nuclear alert. Once bitten twice shy, says the proverb." Sharp critique of Kissinger continued. Kosygin said: "Kissinger lied to us when he was here. He preferred to fraternize with the Israelis." "He is not playing by the rules," grumbled Andropov.

As for the question of whether the Soviet Union was prepared to engage in a war with the United States, most answered with a definite no. Kosygin: "It is not reasonable to become engaged in a war with the United States because of Egypt and Syria." Andropov: "We shall not unleash the Third World War." Kirilenko: "The steps we take should not lead us into a war." Ponomarev: "We do not need another war." Gromyko, Podgorny, and others expressed similar opinions.

At the same time, the majority held that the American nuclear alert had to be considered as a challenge to the Soviet Union and required a response, but opinions differed on the nature of the response. Grechko's position was the toughest. He insisted that measures be taken, mainly in the military sphere, and recommended that a decree be issued to recruit 50,000 to 70,000 men in the Ukraine and in North Caucasus. Suggesting also a partial mobilization, Grechko at the same time warned that it would be a costly undertaking. Andropov liked Grechko's idea. "We should respond to mobilization by mobilizing," he said. Kirilenko favored declaring an increased state of readiness in several military districts in the Soviet Union, a proposal that was supported by Ustinov and Katushev.

The idea of sending Soviet troops to the Middle East was expressed only by Grechko, although with some hesitation and reservation. In a heated discussion he stated: "In the past we have never asked anybody if we could send out troops or not, and we should not do so now." He reminded us that there were 1,500 troops in Syria and that in order to save Syria, he believed, Soviet troops should occupy the Golan Heights.

Kosygin rejected absolutely the idea of sending Soviet troops to the Middle East. "Suppose we send two divisions to the Middle East," he said. "In response, the Americans will send two divisions as well. If we send five divisions, the Americans will send their five. Neither side would be frightened. The United States will not start a war and we have no reason to start it." And here Kosygin stated emphatically: "I told Sadat that we would not become engaged in the war." As I mentioned in Chapter 4, I never found any proof that Kosgyin even made such a statement in Cairo, but one cannot totally exclude the possibility that he said it during a tête-à-tête with Sadat. Or perhaps he was pretending to have made such a statement, in order to demonstrate his toughness—that was always welcome at the Politburo.

Gromyko believed that sending troops to the Middle East would inevitably lead to a confrontation with the United States. "Where is the brink, the line between peace and a new, nuclear war? Who can draw that line?" he asked his colleagues. "We have to act in accordance with the agreements with the Americans. We have to show that the nuclear alert did not frighten us." Andropov, Kirilenko, Katushev, and Ustinov, while supporting a state of increased readiness in several regions of the Soviet Union, opposed sending troops to the Middle East.

Most at the meeting preferred political measures, and Kosygin came up with a set of such steps. He proposed sending Gromyko, with military advisers, to Washington for talks with Nixon, at which Gromyko would express the Kremlin's bewilderment over the military measures taken by the United States and resume the dialogue with the Americans. The main subject of the talks would be the dispatch of Soviet and American military contingents in the Middle East. From Kosygin's point of view, the Soviet military advisers, together with their American counterparts, would be in a position to work out an effective joint operation aimed at implementing Security Council decisions. Having in mind the urgency of the situation, Kosygin suggested that Gromyko leave for Washington immediately. In addition, Kosygin believed that the United Nations opportunities had to be used fully, that the Soviet Union should come forward with a program of concrete measures. What he had in mind was not clear—perhaps calling a Special Session of the General Assembly, as was the case in 1967 when he headed the Soviet delegation.

Katushev was also in favor of a more active Soviet policy in the United Nations. He believed that the Soviet Union should support the idea of setting up United Nations Emergency Forces and express readiness to participate in it, recalling the precedent created by the use of United Nations Emergency Forces during the Korean War. "This is in case either the Americans or the Chinese veto an appropriate resolution in the Security Council," he explained. Ponomarev also believed that the machinery of the United Nations could be used more fully. "If the Security Council could send ten thousand soldiers of the United Nations Emergency Forces, it would be useful," he said. Rather skeptical about the establishment of United Nations Emergency Forces was Ustinov, who believed that before these forces were set up, Cairo and Damascus would fall and Egypt and Syria would surrender.

Other participants touched on the issue of the United Nations too, sometimes showing a very poor knowledge of the United Nations Charter and its mandate. That forced Gromyko to explain to his colleagues the basic rules of United Nations activity and to speak against any proposal that violated the United Nations Charter. He rejected the idea of calling a Special Session of the General Assembly, which would only provoke international tension. He once again pointed out the difference between guarantees that the Security Council resolution would be implemented and the term "appropriate auspices," under which the negotiations between interested parties should be conducted.

Kosygin's suggestion concerning an urgent visit by Gromyko to Washington received no support. Brezhnev believed that to send a Soviet representative to Washington during the American nuclear alert would be interpreted as a demonstration of Soviet weakness. Most of the participants believed that the time for a Gromyko visit to the United States had not yet come. Andropov suggested that instead of Gromyko going to Washington, Kuznetsov should go to the Middle East on a special mission. For his part, Gromyko did not want to go to Washington: "What is the point of me or of any other Soviet representative's going there now? Would it change the military situation in the Middle East?"

Almost two hours had passed since the meeting began. I was making notes and wondering what the final result of the discussion would be. Would the case for a tough response to the nuclear alert prevail? And what kind of response—military or political? The answer surprised me.

When the discussion was at its height, Brezhnev suddenly suggested: "What about not responding at all to the American nuclear alert? Nixon is too nervous—let's cool him down." Because many participants had insisted on asking President Nixon to explain why he had decided to take such a brash and risky step, Brezhnev suggested: "Let Nixon explain the reason for the nuclear alert first." That idea sounded reasonable. Neither previous correspondence with Nixon nor the talks with Kissinger had hinted at such an unexpected turn of events, at such a dramatic decision by Nixon. But how could the Soviet leaders know that while the National Security Council decided on a nuclear alert Nixon had been alseep?

Brezhnev was in a rather complicated situation. He felt that the majority of the participants favored a response to Defcon III—some military, others political. Even Kosygin did not oppose limited military activity on Soviet territory. Brezhnev did not want to confront the majority: "I also was in favor of declaring an increased state of readiness, but then I thought it would be a retreat from our principal policy. If we take mobilization measures, the people would start to worry. The Soviet Union's credibility as the main proponent of world peace and stability would be jeopardized. No matter how complicated the situation might be, our wish is to develop our relations with the United States." Brezhnev spoke out several times. He was in favor of a solid and cautious response to the nuclear alert, because the Soviet Union had given the United States no grounds for such a decision. "Yesterday," he said, "I even gave instructions to break off the airlift for some time. We have to take up the whole issue with the Americans. We should not be provoked by American irresponsibility. I am not inclined to take measures to make Soviet troops ready for action."

Brezhnev's alternative—not giving any response to the American nuclear alert—was welcomed first by Podgorny, Gromyko, and Deputy Prime Minister Kiril Mazurov, and then by other participants as well. All agreed that such a response would be fully consistent with the policy of détente and with peaceful coexistence, one of the main principles of Soviet foreign policy.

In addition, Brezhnev proposed sending a message to Kissinger in Gromyko's name, reminding the American side of the Soviet-American commitment to try to bring the war to an end. Brezhnev insisted that Kissinger and Nixon had not kept their promise to exert their influence on Israel in order to stop the fighting. "It was their solemn promise, but they did not keep it, and I am ready to state that at the Congress of Peace Forces." He believed Gromyko's message should repeat the Soviet proposal to send 200 to 400 Soviet and American military observers to the Middle East. "We can agree with participation of contingents of other states too," he added. Brezhnev summed up the main contents of the new Soviet message this way: "Nixon should know that we are ready to send contingents of the Soviet Union and the United States to the Middle East in order to guarantee the cease-fire, and we do not insist on removing troops from the positions they occupy at present." The decision was made to send a message along these lines to Kissinger, but some new developments would require a revision.

I was glad of the decision and sighed with relief—not because I thought a new message to the White House would lead to a consensus on sending Soviet and American contingents, but because it evidenced the first step toward de-escalation of the conflict.

## "OUR CONSCIENCE IS CLEAR"

A lengthy discussion about the relations between the Soviet Union and the Arab states followed. All participants believed that the Soviet line with respect to the Arabs was entirely justified and correct, and that both the attempt to attain the return of Arab land occupied by Israel, by political means, and the flow of arms supplies to Arab countries, should be continued. The results of military operations on both war fronts were estimated as being very unfavorable to the Arabs. "It would be difficult to smoke the Israeli troops out of the western bank of the Suez Canal," Brezhnev said. He predicted the fall of Ismailia in the next few hours. "We must tell Sadat we were right, that we sympathize with Egypt but we can't reverse the course of military operations." Andropov was of the same opinion: "Our conscience is clear. We tried to hold the Arabs back from starting military operations, but they did not listen. Sadat expelled our military advisers, but when the Arabs started the fighting, we supported them."

Despite the difficult and "hopeless" situation of Egypt and Syria, as one participant called it, the need to give broad support to the Arabs was stressed. There was concern about the decreasing popularity of the Soviet Union in the Arab states. Brezhnev informed the Politburo of demonstrations in Cairo with anti-Soviet slogans. "We have to save the healthy, friendly forces in Egypt," said Grechko emphatically. Katushev was of the opinion that "since Egypt has lost the war" the Soviet Union should concentrate its attention on Syria and that priority assistance should be given to Syria and Iraq. He suggested advising Iraqi leaders to keep their forces in Syria and assuring Assad of the Soviet Union's enduring friendship. At the same time the Syrians should not be encouraged to violate the cease-fire. Ponomarev shared Katushev's views, expressing concern about Assad's position if the Iraqis were to withdraw their troops.

From Brezhnev's point of view, the main area of Soviet-Arab cooperation in the present circumstances should be implementation of Resolution 242, perhaps with some "minor corrections." What he meant by "minor corrections" he did not elaborate. At another point he remarked, "Maybe Sadat will make a statement concerning the territorial corrections," again without elaboration. Nobody touched this delicate question. Several times Brezhnev referred to the weakening position of Sadat in Egypt, spoke about the threat to his regime, and so on. He thought Sadat could survive only if the Israelis withdrew from the western bank of the Suez. Brezhnev supported Andropov's suggestion of sending Kuznetsov to Egypt and Syria. One of Kuznetsov's tasks would be to convince Sadat of the usefulness of Soviet advisers. He also agreed to pay special attention to relations with Assad and to ask Bakr of Iraq to keep Iraqi armed forces in Syria. Our task force was instructed to draft messages to Assad and Bakr in Brezhnev's name.

The members of the Politburo believed that their decisions—aimed at strengthening relations with the Arab states and helping them to continue their struggle against the common enemy, imperialism—fully complied with the other basic Soviet foreign-policy principle: proletarian internationalism.

## "SOMETHING IS WRONG WITH THE AMERICAN LOGIC"

During Brezhnev's concluding remarks, Chernenko passed him a document that turned out to be Nixon's letter dated October 25, which had been delivered to Dobrynin at 6:00 A.M. Washington time. It was not until almost 2:30 P.M. Moscow time that Brezhnev started to read the letter, which was relatively short, some two pages. (The document was circulated in Russian, and some portions of Nixon's message omitted in the President's memoirs and cited below are my own translation from the Russian text.) While reading the letter, he and his colleagues made some comments. Brezhnev liked the fact that Nixon agreed with him that "our understanding to act jointly for peace is of the highest value" and that "we should implement that understanding" in the complex Middle East situation.[5] "That is exactly what we are trying to do, and we are inviting them to follow suit," Brezhnev remarked. Nixon's assertion "that your proposal for a particular kind of joint action, that of sending Soviet and American military contingents to Egypt, is not appropriate in the present circumstances" elicited no comment.[6] But one of the next sentences, unfortunately omitted in Nixon's memoirs, was welcomed. It read:

> We are ready to undertake every effective measure in order to guarantee the implementation of the cease-fire and *we are already in close contact with the government of Israel aimed at ensuring its full compliance with the provision of the Security Council decisions* (emphasis added).

"They should have done that long ago," someone remarked. "Finally the Americans got the message! They understood that we won't permit arbitrariness on Israel's part" was another comment, almost quoting verbatim Brezhnev's "menacing" message.

Nixon's message did not clarify what steps the White House had taken to force Israel to stop the fighting, but that was not important for the Kremlin. Nixon's message to Brezhnev on the eve of Kissinger's arrival in Moscow, in which he urged the Soviet leader to achieve peace by providing strong leadership that "our respective friends in the area will find persuasive," was well remembered in Moscow. Israel was an American fish to fry—that was the general opinion at the meeting. What was important for the Kremlin was the information from Washington that the Americans were already in close contact with the Israeli government and that the goal was to ensure Israel's full compliance with the Security Council resolution. That was the core of the issue.

It is therefore confusing to read in some literature that in the face of the Soviets' "menacing" message the United States had subtly encouraged Israel to escalate its military action. Some American officials, too, confirmed that the United States did not pressure Israel during this critical period. In a private interview many years later, Kissinger himself claimed: "After the Soviets threatened, I asked the Israelis to develop an option to defeat the Third Army. Only after I knew that the Russians were caved in, did I press the Israelis really hard on Friday (October 25)."⁷ October 25, 1973, however, was a Thursday.

Are we to understand that Kissinger was both writing in Nixon's name to Brezhnev (at 12:30 A.M., October 25) that Washington was ready to take every effective measure in order to guarantee implementation of the cease-fire, and at the very same time (at 11:25 P.M., October 24, 1:35 A.M. and 1:45 A.M., October 25) talking to Ambassador Dinitz of Israel and urging him to develop an option to defeat the Third Army? Or another question: How could Kissinger know at 12:30 A.M. Washington time, October 25—when he was assuring the Soviet government that Washington was already in close contact with Israel in order to ensure its full compliance with the cease-fire resolution—that the Soviet Union was "caving in"? The Politburo made a decision to ignore the Defcon III seven or eight hours later than Kissinger wrote the Nixon message. The decision could well have been a different one. And then, if Kissinger was asking the Israelis to develop an option to defeat the Egyptian army, was the statement in Nixon's message a lie? Why was that important sentence omitted in Nixon's memoirs? Perhaps to prove Kissinger's "pressure-on-Israel-after-the-Russians-have-caved-in" theory?

Something is wrong in the story—not all of the details fit together. I do not know the contents of the communications between the United States and Israel the night of October 25, and unfortunately Kissinger's memoirs and other sources available to me do not clear up the picture. From conversation with diplomats and military leaders who were in Cairo at the time, and from my own analysis, however, I have come to the conclusion that the statement in Nixon's October 25 letter referring to American efforts to ensure Israel's compliance with the cease-fire most accurately reflects the truth. The "pressure-on-Israel-after-the-Russians-have-caved-in" theory does not sound serious and seems to have been invented later, probably for some domestic reasons.

Nixon's letter continued:

> In these circumstances, we must view your suggestion of unilateral action as a matter of the gravest concern involving incalculable consequences. It is clear that the forces necessary to impose the cease-fire terms on the two sides would be massive and would require closest coordination so as to avoid bloodshed. This is not only clearly infeasible but it is not appropriate to the situation.[8]

Here Grechko commented: "First of all, why is it infeasible? Why could we not coordinate our action? Second, a gesture of Soviet-American joint action would have led to an immediate halt to the fighting. Is it not clear? The Americans want to impose their own scenario." Nixon's agreement that some American and Soviet personnel be sent to the area as part of an augmented United Nations force was considered to be in the same spirit as the Soviet proposals.

The President's appeal "for acting not unilaterally but in harmony and with cool heads" caused a lively reaction. Does unilaterally putting American troops all over the world on alert mean acting in harmony and with cool heads? asked many at the meeting. Brezhnev responded: "We only said that if the Americans don't agree to act jointly in accordance with our mutual commitments we would have to consider [and Brezhnev repeated "consider"] the question of taking steps unilaterally. And now, after having unilaterally declared a nuclear alert, they dare to criticize us! Something is wrong with the American logic."

Nixon proposed augmenting the existing United Nations observers' mission with Soviet and American personnel and military equipment, which he believed to be "consonant with the letter and spirit of our understanding." He concluded, "This will be a starting point for the negotiations provided for in Security Council Resolution 338, which we together will organize." This welcome statement (also omitted in the memoirs) was also taken as an expression of Nixon's interest in further cooperation with the Soviet Union.

In general, Nixon's letter caused a dual response in the Politburo: on the one hand, satisfaction with the declared readiness of the United States to act jointly with the Soviet Union and to follow the line of détente, but on the other hand, great surprise at the absence of any explanation of the nuclear alert.

Many participants in the Kremlin discussions emphasized that the nuclear alert was in no way consonant with the character of current Soviet-American relations, the letter and spirit of the 1973 summit, or the talks with Kissinger in Moscow a few days before the nuclear alert. They were quite certain that neither Nixon nor Kissinger believed the Soviet Union would intervene in the war in the Middle East, let alone do anything to provoke a military confrontation with the United States. Besides, in the Kremlin's view, the information the Americans had did not give them any real reason for concern regarding a Soviet military action.

The lack of any explanation in Nixon's message of the decision to place American armed forces on alert gave an additional reason for all of us who worked in the Kremlin at that time to believe that the decision to order Defcon III was determined mainly by the pressures of domestic politics. There was no evidence whatsoever that the unambiguous statements by Brezhnev and Gromyko to Kissinger while he was in Moscow—that the Soviet Union would not get involved in the war in the Middle East—had been revised. What are the American diplomats doing? we asked ourselves. Did they have any indication that the Soviet Union was on the eve of a war? Did not the huge Soviet propaganda machine prove the contrary: that the Kremlin leaders were engaged in a large-scale "peace-loving" performance? Our colleagues in the U.S. embassy are getting paid for nothing if they have recommended a nuclear alert to Washington, one of us joked.

In any case, Nixon's letter did not play any significant role in the Kremlin's decision to disregard the American nuclear alert. It was accepted with some relief and gave Brezhnev good reason, before adjourning the meeting, to state that the "strong words" in his previous message to Nixon had finally compelled the Americans to agree with the Soviet idea of acting jointly and putting real pressure on Israel in order to stop the extermination of the Egyptians. "And that is exactly what we wanted," he concluded.

Only much later did we learn that at almost the same time Brezhnev was wrapping up the Politburo meeting, Kissinger was informing Nixon that several hours earlier the American armed forces had been placed in Defcon III readiness and that a message in his name had been sent to Moscow—a message that he read later than the addressee did. "Nixon was not part of the decision-making process that night, nor was he briefed," wrote Walter Isaacson.[9]

Many times I asked myself what would have happened had the Kremlin responded to Defcon III with a Soviet nuclear alert and initiated military action in the Middle East or elsewhere. Certainly it was difficult to imagine that the Kremlin leaders would resort to a large-scale military action, knowing their mood at that time. But who knows? There had already been so many surprises during this war that another one could not be ruled out. Fortunately it did not happen.

The Kremlin's calm, restrained response to the nuclear alert was characterized by Kissinger as a Soviet retreat, a sign that the Soviets had been cowed by American resolve,[10] but the proceedings in the Kremlin on October 25 refute such an interpretation. The deputy prime minister of Egypt, Abdel Qadr Hatem, was very close to the truth when he stated a few days later: "The Soviet threat to send troops to the Middle East was an escalation to force the United States to pressure Israel to observe the cease-fire."[11]

Leaving the conference room, Brezhnev reminded his colleagues that in half an hour the World Congress of Peace Forces would open, and he invited everyone to attend the session. Our task force was instructed to prepare, with Brezhnev's aides, a large set of documents: Brezhnev's reply to Nixon (instead of a letter from Gromyko to Kissinger, as previously suggested by Brezhnev) and messages in Brezhnev's name to Assad and Bakr and to leaders of socialist countries and of a number of major states.

We had a lot of work to do.

## WAS THE SOVIET UNION READY TO INTERVENE?

How could the rather aggressive mood favoring retaliation against the Americans, demonstrated by almost all the Kremlin leaders at the beginning of the Politburo meeting, have turned into the conciliatory mood manifested by the decision to disregard Defcon III? Was it the result of Brezhnev's power—his indisputable authority—or was it fear caused by the American nuclear alert?

To answer these questions, one must keep a few things in mind. A war in the Middle East did not fit into the Kremlin's current policy of promoting the advantages of political means in the settlement of the Middle East conflict. After the Kremlin leaders had failed to talk Sadat and Assad out of launching a war, they made an unequivocal and firm decision not to get involved in it. Consequently, no necessary military measures aimed at involving the Soviet Union in the war had been taken. The Soviet Union was also not prepared, politically or psychologically, to be engaged in a war that could easily turn into a nuclear confrontation with the United States. The Soviet leaders, including the military, had known that better than anyone else. That was the main reason the Kremlin decided to disregard the American nuclear alert.

Then how can one explain a number of Soviet military actions that allegedly caused Defcon III? At a news conference on October 26, Secretary of Defense James Schlesinger was asked: "Can you tell us what steps the Soviet Union was taking that led us to a military alert?" He answered, "I'll mention a number of them. . . . We were aware that the Soviets had alerted comprehensively their airborne forces. In addition, the Soviet airlift was stood down, I believe, starting on Monday, and diminished to zero flights on Tuesday."[12] On October 23 an intelligence report submitted to Nixon claimed that four more Soviet airborne divisions had been placed on alert, bringing the total to seven divisions (roughly 50,000 troops), and that Soviet naval forces in the Mediterranean had been enhanced to eighty-five ships.[13] In addition, establishment of an airborne command post in the southern part of the Soviet Union[14] and the firing of SCUD missiles at Israeli troops, "coupled with the transport of nuclear material through the Bosporus,"[15] were among the Soviet military actions that were said to prove the Soviet Union's readiness for military involvement in the war and to justify Defcon III.

Indeed, from the first days of the war the Soviet Union had taken some normal precautions under circumstances of extreme international tension and a war in its direct neighborhood. There were several local military alerts of Soviet forces during the Middle East crisis in the years preceding the Yom Kippur War. An unprecedented airlift and sealift carried out mainly by the Soviet armed forces and under full responsibility of the Defense Ministry had to be protected, especially because Soviet aircraft resupplying the Arabs were overflying East European states, where Soviet troops had been deployed. Therefore, almost simultaneously with the start of the airlift, several Soviet divisions in Eastern Europe were put on a state of increased readiness. Additional measures were carried out in the navy and in some airborne divisions after the Israeli air raid on Damascus and the sinking of the merchant ship *Ilya Mechnikov*. After Sadat appealed to Brezhnev and Nixon, urging them to send Soviet and American contingents to the Middle East, certain movements of a group of Soviet ships in the Mediterranean were ordered by the Ministry of Defense. Sadat acknowledged that Soviet response.[16] Previously planned maneuvers were held in the Carpathian and Transcaucasian military districts. All these actions were detected by the United States and by other countries. However, no serious movement of Soviet troops took place during the war. "The Soviets did not move any forces," acknowledged Schlesinger.[17]

The increase in the Soviet Mediterranean naval flotilla by some twenty vessels was mainly a response to the buildup of American ships in the Mediterranean and to the Sixth Fleet's movements eastward. After the war, I talked with a commander of a Soviet nuclear submarine, who told me that in the second week of October he was ordered to bring his boat into the Mediterranean and start trailing the American aircraft-carrier *John F. Kennedy*, which had been ordered from the Atlantic to the Mediterranean with her fighter bombers. Many other American ships were targeted for instant attack too. Did the Americans know that they were traced and targeted? I wondered. The commander believed so, but what could the Americans do? At the same time, he was warned by the commander-in-chief of the Soviet Mediterranean naval flotilla to be careful and restrained. Any firing without a special order from Moscow was prohibited. A similar warning was dispatched to other submarine commanders. But the order from Moscow never came, the commander added. "Was he sorry about that?" I asked him. "Certainly not," he replied, but I understood that he would have obediently carried out the order if Moscow had decided to respond to Defcon III in a hawkish way. It was not difficult to imagine the consequences of such an order.

The reason for the pullback of Soviet transport aircraft on October 24 was explained by Brezhnev at the Politburo as a sign of Soviet goodwill and interest in cooling down the tension in the Middle East. Was he speaking the truth? If not, he could be challenged by any other participant who would have known of other reasons for the decision to diminish or stop the flights. Kissinger claimed later that he had learned during the evening of October 24 that eight Soviet Antonov transport planes—each capable of carrying 200 or more troops—were slated to fly from Budapest to Egypt in the next few hours.[18] The discussion at the Politburo did not contain even a hint of such a move.

As far as the October 22 firing of SCUD missiles is concerned, it was in no way designed to demonstrate Soviet readiness to be involved in the war. Judging from the results, though, I am afraid it came closer to demonstrating the contrary!

Now a few words about the role of the Politburo in carrying out military measures during the Yom Kippur War. By the Politburo's mandate and its established practice, it made decisions only on important, large-scale military actions, such as mobilizations general or partial; substantial movements of troops, particularly from one military district to another; large maneuvers, especially unplanned ones; deployment and use of any type of weapons of mass destruction; putting on alert all Soviet armed forces, or forces in one or several military districts; and some other matters. None of these issues came up during the Yom Kippur War. Declaring increased states of readiness of one or several divisions, movements, and planned maneuvers within a military district or group of Soviet troops abroad (for example, in East Germany or Hungary) was within the jurisdiction of the defense minister. Even for a military show of strength without reinforcements in personnel and armaments, there was no need for Politburo clearance. Even in the years of Stalin's dictatorship, on the eve of Hitler's attack on the Soviet Union in June 1941, the People's Commissar for the Navy, Nikolai Kuznetsov, had put the Soviet navy on an increased state of readiness without clearance from Stalin.

Because the Kremlin had made the political decision that the Soviet Union should stay out of the war, the Defense Ministry had to limit its activities to carrying out precautions whose scope and character were to be defined by the ministry itself. This was the reason the Soviet military actions mentioned above were not discussed broadly at the meetings of the Politburo. I remember that, in response to some reports in the Western press that "large units of Soviet troops are moving in Central Europe," Grechko once stated that such movements in a number of countries are "routine autumn maneuvers." It is also true that some delicate issues related to Soviet military activity were discussed in a very narrow circle, sometimes, perhaps, by Brezhnev and Grechko alone, but not by the Politburo.

Being Brezhnev's favorite, Grechko had comparatively broad freedom of action. He had a habit of answering questions from his colleagues on the Politburo concerning the war in the Middle East by saying: "I just informed Leonid Ilyich [Brezhnev] about it." And that was it. Certainly he was one of the "hotheads" in the Defense Ministry who believed that the Soviet armed forces must have the world situation in general under control, not only by their overall superiority but also by their presence in different parts of the world—and the Middle East in particular. Some of his actions and statements (the order to fire the SCUDs, the proposal to occupy the Golan Heights) were of a provocative character, but they were not supported in the Politburo or by Brezhnev himself. In fact, Grechko did not dare confront the "team," with its "collective leadership," and as a rule backed down from his positions. After being very aggressive at the beginning of the notable Politburo meeting of October 25, he was forced to agree that the Soviet armed forces were not ready to intervene, and he joined Brezhnev's proposal to abstain from any military demonstration in response to Defcon III.

The Soviet military actions, some of them grossly exaggerated in the West, did not give sufficient reason to suspect that the Soviet Union would intervene unilaterally. Alexander Haig was correct to say "They're [the Soviet leaders] not going to put forces in at the end of a war. I don't believe that."[19] A Pentagon official confirmed Haig's analysis: "The activities of Soviet forces on October 24 by themselves had caused no undue alarm of the Defense Department."[20]

Kissinger later wrote that he and his colleagues had to respond to the mention of possible Soviet unilateral action in a manner that would shock the Soviets into abandoning it, but actually the only material result of Defcon III was that Brezhnev postponed his statement at the World Congress of Peace Forces for one day. He made the statement on October 26.

After the Politburo meeting, members of the task force and some of Brezhnev's aides and advisers went to the Kremlin dining room. During our late lunch, we talked about Defcon III, Nixon's message, and the Politburo's decision. We were very far from agreement, and most of us were still puzzled by the American nuclear alert. It was difficult to believe that, after effective Soviet-American talks in Moscow and fruitful cooperation in the Security Council leading to adoption of the two cease-fire resolutions, Washington would carry out a major anti-Soviet military action. To some of us, Nixon's message also sounded very strange. It did not contain any explanation of Defcon III and, indeed, acknowledged the usefulness of certain suggestions Brezhnev had made in his latest letter. Finally, Nixon did not ask Brezhnev to cancel or refrain from any Soviet military activity. Despite our doubts, however, there was a consensus that the main reason for Defcon III was American fear of Soviet unilateral action in the Middle East. "That is not bad," one of my colleagues said. "The more the Americans are frightened by us, the more the rest of the world will respect us." Many of the participants even found comfort in the Americans' "panic."

What did concern me was the attitude of many participants in that chat toward the Politburo's decision to ignore Defcon III. They would have preferred a tough response. One, a relatively young man from the Central Commitee, claimed that if the Soviet Union wanted to help the Arabs, troops should be sent without delay. He was confident that the Americans would "swallow" Soviet intervention in the Middle East the same way they had during the Hungarian or Czechoslovakian crises. I did not share these views and wholeheartedly supported the Politburo's decision to disregard the nuclear alert, but I did not like the fact that there were quite a number of outspoken hawks among the younger generation of the Soviet bureaucracy. I was even more surprised when in the evening of the same day, while chatting with my friends at the Foreign Ministry, I heard a similar assessment. "These gerontic leaders are good for nothing," one of my deputies stated. "They are cowards. They should have responded to the American challenge at least the same way."

## BUSINESS AS USUAL

At 4:00 P.M., October 25, the World Congress of Peace Forces opened at the Kremlin's Hall of Congresses. The Congress was attended by more than 3,000 delegates from 144 countries, representing about 1,100 political parties, organizations, and movements and including heads and representatives of more than 120 international and national organizations. Those figures gave the organizers reason to claim that the World Congress was "an unprecedented event in the history of the peoples' movement for peace, thanks to the number of organizations giving it their support and the importance of the program which embraces all problems concerning world peace, and the increasingly favorable prospects for joint action."[21]

In the balcony box sat Brezhnev, his dark-gray suit with full rows of highest Soviet decorations. With him were Kosygin, Podgorny, Gromyko, Kirilenko, and almost all the other Politburo members, with two important exceptions. Andropov and Grechko did not attend the opening session—they had been asked by Brezhnev to stay back and mind the store. "Who knows what one can expect from the unbalanced Americans," said one military expert participating on our task force.

The chairman of the Prepcom—the secretary general of the World Peace Council, Romesh Chandra of India—opened the Congress by addressing "Dear Leonid Ilyich Brezhnev" and expressing gratitude for the Soviet initiative in "preserving peace and justice all over the world." Brezhnev was pleased by the greetings he received at the opening session. From time to time during the session, information about the latest consequences of Defcon III and the situation in the Middle East was delivered to the balcony box. No disturbing news had come in, and that made him happy.

Meanwhile, we were drafting the documents to be sent in Brezhnev's name to a number of heads of state. The most important and at the same time the simplest was Brezhnev's message to Nixon. In drafting the message, we were guided by the points in Brezhnev's concluding remarks at the Politburo: (1) The Soviet Union throughout the war always constantly and strongly supported joint Soviet-American action. (2) The Soviet leaders had stated that they would be forced to consider unilateral measures only if the United States rejected joint action. (3) Because Nixon had now agreed to act together with the Soviet Union in sending a group of American and Soviet observers to Egypt, the need for Soviet unilateral action had evaporated. (4) The Soviet side took note of Nixon's pledge to secure Israel's full compliance with the Security Council decision. (5) Finally, the Kremlin expected a full explanation from the American side concerning the reason for the nuclear alert.

The message was sent to the Hall of Congresses for Brezhnev and Gromyko to see. They deleted paragraphs four and five of the draft ("Let the Americans themselves try to justify their unruly conduct," Gromyko explained), and the message was sent to Washington the evening of October 25. The key sentence was "Since you are ready now, as we understand, to send to Egypt a group of American observers with the same task [to guarantee implementation of the Security Council resolutions], we agree to act in this question together with you." The Kremlin's calm reaction to Defcon III immediately became headline news and was welcomed in the West. Many observers attributed the easing of the crisis to the Soviet Union's willingness not to send armed units to the Middle East and the concurrent agreement of the Americans to joint participation in the observer force.[22]

The Soviet embassy in Washington also reacted calmly to the dramatic events of the night of October 24. Dobrynin recalled that neither he nor his embassy colleagues had exaggerated the potential negative consequences of Brezhnev's "threatening message" or the American nuclear alert. They believed that these events were created artificially and were caused partly by personal ambitiousness. Dobrynin thought that Kissinger, by dramatizing Brezhnev's warning of unilateral action, was trying to make the Israelis become more cooperative and that Defcon III was the result of his desire to please the Israeli lobby by demonstrating strong American support of Israel. In Dobrynin's view, expressed years after the war, if Kissinger had really believed that unilateral Soviet military action was imminent he would never have risked taking responsibility for the decision of the National Security Council without Nixon's participation. Dobrynin was of the opinion that if Nixon had chaired the meeting of October 24 the decision to go to Defcon III would not have been made, that Watergate did not play any substantive role in the decision on Defcon III. That was more Kissinger's baby than Nixon's, he felt.

The number-two man at the Soviet embassy, Vorontsov, shared this view. He saw Defcon III as a "win-win option" for Kissinger. The secretary of state knew very well that the Soviet Union would not intervene in the Middle East, and at the same time he would be considered Israel's savior. Dobrynin recalled that at a reception on October 25 he expressed to Kissinger his displeasure at and disapproval of Defcon III. "Take it easy, Anatoly," Kissinger responded. Vinogradov, for his part, claimed that when he asked Kissinger during the latter's visit to Cairo in November 1973 about the reason for the state of alert, the answer was, "It was the result of Nixon's nervousness."[23] To be honest, the decision-making mechanism on Defcon III has yet to receive the kind of comprehensive analysis it deserves.

Whatever the reasons for Kissinger's attempts to put full responsibility for Defcon III on Nixon, the firm belief in Moscow was that Watergate had diverted Nixon's attention from the Yom Kippur War. Different assessments by Nixon of the events of October 24 and 25 were also noticed in Moscow. Talking to Dobrynin at the end of October 1973, Nixon noted, "All that has happened is just an episode," and added: "If I speak as an ordinary human being, it's very hard for me sometimes." Publicly, however, he gave a different assessment. "It was a real crisis," he emphasized at his press conference on October 26. "It was the most difficult crisis we've had since the Cuban confrontation of 1962."[24]

On the day of the nuclear alert, October 25, Kissinger gave Dobrynin his preliminary views on the future Middle East conference. He proposed convening the conference in Geneva in two to three weeks, with the participation of Egypt, Syria, Jordan, and Israel. A high-ranking U.S. official would represent President Nixon at the opening session and during the most important parts of the negotiations. He said the person to lead the U.S. delegation had not yet been chosen but that it could be a well-known public figure or an experienced diplomat.

Kissinger informed Dobrynin that Golda Meir finally accepted the "Understanding" reached in Moscow regarding the phrase "under appropriate auspices" in paragraph three of Resolution 338. It was taken to mean that the negotiations between the parties concerned would take place with the active participation of the United States and the Soviet

Union at the beginning and thereafter in the course of negotiations when key issues of a settlement were dealt with. At the same time, she told Kissinger that any negotiations must be preceded by a full exchange of prisoners of war.

According to Kissinger, the State Department was trying to find an appropriate United Nations procedure to make the Soviet-American "Understanding" a legally binding document. Because a straightforward approval of the "Understanding" by the Security Council could be blocked by a Chinese veto, the State Department preferred a decision by consensus. The president of the Security Council would make a statement literally repeating the text of the Soviet-American document and suggesting that it reflects the opinion of the Council. Kissinger said that there was another alternative: Israel and the Arab states could appeal separately to the United States and the Soviet Union, requesting that they act in accordance with the "Understanding" reached between them. Then the Security Council could adopt a resolution approving the appeal of the parties concerned and the consent of the United States and the Soviet Union to the appeal. At the same time, Kissinger had some doubts about whether the belligerent states would agree to recognize openly the special role of the United States and the Soviet Union—they might pretend to be opposed to accepting such a procedure.

There were some other minor issues and contacts between the Soviet and American officials in Washington and Moscow on that day, but apart from Dobrynin's remark at a reception and Kissinger's "take it easy" reply, the subject of the nuclear alert did not come up at all. Business was as usual.

## FRIENDSHIP AS USUAL

We prepared several cables to send to the leaders of the Arab states during the afternoon of October 25.

Communications with Sadat continued almost non-stop. On that day, Vinogradov, as in the preceding days, spoke with Sadat several times. According to the ambassador, Sadat appraised the American nuclear alert as cheap blackmail that could not frighten anyone. He informed Vinogradov that the Americans had rejected a joint Soviet-American force and had asked the Soviet government to agree with setting up a United Nations Emergency Force with the participation of the Soviet military. Sadat did not, however, tell Nixon that Egypt had requested the participation of Soviet armed forces in the United Nations Emergency Force. Sadat once again expressed gratitude for the dispatch of Soviet military observers to Cairo.

Vinogradov also raised the question of prisoners of war and pointed out that the Americans attached great importance to it. Moscow believed, he said, that a solution to the problem could facilitate progress on other issues, but Sadat replied that the Americans should instead attach priority importance to Israel's compliance with the cease-fire. Sadat charged the Israelis with attempts to isolate the Third Egyptian Army and force it to surrender. He would be obliged, he said, to take unilateral action to reopen the supply lines, and hoped the Soviet Union would support him. Vinogradov responded with full understanding and stated that the 400 Soviet tanks arriving in Egypt were the best proof of the durability of the Soviet-Egyptian friendship.

A comprehensive message to Assad was drafted, and Mukhitdinov was ordered to see Assad immediately and convey to him that the Soviet leadership, guided by its "sincere wish to render full support to Egypt and Syria," had just taken some additional steps: On October 24 the Kremlin had contacted the White House several times to urge that the United States put the necessary pressure on Israel to force Tel-Aviv to comply with the cease-fire.

> More than that [the draft went on], we have proposed that Nixon immediately participate in effective steps by the United States and the Soviet Union, including sending American and Soviet military contingents with the goal of putting an end to the arbitrariness on the part of the Israeli ruling circles and securing implementation of the Security Council decisions of October 22 and 23 regarding the cease-fire and the cessation of all military activity.

With the latest developments in mind, the issue of an eventual Soviet unilateral action, which had just caused a near disaster, was not mentioned. Assad was also informed that a group of Soviet military observers was on its way to Cairo.

An important point in the message to Assad was the promise to continue the flow of military equipment and weaponry, in the hope that these would be "appropriately used to strengthen the Syrian armed forces." Assad was informed that the Soviet leaders intended to urge

Iraqi President Bakr to continue giving full support to Syria in its "courageous struggle against the Israeli aggressor" and "to refrain from withdrawing Iraqi troops from the Syrian-Israeli front." In conclusion, the Kremlin reiterated the steadiness of the Soviet Union's political course of full support of the just case of the Arab states. Because of Assad's known resentment over the failure to secure an early cease-fire, the message ended with a declaration of friendly feelings and very best wishes and personal regards.

The message to Bakr was shorter and very much to the point. First, it acknowledged with appreciation the substantive contribution of the Iraqi armed forces to the "joint struggle of the Arab states against the Israeli aggressor." The situation at the Syrian-Israeli front remained very tense, however, the message acknowledged, and one could not exclude an Israeli provocation there. Therefore the message emphasized the utmost importance of readiness to rebuff any new military adventures on the part of Israel.

> We express our hope [said the message] that in this crucial hour the armed forces of Iraq would not be withdrawn from the Syrian-Israeli front. Their withdrawal would weaken the joint front of the Arab armed forces, which could be used by the Israeli aggressor as an opportunity to strike Syria and other Arab states.

Moscow assured Bakr that the Soviet Union would continue its full cooperation with and assistance to Iraq, including military assistance.

Thus, while assuring the Arab leaders of the Soviet Union's continuing military support of the Arab states in their struggle against Israel, the Kremlin leaders were simultaneously discussing with Kissinger the details of a peace conference designed to build a stable peace and cooperation in the Middle East. Friendship as usual.

## HOW THE SECURITY COUNCIL DEALT WITH THE NUCLEAR ALERT

As I was participating in the drafting of messages and other documents, I had to keep my eye on developments in New York. We learned from Vinogradov, and later from Dobrynin, that Sadat had yielded to

American pressure and accepted United Nations forces composed of nonpermanent members of the Security Council. The sponsors of the new resolution (Resolution 340), eight nonpermanent members of the Council—Guinea, India, Indonesia, Kenya, Panama, Peru, the Sudan, and Yugoslavia—had been forced to amend their original draft and on the morning of October 25 to submit a revised text of paragraph three, which now stated that the Security Council

> decides to set up immediately, under its authority, a United Nations Emergency Force to be composed of personnel drawn from Members of the United Nations except the permanent members of the Security Council, and requests the Secretary General to report within twenty-four hours on the steps taken to this effect.[25]

We in Moscow did not like the amendment, and, we learned later, neither did the British or the French. The latter even insisted on a separate vote regarding paragraph three and abstained. But because the formula was acceptable to the Egyptians and formally proposed by the nonaligned states, Malik was instructed to vote in favor. He was also advised to stop his threats of sanctions against Israel, and his appeals to sever diplomatic relations with her, and so on—which gave Huang Hua of China occasion to point out that at the previous meeting Malik had "pretentiously said he was instructed by his government to issue a 'solemn warning' to Israel" but that now it was apparent that this was only "an obnoxious, ugly performance."[26] Malik, as I have mentioned, had no instructions to propose sanctions or severing of diplomatic relations with Israel, so he deserved the tongue-lashing he got.

The main reason the Soviet Union supported Resolution 340, however, was the belief that the new resolution, which was sponsored by a large group of nonaligned countries, would finally bring the hostilities to an end—allowing the World Congress of Peace Forces to be convened in conditions of peace and thereby manifesting the superiority of political solutions, rather than military ones, in settling international conflicts.

To be honest, we were not especially concerned with the results or even with the wording of the new resolution. What had seriously troubled us was the possibility that there might be a Security Council debate over the American nuclear alert, which would have occurred if any United Nations member state had requested that the council take up that issue. The reason for our concern was that at that moment the

Kremlin had decided to disregard the nuclear alert and Malik had been ordered to wait for further instructions. But if the Security Council were to start a lengthy discussion on Defcon III, it would hardly be possible for the Soviet representative to remain silent, and an open and heated Soviet-American confrontation would be inevitable, complicating the Middle East settlement. In addition, the atmosphere of the World Congress would be poisoned. I remember a conversation with Gromyko that day. Very concerned, he asked me how to avoid another messy discussion in the Security Council. I predicted a heated debate with Malik starring. Fortunately I was wrong. One can imagine our relief when we got the news that during the seven-hour-long session of the Security Council only one speaker—the representative of Panama, Ambassador Aquiliano Boyd—mentioned the "alarming news" that the U.S. strategic forces had been put on alert.[27] The world was on the verge of a serious Soviet-American confrontation that could easily become a nuclear one, but the Security Council kept silent.

Afterward, our task force discussed the outcome with Gromyko. Two explanations for the Security Council's passivity were offered. One was that Defcon III had not been taken seriously by the world leaders, who considered it blackmail, a step taken for the benefit of the American audience. The other theory was that in the years of the Cold War the Security Council had proved to be so impotent that it could not even respond to an attempt to initiate consideration of a nuclear alert. Most of us supported the first theory.

## A RESPONSE TO THE ALERT BECOMES NECESSARY

Late in the evening of October 25, first reports of a press conference held by Secretary of State Kissinger began to reach Moscow. Although Kissinger's tone was calm and his answers to questions were reassuring ("We are not seeking an opportunity to confront the Soviet Union"),[28] even the few in the Kremlin who had some doubts about the nature of Defcon III now got the message: The American nuclear alert was a challenge to the Soviet Union. This became even more obvious in the press conference held by President Nixon on October 26, when the President claimed Washington had information that led the White House to believe the Soviet Union was planning to send a substantial military force to the Middle East. (Defense Secretary Schlesinger, on the same day, gave a slightly different description: "There were . . . some [Soviet] actions that increased our wariness and some ambitious diplomatic signals to which Dr. Kissinger referred, but those events [Soviet troops moving into the Middle East] did not take place."[29]) Nixon continued:

> I ordered shortly after midnight on Thursday morning an alert for all American forces around the world. [Kissinger claims that Defcon III was ordered by Admiral Moorer at 11:41 P.M. Wednesday evening, following the decision of the National Security Council chaired by him.] This was a precautionary alert. The purpose of that was to indicate to the Soviet Union that we could not accept any unilateral move on their part to move military forces into the Mideast.[30]

Cables from Soviet embassies all over the world confirmed the unequivocally anti-Soviet character of the White House decision. The question of how to respond was discussed again in the Kremlin on Friday, October 26, although I do not remember any formal meeting of the Politburo on that day. Brezhnev had to deliver his long speech at the World Congress of Peace Forces that afternoon, so he was quite busy in the morning. In a number of telephone conversations with his closest associates, a consensus was reached on the following steps: sending a message to Nixon expressing profound disappointment and dissatisfaction with the nuclear alert; addressing heads of leading nonaligned and Western states on that issue; informing the leaders of socialist states of the "provocative character" of the nuclear alert; issuing an official statement through Tass; including in Brezhnev's speech at the World Congress a condemnation of the nuclear alert; and finally, encouraging a public campaign criticizing the action of the United States. Explaining to the task force what we were to do, Gromyko cautioned us: "But do not overplay it, please. Remember our principal policy—we want peace restored in the Middle East and détente preserved."

In the meantime, new and alarming cables from Cairo came in. Vinogradov was reporting the desperate situation of the encircled Third Army: the Israelis were blocking convoys of medical supplies, water, and food. Sadat told Vinogradov he had sent a message to Nixon warning that Egypt would be forced to reopen the supply lines by unilateral military action. He was asking Moscow to support him and "put pressure on Nixon" to force the Israelis to comply with the latest

Security Council resolution and let the convoys through. Our task force was asked to deal with both these issues in Brezhnev's message to Nixon.

Our draft message labeled the reference American officials made to "certain Soviet military steps" as justification for the alert as absolutely groundless and absurd. The alert was characterized as unprovoked action that was not conducive to the relaxation of international tensions and a violation of the bilateral pledge to act in a calm and restrained way. The message also strongly condemned Israel for jeopardizing the interests of universal peace and security. Brezhnev urged Nixon to take necessary measures to resolve the problems raised by Sadat in his latest correspondence with Moscow and Washington. The draft included a threat that if no necessary steps were taken by the American side a new problem would inevitably arise: an international action providing the Egyptian Third Army with supplies. This matter, the draft concluded, had to be settled in a matter of hours. The final version of the message differed slightly from the original. Brezhnev made the nuclear alert criticism milder and deleted the threat of action in connection with the desperate situation of the Third Army.

Kissinger called Brezhnev's message a strange one.[31] It was indeed strange, but that was because of the strange character of the American nuclear alert to which Brezhnev had to respond. The vague, indefinite character of Brezhnev's message—he wrote about threats to international peace and security, but did not suggest any practical measures to prevent them—was partly the result of Kissinger's conciliatory press conference, which got positive coverage in the Soviet press and was considered a signal to close the case. Our message went out after Kissinger's press conference but before Nixon's.

Reading the text of Nixon's press conference, I was struck by the tough and hostile language he used (for example, "What Mr. Brezhnev does understand is the power of the United States" and "It was the most difficult crisis we've had since the Cuban confrontation of 1962"[32]). It differed greatly from the conciliatory tone of most of the messages Nixon had sent to Brezhnev during the war, including the one received in Moscow after Defcon III. However, I understood that the tough tone was mainly for domestic consumption—such double standards were used by Soviet leaders too from time to time. But how would Brezhnev and his colleagues react? I had no doubt that if such hawkish statements had been made before the Politburo's decision on Defcon III, the character of that decision would have been quite different.

A dismissal of Nixon's press conference remarks was put out in a statement by Tass. When Brezhnev was shown extracts of Nixon's press conference, he was angry enough to order Central Committee Secretaries Ponomarev, Katushev, and Vladimir Dolgikh, with my participation, to draft a response. I suggested using our tough version of the message to Nixon, which Brezhnev had softened, as a basis for the Tass statement. The Tass statement rejected Washington's explanation of the alert as "absurd, since the actions of the Soviet Union are aimed solely at promoting implementation of the decisions of the Security Council on a cease-fire and the restoration of peace in the Middle East." It added that the U.S. action did not promote the relaxation of international tension and was taken "obviously in an attempt to intimidate the Soviet Union." Implying that the Kremlin did not intend to be intimidated, the statement concluded: "But those who are behind this step should be told that they have chosen the wrong address."[33] Nixon's name was not mentioned in the statement, but he was nonetheless its target. This was the sharpest criticism of the American President in the time of détente.

A number of messages in Brezhnev's name along the lines of the Tass statement were sent to world leaders during the following days. Among the addressees were President Tito of Yugoslavia, Prime Minister Indira Gandhi of India, Prime Minister Edward Heath of England, President Georges Pompidou of France, Chancellor Willy Brandt of West Germany, and Prime Minister Mariano Rumor of Italy. The messages were cut-and-dried, with only a few nuances and emphases that were tailored to the different recipients. The events of the last few days, the messages claimed, once again clearly demonstrated that the actions of the United States are guided exclusively by selfish interests for certain domestic political dividends and have nothing to do with establishing a just and durable peace in the Middle East. Satisfaction was expressed that in a number of countries, including the country of the addressee, the needless deterioration of the international situation had caused disappointment and even strong disapproval.

The messages ended on something of a mysterious note: "The Soviet Union could not, certainly, remain indifferent to this step by the United States, and reached appropriate conclusions." What kind of "appropriate conclusions" was not clear, I am afraid, even for the authors. I have to confess that this set of messages was not exactly an ideal example of diplomatic correspondence. One reason for that was the ambiguity of the very idea of addressing world leaders with complaints against the United States at the time when the war had finally been stopped thanks in large degree to Soviet-American cooperation.

The drafts prepared by the task force in cooperation with a number of experts were circulated in the Politburo. In response, we received a list of amendments and comments, some of them contradictory and opposing. We prepared a second version and showed it to Gromyko. After he talked with Brezhnev, the decision was made to instruct the Soviet ambassadors to inform the addressees of the Kremlin's dissatisfaction with the American nuclear alert verbally. In the whirlwind of events of those days, I did not see the final version of the instructions.

As one might expect, the noisiest and toughest Soviet reaction to Defcon III was displayed by Malik. It was the first time during the Yom Kippur War that an open Soviet-American confrontation had erupted in the United Nations, and the Soviet media had begun to run stories about a "wave of indignation" all over the world in connection with Washington's "irresponsible decision" to put its armed forces on alert.

This propaganda warfare, portraying the American action as irresponsible and provocative, was an inevitable part of the process of de-escalation. The main result was that both sides got what they wanted in terms of public relations from the escalation of the conflict. The Kremlin, by threatening to undertake unilateral action it never actually planned, had succeeded in dramatizing the situation, thus pushing the United States and Israel to speed up the actual end of war and saving Egypt from a humiliating surrender. The White House, on the other hand, both prevented an unacceptable development in the Middle East, which could have led to further Soviet political and military expansion, and succeeded in demonstrating the special role of the United States in the Middle East peace settlement.

## THE TRIUMPHANT BREZHNEV

In the end, the de-escalation bore fruit. According to the information from Cairo, on October 26 not a single shot was fired on the Egyptian-Israeli front. The cease-fire took hold on the Golan Heights as well. The next day, representatives of Egypt and Israel met at the 101-kilometer mark of the Cairo-Suez road, and for the first time in decades direct negotiations between the belligerents had started. The Yom Kippur War was over.

The events in the Middle East faded into the background. Now the Soviet media were full of reports from the World Congress of Peace Forces. The headlines in the papers were typical: "Unity and Solidarity," "Cheery Optimism," "In the Interests of All Peoples," "The Epoch of Great Changes," "Strengthening of Peace the Most Important Task of the USSR," and so on.

The highlight of the Congress and, I believe, of world affairs that day was Brezhnev's address. I have already mentioned the importance the Kremlin leaders and Brezhnev personally attached to the Congress. I saw Brezhnev for a few moments that morning. He was excited and inspired by his speech, and pleased to learn that the Security Council had approved a resolution establishing an emergency peace force and that the cease-fire was taking hold on both fronts for the first time since the war started. A group of his speechwriters were making the final revisions in the text.

Within the last few days, the part of the speech that was devoted to the Middle East had been revised several times, and some of the points were inserted by Brezhnev himself. For example, Brezhnev wanted to remind his audience that in recent years the Soviet Union had often warned that the Middle East situation was extremely dangerous. He was eager to make clear that from the very beginning of the hostilities the Soviet Union had taken "all political measures to bring about the end of the war." Recent events, he stated, had forced the Soviet Union to be vigilant and to take urgent and decisive steps to guarantee that the terms of the resolution on the cease-fire and troop withdrawal were met.

Brezhnev did not want to mention his message to Nixon suggesting sending joint Soviet and American contingents to Egypt, or only a Soviet contingent. Neither did he want to go into the details of Sadat's appeals to him, and of Nixon's claim that Sadat had asked only to have representatives sent to the region to observe the implementation of the cease-fire. And Brezhnev decided to downgrade the American nuclear alert (his speech was given a few hours before Nixon's press conference), saying only that cooperation in the Middle East "cannot, of course, be helped by actions undertaken in recent days in certain circles of NATO countries [what anonymity!], such as the artificial intensification of passions by distributing fantastic rumors about the intentions of the Soviet Union in the Middle East."

Rejecting the allegation that the Soviet Union was opposing negotiations, Brezhnev stated that it was impossible to exaggerate the importance of negotiations between interested parties, which must begin immediately under appropriate auspices. Finally, he confirmed the Soviet stand that all states must be guaranteed peace, security, and inviolability of frontiers and that the Soviet Union was ready to participate in the guarantees.[34] Twice in his speech Brezhnev referred to the "Palestine problem," emphasizing the need to ensure the legitimate rights of the Palestinian people. In diplomatic talks during the war the Palestine problem had hardly been mentioned, so the speechwriters were careful to make this speech balanced. Later, Yasser Arafat stated with satisfaction: "We shall never forget that Comrade Leonid Brezhnev has always, whether talking to President Nixon or addressing the World Congress of Peace Forces, . . . spoken in support of the Palestinian people and their legitimate national aspirations."[35]

There was nothing extraordinary in Brezhnev's analysis of the Mideast situation. His purpose was to make it consistent with his main idea that the trend in international relations was toward relaxation of tensions, that détente was irreversible, that political means must prevail over military means in international conflict-management, and that peace must be fought for tirelessly day in and day out because there still were imperialist forces that continued to act in the spirit of the Cold War.

Everyone must admit that he succeeded in his task. His address at the World Congress was characterized in the West as moderate (*New York Times*), mild (*Asahi Shimbun*, Tokyo), and businesslike (*The Times*, London) and was received with relief. In socialist and many nonaligned states, it got the highest marks ("brilliant," "excellent," "outstanding"). The Moscow magazine *New Times* wrote:

> When he finished the profound, comprehensive speech in which he examined with utmost clarity the most important aspects of the people's struggle for peace, national independence, and social progress, and the principles of peace policy consistently pursued by the Soviet Union, the delegates rose with one accord to give him a standing ovation.[36]

Brezhnev had reason to be pleased. He could consider the positive response to his speech all over the world as evidence that his policy, including in the Middle East, was a triumph.

But was it really a triumph? Brezhnev and his closest associates felt that their objective—to prevent another overall defeat of the Arabs and

Soviet involvement in the war and thereby preserve détente—had been achieved. Their interest and personal entanglement in the Middle East problem was significantly diminishing. The weekend of October 27 and 28 was the first weekend in the month Brezhnev did not call for a meeting on the Middle East.

By the end of October, I was advised by the Communist Party bosses of the Foreign Ministry to convene a meeting of my department's Communist nucleus. Suffice it to say that all the almost seventy of my subordinates in the Department of International Organizations were members of the CPSU or the Komsomol (Communist Youth League). I decided to analyze the results of the war in the Middle East and to discuss the prospects for a peace settlement. In my presentation I reminded my colleagues of the main events connected with the Middle East conflict and informed them about some details of Moscow's negotiations with Kissinger and the Politburo's decision to disregard the American nuclear alert. I emphasized the growing role and responsibility of our department in the process of peace settlement in the Middle East, invited my colleagues to come up with fresh ideas and initiatives aimed at an effective convocation of the peace conference, and suggested setting up a departmental ad hoc group to do the preparatory work for the conference. My remarks and analysis were based on Brezhnev's speech at the World Congress, and of course I praised Comrade Leonid Ilyich Brezhnev and Comrade Andrei Andreyevich Gromyko.

My introductory remarks were followed by a rather dull and short discussion. There were no fresh ideas or initiatives for the peace process. The participants mostly repeated Brezhnev's assessments or made general statements along the following lines: The Soviet Union was pursuing a praiseworthy and objective policy in the Middle East, or the Soviet policy was a real embodiment of the principles of Marxism-Leninism, which proceed from the need to eliminate all forms of exploitation, national oppression, and infringement of personal liberties.

Listening to such twaddle, I became very angry. What I really wanted was a brainstorming session, a think-tank on the eve of the peace conference. It did not work. Did none of the young and able diplomats of one of the most prestigious units of the Foreign Ministry have a personal opinion or assessment? Certainly they did. The heated and highly interesting arguments I had with my colleagues on many occasions during the war were proof that among the diplomats there were different assessments and divergent views. But those arguments and discussions were held *informally*. This party meeting was a *formal* one, and that made all the difference. This was quite typical of Soviet society: to be frank, open, and sincere in private and to express only standard opinions in public, especially at party meetings.

So the meeting was a failure (as most such meetings were). After it adjourned, I invited a group of my closest colleagues to my office to continue the discussion. An ad hoc preparatory group was set up, with Vsevolod Oleandrov, who later became ambassador-at-large, as its head. Unfortunately, the second attempt to provoke a creative discussion was not very successful either. There was uneasiness in the air. Although we had done everything right and the results were satisfactory, there was no pleasure in it, no sense of satisfaction. Something was wrong, and I did not know what it was. We knew only that we were not optimistic about the peace process. We agreed that an important chapter of the Middle East crisis, in which the Soviet Union had played a decisive role, had ended. Would the Soviet Union continue to play the same role during the next phase? I did not feel sure of that.

After the hostilities in the Middle East ended, the correspondence with Nixon, Sadat, Assad, and other leaders on Middle East issues continued for some time, but it became increasingly rare and sporadic. The Politburo Commission on the Middle East held several meetings in late October and November; Kuznetsov, as a special representative of the Kremlin, visited Damascus and Cairo; and military delegations were sent to Egypt and Syria. An enormous number of both trifling and serious problems arose: the exchange of prisoners of war, disengagements of troops, troop withdrawals to the positions of October 22, the sending and removing of observers, and, last but not the least, preparation for the peace conference. Most of these issues were discussed and decisions were made in the Foreign Ministry in cooperation with other ministries and government agencies.

But this was routine work for the huge bureaucratic and diplomatic machine of the Soviet Union. The drama of the situation created by the decision of the Egyptian and Syrian leaders to launch an attack against Israel on October 6, which had sharply spotlighted the pros and cons of the Kremlin's policy-making mechanism, gradually dissipated by the end of the month. Each of us on the task force resumed our normal duties. One ordinary weekday full of usual bureaucratic fuss was followed by another one, as if nothing had happened in October 1973.

# CHAPTER 8
## CONCLUSION

The Kremlin leaders—and they were not alone—evaluated the outcome of the war in the Middle East in October 1973 as a triumph of Soviet foreign policy and diplomacy and a political victory for the Soviet Union. In his address to the Indian parliament on November 29, 1973, Brezhnev, praising the growing Arab strength shown during the war, emphasized the "high efficiency of the solidarity and friendly cooperation the Soviet Union, other socialist countries, and many states of Asia, Africa, and other continents had given the Arab people in their just struggle."[1] This assessment was seconded by Podgorny and Kosygin, in their greetings to the Arab summit held in Algiers in late November 1973:

> Today, when international détente is gaining momentum, when Israel and its imperialist backers are finding themselves increasingly isolated in the international arena and the peace forces are giving ever greater support to the Arab peoples' liberation struggle, there are more favorable conditions for achieving a lasting and just peace in the Middle East.[2]

And speaking on behalf of the Politburo at the October Revolution celebration in the Kremlin on November 6, Kirilenko glorified Brezhnev's activity in international affairs and stressed the outstanding role of the Soviet Union in the peaceful settlement of the war in the Middle East.[3]

The Soviet media disseminated widely any Arab statements and documents that acknowledged the Soviet Union's important role in the Middle East war. In December 1973 the Moscow *New Times* magazine said: "It is significant that the statement of the Arab summit in Algiers noted 'with deep satisfaction' the 'political and military support rendered by the Soviet Union and other socialist countries, and also their economic cooperation with the Arab states.'"[4] The central Soviet newspapers published the message of the Egyptian parliament to the Supreme Soviet of the Soviet Union dated December 8, 1973, which stated: "We welcome and highly appreciate the position of the friendly Soviet Union, which by its support has confirmed its glorious friendship with our people, a friendship that we are proud of and that we would respect highly and truly."[5] Egypt's vice prime minister, Abdel K. Hatem, was quoted as saying in December 1973: "The political and economic assistance which the Soviet Union has rendered to the Arabs, and the Soviet weaponry with which we resisted the aggression, will be one of the strongest factors of the friendship between our two great nations."[6]

A great many Soviet journalists, political scientists, and commentators followed suit and magnified "another great victory of the Leninist foreign policy of the Soviet Union." For example, E. Dmitriev and V. Ladeikin wrote: "An indisputable political result of the October 1973 events was the sharp increase in the Soviet Union's authority in the Arab states, and the strengthening and further broadening of friendly Soviet-Arab relations."[7] Colonels N. Nikitin and S. Petrov claimed that the successes of the Arab states were possible only because of the "tremendous assistance of the Socialist states, and primarily the Soviet Union."[8]

The Kremlin leaders were satisfied not only with the political results of the war but also with the performance of their numerous aides, many of whom—including our task force—were promoted. In a few years, Kuznetsov was nominated to the high post of first deputy to Brezhnev when the latter replaced Podgorny as formal head of the Soviet Union; Kornienko became a deputy foreign minister; Sytenko was appointed under-secretary general of the United Nations, replacing the defector A. Shevchenko; and I became a member of the Collegium of the Foreign Ministry.

Indeed, on the surface everything seemed fine. Despite the Kremlin leaders' disapproval of the decision by Sadat and Assad to start the war, the Soviet Union gave Egypt and Syria all kinds of support—military, diplomatic, and economic. In the initial stage of the war, first-class Soviet military hardware was one of the main prerequisites for the Egyptian and Syrian successes, and the permanent flow of Soviet supplies by sealift and airlift guaranteed Arab resistance when the tide of the war had turned. The international actions of the Soviet Union contributed significantly to prevention of an Arab surrender in the last week of the war. Thus it appeared that the Soviet Union had strictly and successfully followed the principle of proletarian internationalism and constant support of "peoples fighting imperialism."

At the same time, the Kremlin did not give up its idea of spreading the détente to the entire world and strengthening the Soviet Union's cooperation with the capitalist world. Even during the Yom Kippur War, the Soviet Union was visited by a number of Western leaders who expressed keen interest in developing cooperation with the USSR. Perhaps the most important result of the war was that Soviet-American détente did not blow up, in spite of divergent views and competing goals of Moscow and Washington. Almost daily communications between the Kremlin and the White House, joint diplomatic actions in the Security Council, and mutual interest in avoiding the spread of the war—these were said to have been motivated by, and to have proved the advantage of, the policy of peaceful coexistence—which was another cornerstone of the Leninist foreign policy.

While strongly supporting Egypt and Syria, the Kremlin did not want the Soviet Union to be directly involved in the war. Although by the third week of the war the situation of the Arabs was hopeless and Defcon III was an obvious American military challenge to the Soviet Union that could be used as a pretext for a further escalation of superpower confrontation, the Kremlin succeeded in avoiding Soviet participation in the war.

So was it a victory? In history only the final result can be seen to have been inevitable and important, and usually years or decades have to pass before an evenhanded assessment of any event or of any policy can be given. In this instance, however, there was no need for much time to pass. Many of us Soviet diplomats did not feel triumphant when the war ended. We felt it was a hollow victory.

We knew that relations with Egypt and Syria had not improved. In fact, they had deteriorated during the war, notwithstanding some false-hearted and untrue Arab and Soviet statements to the contrary. Sadat's growing contacts with the Americans, only some of which were known to Moscow, proved that Egypt had embarked on an entirely new foreign policy, which was pro-American and anti-Soviet. The Soviet failure to meet Assad's request for an early cease-fire damaged Soviet-Syrian relations substantially. His hesitation in accepting the Soviet-American resolution in the Security Council, and his refusal to participate in the Geneva Peace Conference, showed a serious shift in his attitude toward the Soviet Union. As a result of these developments, the Soviet Union—which had played a central role in the sequence of events in the area from the outbreak of the war to the adoption of Security Council Resolution 340—was losing its role. There was no increase whatsoever in Soviet authority and influence in the Arab world as a result of the war, as some commentators have claimed. We felt that the peace process was shifting from Moscow to Washington, particularly after Sadat's drift toward cooperation with the United States. So much for implementation of the principle of proletarian internationalism and common struggle against imperialism during the Yom Kippur War.

I do not think that the policy of détente gained strength during the war either. It is true that détente between the superpowers helped prevent a nuclear confrontation, but the war had proved the weakness and insecurity of détente too. It showed that—détente notwithstanding—mutual mistrust, suspicion, and fear prevailed in the relations between the superpowers. Détente was undoubtedly cherished by the Kremlin in hopes that in response the Soviet Union would be able to have a new trade relationship with the United States, and especially that the USSR would receive the most-favored-nation trade status Washington had promised Moscow in 1972. Although the Kremlin leaders showed a certain restraint in the Yom Kippur War, which was recognized all over the world, the most-favored-nation trade agreement was not approved by the U.S. Congress. A large number of Americans openly opposed Nixon's détente with the Soviet Union, and the trade and arms-control policies that went with it. There was no open criticism of détente in the Soviet Union, of course, but obvious disappointment with it was expressed by the Soviet propaganda machine, which began to emphasize the task of "exposing the policy of the U.S. imperialist circles that were threatening peace." The Yom Kippur War marked the beginning of détente's decline, which gradually progressed throughout the 1970s.

Certainly the Soviet Union had made a number of gains as a result of the war, as some analysts correctly asserted.[9] The most significant were NATO's deep political crisis caused by the West European opposition to supplying Israel from U.S. bases in Europe, the Arab oil embargo, and a split within the European Economic Community. But these developments were the consequence of the other superpower's policies and had nothing to do with Soviet foreign policy.

As for the Soviet Union's foreign policy—which by the way I felt was executed quite well by the professionals involved—it could never have produced anything but a hollow victory, because its very foundation was untenable. The goal of Soviet policy was to implement simultaneously two incompatible principles: peaceful coexistence and proletarian internationalism. If international cooperation meant reaching mutually beneficial agreements that would bring positive rewards to both sides—socialist and capitalist partners—the class struggle and proletarian internationalism were aimed at weakening (ideally, annihilating) their opponent, the same capitalist partner. In the present case, during the Yom Kippur War the Kremlin tried to cooperate with the United States, the leader of the "imperialist camp," and at the same time did its best to help the Arabs defeat Israel and "those imperialists who were backing it"—the same United States. Such mutually exclusive, contradictory principles could not help but bring substantive losses.

I do not share the opinion of those who claim that during the Yom Kippur War the Soviet Union appeared to be more interested in détente than in what would be in the interests of their allies, Egypt and Syria. It is true that a confrontation with the United States threatened Soviet security interests more than the conflict in the Middle East did, but the point is that the Kremlin tried to sit on two chairs. It tried to develop cooperation with the United States while challenging the U.S. position in the Middle East by supporting the Arab states against Israel.

Several Soviet miscalculations and political blunders during the Yom Kippur War were caused by the Kremlin's orthodox and dogmatic mode of thinking, which presupposed that the destruction of capitalism as a political-economic system was inevitable and that the victory of socialism and communism was unavoidable. The imposed breakaway of more than a dozen European and Asian countries from capitalism, and the emergence of the "socialist camp," was considered irrevocable. The Arab states and the rest of the developing countries were categorized either as "progressive" (those that embarked on the road of socialist development) or as "reactionary" (those that did not). The progressive Arab countries—and, at that time, Egypt and Syria were among them—

were supposed to be united with the Soviet Union by a common position regarding domestic and international policy.

The Kremlin was convinced that Egypt and Syria had a vital interest in maintaining the closest relationship with the Soviet Union and would never depart from their friendly stance toward it. Any important move in domestic or foreign policy by the "progressive" countries not cleared by Moscow was met with suspicion and considered treason. The importance of military cooperation was greatly exaggerated. The fact that the Soviet Union provided Egypt and Syria with all kinds of weapons and military training inspired a belief that these countries were bound to Moscow forever.

The multicolored mosaic picture of the world was seen by the Kremlin leaders only in white and black. If the reality did not fit the Communist dogmas, the reality was neglected—and agreements worked out in negotiations were interpreted frivolously and one-sidedly in conformity with the dogmas. The Kremlin's orthodox dogmatic approach underestimated, and sometimes ruled out, any manifestation of national, religious, or historical identities in international relations. This mentality determined how Soviet foreign policy was conducted both in general and during the Yom Kippur War, and it accelerated the decline of the Soviet Union's role and influence in the Middle East after the war.

There were no winners in the Yom Kippur War—none of the participants and neither of the superpowers came out ahead. Only some politicians scored a few gains in their domestic struggles for power and international standing. In the Soviet Union, the big winner was undoubtedly Brezhnev himself. As a result of the war, his rating in the Soviet Union and in world politics increased significantly. One delegate to the World Congress of Peace Forces described Brezhnev's activity as "a ray of light at a critical moment, a moment that seemed tragic."[10] The position of two other members of the post-Khrushchev ruling Troika—Kosygin and Podgorny—consequently weakened.

The losses resulting from the Yom Kippur War were much more impressive. The Arab and Israeli casualty figures tell a frightening story. According to data considered by the Soviet Ministry of Defense as reliable, Egypt's and Syria's casualties totaled 28,751 men, 4,902 of them killed, 14,265 wounded, and 9,584 captured or missing. Israel's casualties totaled 16,800: 4,000 killed, 12,000 wounded, and 800 prisoners of war or missing.

Aircraft and tank losses by the belligerents were severe. They exceeded the losses of many of World War II's largest battles—the Battle of Kursk (1943), for one. The Arabs, including the Iraqis, lost 334 planes and 53 helicopters, and the Israelis lost 252 planes and 10 helicopters. Arab tanks destroyed came to 2,000, while the Israelis lost 1,084. The Yom Kippur War apparently cost Israel about $250 million a day, or a total of approximately $6 billion.[11] The Arab states' expenses were apparently much higher. All these figures mean that every day the cease-fire was delayed by the superpowers in particular resulted in approximately 420 killed and 1,200 wounded Arabs and Israelis, and that one hour of meaningless babble in the Security Council increased the war spending of the belligerents by several millions of dollars.

The genesis and the course of the Yom Kippur War are well known. One of the bloodiest wars in the entire post–World War II period lasted only three weeks. On the battlefield, the war was fought by the Israelis and the Arabs. The outcome of the war, however, was to a great degree determined by the policies of the superpowers: The cease-fire agreement resulted from negotiations between them, the fighting was finally stopped after some tough political and military steps by them, and it was they who decided to convene a peace conference, determining what its format would be and who would attend. Everything about the war depended on the readiness of the superpowers to find an end to the conflict that was *satisfactory for them*.

Surely there was a good chance for a powerful and speedy superpower intervention aimed at an immediate cessation of the fighting. Several bilateral and multilateral documents could have served as guidelines for joint actions: the "Basic Principles of Mutual Relations Between the USSR and the USA," signed on May 29, 1972; the understanding between Brezhnev and Nixon concerning the Middle East reached at the Soviet-American summit in the summer of 1973; Resolution 242 of the Security Council; and others. Besides, the détente "honeymoon" created a favorable atmosphere for effective cooperation between the United States and the Soviet Union.

Finally, both superpowers were indeed eager to avoid a war in the Middle East, at least in the fall of 1973, and both were interested in establishing peace in the region. But the problem was that each of the superpowers wanted to impose its own version of peace in the region: the Kremlin an anti-American peace, the White House an anti-Soviet peace. All the discussions in the Kremlin concerning the war finally focused on the impact any Kremlin decision would have on the standing and reputation of the United States in that region. The Kremlin hemmed and hawed on the issue of a cease-fire in the first days of the war not only because Sadat rejected the idea but also primarily because a successful Arab advance and Israel's defeat would seriously jeopardize American positions. When the Israelis began their offensive and the Arabs were about to lose the war, however, the Kremlin became very cooperative on the cease-fire issue—because it wanted to save the Arabs, but also because it was eager to prevent the rise of U.S. influence in the Middle East as a result of an Israeli victory. Nixon, Kissinger, and other American participants in the events have confessed that the White House was guided by the same philosophy: pressuring for an early cease-fire in the first days of the war and temporizing later when the tide of the war had turned. Thus, in spite of détente and bilateral and multilateral commitments, both superpowers were disposed to take extreme steps in order to prevent the other superpower from gaining political and military advantage in the region. Both bluffed—the Kremlin politically (Brezhnev's message threatening to intervene in the Middle East unilaterally) and the White House militarily (by declaring Defcon III). The difference was that the Soviet people did not have to pay a single ruble for the Kremlin's bluff, while the American taxpayer had to take care of the White House's bluff, which cost the United States coffers a pretty penny.

When each superpower believed that its counterpart was not ready to come off a loser, it tried to end the diplomatic game in a draw. That is how the joint draft of the cease-fire resolution, the bilateral "Understanding," and the decision to convene a peace conference came into being. But even the decisions worked out by the superpowers jointly were obscure and ambiguous. They did not lay out practical and realistic approaches for peaceful settlement of the Middle East conflict, and they did not help to begin a comprehensive peace process. Many of these decisions were stillborn babies. The Geneva Peace Conference held in December 1973 was a pitiful event. As a member of the Soviet delegation to the conference, I got the impression that the most significant event at the conference was Gromyko's acceptance of being seated at the conference table next to Abba Eban although it violated the alphabetical order in accordance with which the delegations were seated at international conferences.

In addition, there was another serious flaw in Soviet-American relations: each side showed a basic lack of understanding of how the other side perceived things. This led to a number of miscalculations and false decisions. Brezhnev and his colleagues did not realize the seriousness of

Watergate for President Nixon and for the American decision-making process. Nixon and Kissinger, for their part, completely ignored how important it was for Brezhnev and his supporters to gain a reputation as leaders of "peace-loving forces" all over the world by orchestrating a great propaganda show in Moscow in October 1973.

The peace process in the Middle East was delayed for decades mainly because of the Soviet-American confrontation during the Cold War. If the Soviet Union and the United States had complied responsibly with their international obligations and had been guided by the noble task of helping the Arabs and the Israelis live in peace and prosperity, the Yom Kippur War could have opened up great opportunities for establishing a genuine peace in the Middle East. In harmony and cooperation the two superpowers could have imposed a cease-fire and stopped the fighting in the first days of the war, thus saving thousands and thousands of Arabs and Israelis. The superpowers could have initiated a fair and comprehensive peace process that could have prevented the subsequent military conflicts, confrontations, and hostilities in the Middle East. They had all the power and influence and the world community's broad support needed for implementing that great mission. Instead, they provoked the Arabs and the Israelis, thereby making the difficult peace process even more difficult.

Therefore, as it seems to me, neither the politicians and diplomats nor the military leaders who participated in the political game of the Yom Kippur War could have been happy with and proud of its results. Not all is well that ends well.

# NOTES

## CHAPTER 1: ON THE EVE OF THE WAR

1. Radio Moscow, October 5, 1973.
2. *Pravda*, October 6, 1973.
3. Alvin Z. Rubinstein, *Red Star on the Nile: The Soviet-Egyptian Relationship Since the June War* (Princeton: Princeton University Press, 1977), p. 255.
4. Ibid., p. 254.
5. Ibid.
6. Mohamed Heikal, *The Road to Ramadan* (New York: Quadrangle / New York Times Book Co., 1975), p. 35.
7. Marvin Kalb and Bernard Kalb, *Kissinger* (Boston: Little, Brown, 1974), p. 453.
8. Heikal, *The Road to Ramadan*, p. 214.
9. Ibid., p. 209.
10. Gerald S. Strober and Deborah Hart Strober, *Nixon: An Oral History of His Presidency* (New York: Harper Collins, 1994), p. 145.
11. Richard M. Nixon, *The Memoirs of Richard Nixon* (New York: Grosset & Dunlap, 1978), p. 921.
12. Henry A. Kissinger, *Years of Upheaval* (Boston: Little, Brown, 1982), p. 463.


## CHAPTER 2: SEARCHING FOR AN EARLY CEASE-FIRE

1. Kissinger, *Years of Upheaval*, p. 472.
2. *Istoricheskii Archiv*, no. 6 (1993): 142.
3. Andrei Gromyko, *Memoirs* (New York: Doubleday, 1989), p. 271.
4. United Nations Security Council (hereafter UNSC), 1433rd Meeting (June 19, 1968), Official Records, p. 11.
5. Walter Isaacson, *Kissinger: A Biography* (New York: Simon & Schuster, 1992), p. 515.
6. Kalb and Kalb, *Kissinger*, p. 463.
7. Kissinger, *Years of Upheaval*, p. 481.
8. Nixon, *Memoirs*, p. 921.
9. *Pravda*, October 8, 1973.
10. Ibid.
11. *Trud*, October 9, 1973.
12. Heikal, *The Road to Ramadan*, p. 213.
13. Anwar Sadat, *In Search of Identity: An Autobiography* (New York: Harper & Row, 1978), p. 251.
14. UNSC, 1743rd Meeting (October 8, 1973), Official Records, Twenty-eighth Year, p. 7.
15. George Bush, *Looking Forward* (Garden City, N.Y.: Doubleday, 1987), p. 111.
16. UNSC, 1743rd Meeting, Official Records, p. 7.

17. Ibid., p. 8.
18. *Pravda*, October 9, 1973.
19. *Pravda*, October 8, 1973.

## CHAPTER 3: "WE HAVE TO HELP OUR ARAB BROTHERS"

1. Many of Kulikov's assessments were repeated later in an article published in "Lokalnii voini" (Local Wars) (Moscow: Military Academy of the General Staff, 1975), p. 277.
2. Heikal, *The Road to Ramadan*, p. 214.
3. Galia Golan, *Yom Kippur and After: The Soviet Union and the Middle East Crisis* (New York: Cambridge University Press, 1977), p. 85.
4. *New Times* (Moscow), no. 45 (1988): 21.
5. *New York Times*, October 12, 1973.
6. Robert Freedman, *Soviet Policy Toward the Middle East Since 1970*, 3rd ed. (New York: Praeger, 1982), p. 145.
7. See Chaim Herzog, *The War of Atonement, October 1973* (Boston: Little, Brown, 1975), p. 195.
8. V. A. Mazulenko, "Distinctive Features of the Military Conduct in Local Wars in the Middle East" (in Russian), *Woenaya Misl*, no. 7 (1977): 78.
9. *Pravda*, October 14, 1973.
10. *Trud*, October 13, 1973.
11. UNSC, 1744th Meeting, October 9, 1973, Official Records, p. 9.
12. Ibid., p. 13.
13. Ibid., p. 18.
14. *Pravda*, October 14, 1973.
15. *Krasnaya Zvezda*, October 13, 1973.
16. Kalb and Kalb, *Kissinger*, p. 478.
17. Vladimir Vinogradov, "Egypt: Time of Sedition," *Znamya*, no. 12 (1989): 190.
18. Kissinger, *Years of Upheaval*, p. 519.

## CHAPTER 4. KOSYGIN'S VISIT TO CAIRO

1. *Pravda*, October 16, 1973.
2. Ibid.
3. *New York Times*, October 16, 1973, p. 18.
4. *New York Times*, June 15, 1973, p. 1.
5. *New Times*, no. 48 (1973): 21.
6. *Krasnaya Zvezda*, October 19, 1973.
7. *New Times*, no. 45 (1988): 22.
8. *Pravda*, October 19, 1973.
9. Ibid.
10. Tass, October 17, 1973.
11. *Pravda*, October 19, 1973.
12. *Trud*, October 17, 1973.

13. *New York Times*, October 19, 1973, p. 1.
14. Sadat, *In Search of Identity*, p. 259.
15. Ion D. Glassman, *Arms for the Arabs: The Soviet Union and War in the Middle East* (Baltimore: Johns Hopkins University Press, 1975), p. 153.
16. Heikal, *The Road to Ramadan*, p. 235.
17. "October War Counter Claims," *Journal of Palestine Studies* 3 (Summer 1974): 163. Reprinted from *Al-Safir* (Beirut), April 16, 1974 (talk given by V. Vinogradov to Egyptian officials and political personalities).
18. Sadat, *In Search of Identity*, p. 258.
19. Ibid., p. 259.
20. Ibid., p. 260.
21. Heikal, *The Road to Ramadan*, p. 246.
22. Herzog, *The War of Atonement*, p. 244.
23. *New York Times*, October 20, 1973, p. 12.

## CHAPTER 5: KISSINGER IN MOSCOW

1. *Izvestia*, October 19, 1973.
2. Kissinger, *Years of Upheaval*, p. 534.
3. Ibid., p. 532.
4. Ibid., p. 542.
5. Ibid.
6. Henry A. Kissinger, *White House Years* (Boston: Little, Brown, 1979), p. 1141.
7. Kisa: pussycat.
8. Kissinger, *Years of Upheaval*, p. 547.
9. Stephen E. Ambrose, *Nixon*, vol. 3 (New York: Simon & Schuster, 1991), p. 245.
10. Ibid.
11. Kissinger, *Years of Upheaval*, p. 550.
12. Nixon, *Memoirs*, p. 933.
13. Sadat, *In Search of Identity*, pp. 264–65.
14. Kissinger, *Years of Upheaval*, p. 553.
15. Jonathan Aitken, *Nixon: A Life* (Washington, D.C.: Regnery, 1993), p. 508.
16. Moshe Dayan, *Story of My Life* (New York: Morrow, 1976), p. 513.
17. Kissinger, *Years of Upheaval*, p. 553.
18. UNSC, Resolution 338.
19. Kissinger, *Years of Upheaval*, p. 555.
20. UNSC, 1747th Meeting, October 21, 1973, Official Records, p. 7.
21. Ibid.
22. Ibid., p. 11.
23. Ibid., p. 10.
24. Kissinger, *Years of Upheaval*, p. 570.
25. Ibid., p. 555.
26. Sadat, *In Search of Identity*, p. 265.
27. Glassman, *Arms for the Arabs*, p. 139.
28. *Izvestia*, October 23, 1973.
29. *Izvestia*, October 19, 1973.
30. *Krasnaya Zvezda*, October 20, 1973.

31. *Pravda*, October 21, 1973.
32. *Krasnaya Zvezda*, October 20, 1973.
33. *Izvestia*, October 21, 1973.
34. *Pravda*, October 21, 1973.
35. Nixon, *Memoirs*, p. 936.
36. U.S. Department of State, "Arab-Israeli Conflict," Foreign Policy Outlines, November 1973.
37. Walter Laqueur, *Confrontation: The Middle East War and World Politics* (London: Wildwood House, Abacus, 1974), p. 161.
38. David Kimche, *The Last Option, After Nasser, Arafat, and Saddam Hussein: The Quest for Peace in the Middle East* (New York: Charles Scribner's Sons, 1992), p. 24.
39. Kalb and Kalb, *Kissinger*, p. 485.
40. Ibid.

## CHAPTER 6: THE ESCALATION

1. Golan, *Yom Kippur and After*, p. 120.
2. Kissinger, *Years of Upheaval*, p. 574.
3. *The Yom Kippur War*, by the Insight Team of the *London Sunday Times* (Garden City, N.Y.: Doubleday, 1973), p. 401.
4. Ibid., p. 400.
5. Moshe Maóz Asad, *The Sphinx of Damascus: A Political Biography* (New York: Weidenfeld & Nicholson, 1988), p. 95.
6. Doc. S/11040, Security Council, 28th Year, Official Records, Supplement for October, November, and December 1973 (New York: United Nations, 1974), p. 84.
7. Nixon, *Memoirs*, p. 936.
8. Heikal, *The Road to Ramadan*, p. 250.
9. UNSC, 1748th Meeting, October 23, 1973, Official Records, p. 14.
10. Ibid., p. 8.
11. Ibid., p. 9.
12. UNSC, Resolution 339.
13. *Izvestia*, October 24, 1973.
14. UNSC, 1749th Meeting, October 24, 1973, Official Records, p. 16.
15. Ibid., p. 7.
16. Vinogradov, "Egypt: Time of Sedition," p. 193.
17. Heikal, *The Road to Ramadan*, p. 251.
18. Nixon, *Memoirs*, pp. 936–37.
19. William Quandt, "Soviet Policy in the October 1973 War" (RAND, R-1864-1SA, May 1976), p. 33.
20. Alexander M. Haig Jr. and Charles McCarry, *Inner Circles: How America Changed the World* (New York: Warner Books, 1992), p. 414.
21. Kalb and Kalb, *Kissinger*, p. 577.
22. UNSC, 1749th Meeting, Official Records, p. 8.
23. Ibid., p. 9.
24. Kissinger, *Years of Upheaval*, p. 589.
25. Kalb and Kalb, *Kissinger*, p. 493.
26. Kissinger, *Years of Upheaval*, p. 589.

## CHAPTER 7: THE DE-ESCALATION

1. *Pravda*, October 25, 1973.
2. *Izvestia*, October 25, 1973.
3. Ibid.
4. *New Times*, no. 43 (1973): 5.
5. Nixon, *Memoirs*, p. 939.
6. Ibid.
7. Richard Ned Lebow and Janice Gross Stein, *We All Lost the Cold War* (Princeton: Princeton University Press, 1994), p. 271.
8. Nixon, *Memoirs*, p. 939.
9. Isaacson, *Kissinger*, p. 532.
10. Ibid.
11. *The Times* (London), October 29, 1973; as quoted by Glassman, *Arms for the Arabs*, p. 164.
12. *Department of State Bulletin* 69, no. 1795 (November 19, 1973): 617.
13. Nixon, *Memoirs*, p. 937.
14. Rubinstein, *Red Star on the Nile*, p. 275.
15. Glassman, *Arms for the Arabs*, p. 164.
16. Sadat, *In Search of Identity*, p. 266.
17. *Department of State Bulletin* 69, no. 1795, p. 621.
18. Kissinger, *Years of Upheaval*, p. 589.
19. Isaacson, *Kissinger*, p. 530.
20. *New York Times*, November 21, 1973, p. 17.
21. *New Times*, no. 42 (1973): 6.
22. *New York Times*, October 27, 1973, p. 10.
23. Vinogradov, "Egypt: Time of Sedition," p. 193.
24. *New York Times*, October 27, 1973, p. 14.
25. UNSC, Resolution 340.
26. UNSC, 1750th Meeting, October 25, 1973, Official Records, p. 2.
27. Ibid., p. 8.
28. *New York Times*, October 26, 1973, p. 19.
29. *Department of State Bulletin* 69, no. 1795, p. 621.
30. *New York Times*, October 27, 1973, p. 14.
31. Kissinger, *Years of Upheaval*, p. 608.
32. *New York Times*, October 27, 1973, p. 14.
33. *Pravda*, October 28, 1973.
34. *Pravda*, October 27, 1973.
35. *New Times*, no. 48 (1973): 20.
36. *New Times*, no. 44 (1973): 13.

## CHAPTER 8: CONCLUSION

1. *Pravda*, November 30, 1973.
2. *New Times*, no. 48 (1973): 19.
3. *Pravda*, November 7, 1973.
4. *New Times*, no. 50 (1973): 1.

5. *Pravda*, January 30, 1974.
6. E. Dmitriev and V. Ladeikin, *The Path to Peace in the Middle East* (in Russian) (Moscow: IMO, 1974), p. 218.
7. Ibid.
8. *Woenno-Istoricheskii* (Moscow), no. 11 (1974): 83.
9. Freedman, *Soviet Policy*, p. 151.
10. *New Times*, no. 44 (1973): 13.
11. Frank Aker, *October 1973: The Arab-Israeli War* (Hamden, Conn.: Archon Books, 1985), p. 128.

# INDEX

*Agence France Presse,* 6
airlift of military supplies, 57–58, 103, 107, 191. *See also* military supply, Soviet-Arab
Akhromeyev, Sergei, 167, 168
Akopov, Pogos, 11, 110, 166
Aleksandrov, Andrei
   grasping of Brezhnev's political moods, 69
   Kissinger negotiations, 126
   military supply to Arabs, 102–3, 124
Algeria. *See also* Boumedienne, Houari
   and Arab unity, 62, 64, 67
   delegation to Moscow, 84–86
   as "torpedo," 91
*Al-Hawadith,* 110
*Al-Hayat,* 74
Ali, Ahmed Ismail, 100
Allende, Salvador, 6
All-Union Central Council of Trade Unions, 43
All-Union Society of Cultural Relations with Foreign Countries, 69
*Al-Safir,* 48
Amasha, S. M., 63
Ambrose, Stephen E., 125
Andreasyan, Ruben, 98
Andropov, Yuri
   background, 26–27
   Brezhnev-Kissinger negotiations, 90, 91, 131, 133, 135
   defining Israeli withdrawal, 95
   and escalation of war, 152
   as member of Politburo, 23, 31
   military supply to Arabs, 58
   response to nuclear alert, 179–82
   Sadat's request for cease-fire, 132
   Soviet-Arab cooperation, 184
   U.S. supply to Israel, 75–76
anti-intellectualism in the Kremlin, 22
Antonov transport planes, 58, 75, 192

"appropriate auspices," 137, 139, 141–42
   justification for sending troops, 160, 182
   in "Understanding" document, 197
Arab Republic of Egypt. *See* Egypt
Arabs. *See individual countries*
Arab Socialist Resurrection (Ba'th) Party, 74
Arab-Soviet relations. *See* Soviet-Arab relations
Arab unity, 61–66, 77
   coalition, 91
   nonsupport of Syria, 156
   summit, 211–12
Arafat, Yasser, 61–62, 208
Assad, Hafiz, al-. *See also* Syria (Syrian Arab Republic)
   beginning of war, 7, 18
   Brezhnev-Kissinger negotiations, 139, 140
   Brezhnev message to, 199
   cease-fire opposition, 40
   cease-fire request, 43–45, 72–73
   cease-fire terms, 48
   military situation during cease-fire, 155–56
   Moscow's view of, 74
   Sadat's request for cease-fire, 130
   Soviet-Arab cooperation, 185
   Soviet observers, 172
   Syria's strategy, 12–16
Atherton, Alfred, 126
Azimov, Sarvar, 62

Bab al-Mandab, Strait of, 129, 130
Bahrain, 98
Bakdash, Khalid, 74
Bakr, Ahmad Hassan, 62, 185, 200
Bakri, I., 63
Baqi, Murtada Abdul, 63
Bar-Lev, Chaim, 144–45
Bar-Lev Line, 55

## INDEX

Baroody, Jamil, 142–43, 159
"Basic Principles of Mutual Relations Between the USSR and the USA" (1972), 40, 217
Ba'th (Arab Socialist Resurrection) Party, 74
Bazanov, Boris, 90, 110, 112
Belqasem, Sharif, 84
Ben Yahya, Mohammed, 84
Bitter Lakes region, 107, 109
Boumedienne, Houari. *See also* Algeria
 and Brezhnev's message on Arab unity, 62–63
 visit to Moscow, 84–86, 90, 102
Boyd, Aquiliano, 202
Brandt, Willy, 205
Brezhnev, Leonid
 aid to Arab leaders, 102
 Arab-Soviet cooperation, 184–85
 Arab unity, 51, 61–64
 avoidance of war, 18
 Boumedienne visit, 84
 cease-fire, 79, 82
 and escalation of war, 152–54, 164, 166, 169
 as foreign relations spokesman, 121
 Israeli retaliation, 68, 70
 Kissinger negotiations, 90–97, 99, 124, 126, 128–38
 Kissinger relations, 123–24
 Kosygin-Sadat talks, 108–10
 messages to world leaders, 205–6
 Nixon communications, 37–38, 41, 76, 116–20, 157, 204
 nuclear alert response, 182–84
 and the Politburo, xi, 23–25, 30–31
 and "propaganda insurance," 99–100
 Sadat contact, 2, 3, 6–12, 46
 "Understanding" and guarantees, 161
 unilateral action, 188
 U.S. cooperation in Middle East, 160–61, 163–64
 as winner, 207, 211, 216
 World Congress of Peace Forces, 178, 195
Brutenz, Karen, 74
buffer zone, 109
bureaucratic etiquette, 2, 3
Bush, George W., 49

Cairo talks, 87–114
Caradon, Lord (Hugh Foot), 34
cease-fire, 14–15, 21–51, 65. *See also* guarantees
 Assad request for, 74
 Brezhnev address to Nixon, 119
 Brezhnev-Kissinger negotiations, 127, 134, 135–37, 139–40
 compliance and U.S. role, 187
 *de facto*, 97, 99
 and diplomatic game, 77–83
 in effect, 206
 Kosygin-Sadat talks, 87–114
 as result of superpower policies, 217, 218
 Sadat request for, 129–31
 Security Council adoption, 141–43
 status quo ante, 49
 violations, 151–56
cease-fire-in-place, 45, 46, 78, 81
 Kosygin-Sadat talks, 105, 110
 and Soviet draft resolution, 86
Central Committee of the Communist Party of the Soviet Union (CPSU), xvi
 gathering of ideas on peace process, 209
 international policy responsibility, 28
 Israeli "criminal acts," 69
 "October Revolution Slogans of the CC of the CPSU," 77
 and "propaganda insurance," 99–103
 World Congress of Peace Forces, 164–65
Chandra, Romesh, 195
Chernenko, Konstantin, 185
Chiao Khuan Hua, 158–59
Chile, 6
China, 201
 position on cease-fire resolution, 90, 97
 position on Soviet-American action, 162
 Resolution 242, 142
 Resolution 339, 158–59
"Chinese syndrome," 37–38
*Christian Science Monitor*, 103
Cold War, 219
Collegium of the Foreign Ministry, xvi, 212
Communist Party. *See* Central Committee of the Communist Party of the Soviet Union (CPSU); Politburo
Communist Party conference, 102
Communist Party of the United States, 178
Communist Youth League (Komsomol), 209

# INDEX

Council of Trade Unions, 69
Cox, Archibald, 94
CPSU. See Central Committee of the Communist Party of the Soviet Union (CPSU)
"criminal acts," 66–71
Cromer, Lord (George Rowland Stanley Baring), 175

Dayan, Moshe, 67, 133, 171
Day of Atonement (Yom Kippur), xv
de-escalation, 177–210
Defcon III (Defense Condition III), 174–75
 and the media, 177–78
 Soviet reaction to, 179–83, 189–97
 Soviet response to, 202–6
 United Nations Security Council, 200–202
Defense Ministry (Soviet Union), xii. See also Grechko, Andrei
Denmark, 88–89
Department of International Organizations. See also "task force"
 cease-fire resolution draft, 39, 87
 gathering of ideas on peace process, 209
 Israelyan as director of, xvi
détente, 32–33, 37
 Brezhnev assessment of, 126–27
 international, 213
 as justification for joint Soviet-American action, 160
 "propaganda insurance" and, 101
 Soviet commitment to, 89
 status at end of war, 214, 217
 Watergate and, 94
Dinitz, Simcha, 175, 187
Diplomatic Academy, xvi, 22
Dmitriev, E., 212
Dobrynin, Anatolii
 and beginning of the war, 21–22
 Brezhnev-Kissinger negotiations, 120–21, 124, 126, 133
 and Brezhnev speech, 51
 cease-fire, 79–80, 83
 Israeli violations, 170–71
 Kissinger communications, 36, 40, 49, 93, 173–74
 reaction to nuclear alert, 196
dogmatic mode of thinking, 215–16

Dolgikh, Vladimir, 205

Eban, Abba, 171
Egypt. See also Sadat, Anwar al-; Soviet-Arab relations
 beginning of war, xv, 12
 Cairo talks, 87–114
 casualties and losses, 216–17
 confiscation of sample weapons, 75
 Gidi/Mitla offensive, 71–72
 Israeli cease-fire violations, 154–55
 losing of the war, 184–85
 military operations, 54–55
 SCUD missile firing, 143–45
 Soviet relations, 6–10, 73, 216
 Suez Canal and Golan Heights attacks, 21–22
 Syria relations, 67
"Egyptian agreement," 111
Egyptian Second Army, 108
Egyptian Third Army, 107, 108
 Israeli encirclement, 151, 154, 156, 166
 supply cutoff, 165, 199
Emergency Forces, U.N.
 idea of setting up, 181–82, 198–99
 Resolution 340, 201
escalation of war, 151–75
etiquette, bureaucratic, 2, 3
European Economic Community, 215
evacuation of Soviets from Egypt and Syria, 2, 3, 4
 as call for joint preventive action, 17
 question of Sadat's permission, 11

Fahmy, Ismail, 8
Farra, Muhammed al-, 35
Fattah, A., 129
Feisal, Y., 63
Foreign Ministry (Soviet Union), xviii. See also Gromyko, Andrei
Forest, James, 178
Freedman, Robert, 66

Gandhi, Indira, 205
Gareyev, Mahmut, 61, 72
Geneva Peace Conference, 218. See also peace conference
Gidi Pass, 45, 66, 72
Glassman, Jon D., 144
Gluchov, Yuri, 5–6

Golan, Galia, 152
Golan Heights, 14, 21, 22, 46
  Palestinian brigades in, 67
  Syrian attack on, 54, 55
  Syrian hopes of liberating, 72
  Syrian-Iraqi offensive plan, 155
Grechko, Andrei
  background, 27–28
  beginning of war, 51
  Boumedienne visit, 84
  Brezhnev-Kissinger negotiations, 134–35
  Chinese veto of draft resolution, 97
  Egypt and Syria communication, 72
  Egypt firing of SCUD missiles, 143–44
  Egyptian confiscation of sample weapons, 75
  and escalation of war, 152
  Kosygin-Sadat visit, 90, 91
  as member of Politburo, 23, 31
  military operations, 53, 55–56
  military responsibilities, 193
  military situation, 132–33
  and "propaganda insurance," 100–101
  response to nuclear alert, 179, 180
  Soviet-American joint action, 188
  Soviet-Arab cooperation, 184
Gromyko, Andrei
  and Arab unity, 61, 63–65
  avoidance of war, 18
  background, 23, 28–29
  beginning of war, 1–4
  Boumedienne visit, 84
  Brezhnev-Kissinger negotiations, 131, 134–39
  Brezhnev's address to Nixon, 116
  Cairo visit planning, 90, 93
  cease-fire, 79–80, 82, 83
  cease-fire diplomatic moves, 78
  cease-fire-in-place proposal, 81, 82
  cease-fire resolution drafts, 87–88, 95, 96
  cease-fire violations, 151–54
  Israeli retaliation, 68, 69
  Kissinger and Soviet-American cooperation, 163
  Kissinger invitation, 121, 125
  meeting with Egypt and Syria, 7
  as member of Politburo, 31
  military supply to Arabs, 58
  Nixon and Israeli aid, 76
  and no guarantees, 162
  on oil embargo, 97–98
  opinion of Kissinger, 124
  response to nuclear alert, 181, 183
  Sadat's request for cease-fire, 132
  SCUD missile firing by Egypt, 143–45
  Soviet response to nuclear alert, 203, 206
  and task force, 41–42, 202
  and Tito, 140
  on U.N. observers, 158
  United Nations Security Council meeting, 44
  World Congress of Peace Forces, 195
GRU (military intelligence) reports, 115
guarantees
  cease-fire, 106–10, 130, 131, 142; and borders, 111; interpretation of, 147–48; as response to nuclear alert, 184
  Israeli compliance, 142
  Malik statement regarding, 171
  Soviet-American, 139, 157; Sadat claim of, 154–55, 158
  varying interpretations of, 162, 163
  withdrawal of Israeli troops, 140
Guinea, 201
Guiringaud, Louis de, 141

Haig, Alexander M., Jr., 170, 173, 174, 194
Hall, Gus, 178
Hamud, K., 63
Hatem, Abdel Qadr, 190, 212
Heath, Edward, 205
Heikal, Mohamed
  on alleged peace plan, 111
  on Assad and Vinogradov, 47
  on Assad-Mukhitdinov talks, 14–15
  on Israeli crossing of Suez Canal, 113
  on Sadat and Soviet arms, 12
  on Sadat-Vinogradov talks, 158
  on Soviet airlift, 57
  on Soviet intervention, 166
Herzog, Chaim, 114
Huang Hua, 201
Hungary, 26–27
Hyland, William G., 135

Ievlev, Nikolai
  Egyptian firing of SCUD missiles, 143
  military situation, 104, 107, 108
  and Sadat, 72
  Soviet military support, 54, 58
  U.S. weapon samples, 74–75
*Ilya Mechnikov* (ship), 68, 100
imperialism
  anti-imperialist struggle, 62, 213, 215
  Kremlin propaganda, 60
  as Politburo topic, xvii
  U.S. in Hungary, 27
  U.S. policy opposition, 31
India, 201
Indonesia, 201
Iraq
  and Arab unity, 62, 64, 91
  armed forces, 46–47
  support for Syria, 67, 68, 155
Iraqi Communist Party, 101
Iraqi Revolutionary Command Council, 63
Ismail, Hafiz, 15, 82
  Kissinger-Sadat talks, 103, 104, 129–30, 131
Ismailia, 184
Israel. *See also* withdrawal of Israeli forces
  beginning of war, xvii, 12
  blocking of medical supplies, 203
  casualties and losses, 216–17
  cease-fire violation, 151–52, 159
  cessation of military activity, 175
  counteroffensive, 66, 90–91, 115
  and Egyptian Third Army, 151, 156
  infiltration force, 107
  offensive, 46
  Politburo review of military situation, 132
  SCUD missile firing by Egyptians, 143–45
  Soviet blaming of, 41
  Suez Canal and Golan Heights attacks, 21–22
  U.S. military supply, 75–76, 115, 129
Israeli Communist Party, 102
Israelyan, Victor. *See also* "task force"
  background, xvii–xviii
  beginning of war, 1–6, 22–23
  gathering of ideas on peace process, 209
  on Gromyko's position, 88
  on Kremlin attitude to Syria, 73
  as member of Collegium of the Foreign Ministry, 212
  as member of task force, 33, 35
  setting up of observer group, 167
  Syria's cease-fire appeal, 43–45
"Istiqlal" (Moroccan Communist Party), 101
Ivanov, V., 100
*Izvestia*, 70, 116
  handling of nuclear alert, 177–78
  propaganda and Kissinger visit, 145

Jadid, Salah, 74
Jarring mission, 43
*John F. Kennedy* (aircraft carrier), 192
joint military action. *See* observers, military; troops, Soviet-American
Jordan, 64, 67–68
Jorgensen, Anker, 88–89

Kalb, Bernard, 11, 147, 171
Kalb, Marvin, 11, 147, 171
Katushev, Konstantin, 23, 32
  on cease-fire, 80
  response to Nixon's press conference, 205
  Soviet-Arab cooperation, 184–85
  and Soviet propaganda, 77
  support for mobilization, 180, 181
Kenya, 201
KGB, xviii. *See also* Andropov, Yuri
  presence during Cairo talks, 108
  and Sadat's communication with Kissinger, 132
Khaddam, Abd al-, 7, 155–56
Kimche, David, 147
Kirilenko, Andrei
  assessment of Yom Kippur War, 212
  Israeli retaliation, 68
  little knowledge of Middle East, 32
  Politburo meetings, 30, 31
  response to nuclear alert, 180, 181
  World Congress of Peace Forces, 195
Kirpichenko, Vadim
  and Cairo talks, 108, 114
  criticism of Sadat, 166
  Egypt-Soviet relations, 9
  intelligence prediction of war, 16

## 232 INDEX

Kissinger, Henry A.
  activity with Arabs in New York, 5
  background, 122–24
  beginning of war, 22
  Brezhnev letter on Resolution 339, 157
  Brezhnev negotiations, 131, 133, 135–38
  cease-fire, 79, 83
  cease-fire-in-place proposal, 81, 82
  cease-fire status quo ante, 49
  Defcon III responsibility, 196–97
  Dobrynin invitation, 120
  Dobrynin talks, 36, 40
  Gromyko and Soviet-American cooperation, 163
  Nixon letter to Dobrynin, 186–87
  press conference, 202
  reaction to Brezhnev's message, 204
  reaction to Soviet action, 173–75, 194
  on security guarantees, 118
  Soviet criticism of, 160, 171
  Soviet reaction to, 93–94
  "Understanding" (document), 137–38, 161, 198
"Kissinger-Dobrynin channel," 122–23
Komsomol (Communist Youth League), 209
Kornienko, Georgii, 1, 33. *See also* "task force"
  as deputy foreign minister, 212
  Kissinger negotiations, 126
  as member of task force, 34–35
Kosygin, Aleksei
  Arab military supply, 55, 58
  Arab unity, 61, 63
  assessment of Yom Kippur War, 211
  attitude toward Sadat, 112–13
  avoidance of war, 18
  background, 24, 25–26
  Boumedienne visit, 84
  Brezhnev-Kissinger negotiations, 134
  Cairo/Sadat talks, 87–114, 125
  cease-fire, 133
  cease-fire request by Sadat, 131–32
  evacuation of Soviets, 3
  Israeli retaliation, 68
  observer team proposal, 162, 167
  as Politburo member, 23, 31
  and "propaganda insurance," 100–103
  response to nuclear alert, 180–84

  weakening of position, 216
  World Congress of Peace Forces, 195
*Krasnaya Zvezda*, 77, 145
Kulikov, Victor
  analysis of "criminal acts," 66–68
  military expansion, 71–72
  military operations, 53–56
  military situation, 90, 132–33
  Soviet-American troops proposal, 162–63, 167
  U.S. military supply to Israel, 75
Kurdyumov, Nikolay, 103
Kuwait, 67, 98
Kuznetsov, Vasilii. *See also* "task force"
  Arab military preparations, 5
  beginning of war, 1
  Boumedienne visit, 84
  Brezhnev-Kissinger negotiations, 135–38
  cease-fire attempts, 37, 43, 44
  cease-fire resolution, 78, 95
  evacuation of Soviets, 4
  as first deputy to Brezhnev, 212
  on Kissinger, 122
  as member of task force, 33–34
  response to nuclear alert, 180, 182
  Soviet-Arab cooperation, 185
  unilateral action, 169
  on U.S. policy toward Israel, 93
  visits to Damascus and Cairo, 210
Kvadrat missiles, 54, 61

Ladeikin, V., 212
Lebanese Communist Party, 101
Leontyev, A., 145
Libya, 67
*London Sunday Times*, 155–56
Lord, Winston, 126

M-60 tanks, 75
Maitland, Sir Donald (James Dundas), 141
Malek, Reda, 63, 84
Malik, Yakov
  background, 49–50
  cease-fire, 79
  Israeli "criminal acts," 70
  Israeli violations, 170–72
  meeting with Waldheim, 167
  reaction to nuclear alert, 206
  Resolution 339, 157, 158–59

Resolution 340, 201
Soviet-American resolution, 138, 141
as Soviet U.N. representative, 5
Maliutka antitank weapons, 54–55, 59
Mazulenko, V. A., 67
Mazurov, Kiril, 183
McIntyre, Laurence, 170
media, Soviet
  assessment of Yom Kippur War, 212
  end of news blackout, 114
  and Kissinger visit, 145–46
  on nuclear alert, 177–78
  underestimation of Watergate scandal, 94
  and U.S. military support to Israel, 103
  warnings of Israeli aggression, 5–6
Medwedko, Leonid, 60
Meguid, Ismat Abdel, 35, 147
Meir, Golda, 102–3, 171, 197
Middle East. *See also* Egypt; Israel; Syria (Syrian Arab Republic)
  as region of conflict, xvii, 191
Mig aircraft, 59, 61
  reconnaissance, 113
military intelligence (GRU) reports, 115
military losses, 216–17
military readiness, 180, 181, 192–93
military situation
  and cease-fire violations, 155–56
  during Kosygin-Sadat talks, 104, 107, 108
  review of, 90–91, 132–33
military supply, Soviet-Arab, 11, 16, 56–61, 213
  Algeria request for increase, 84–85
  Egypt, 10, 12
  Egypt and Syria, 92–93
  expansion of, 71–75
  as fulfillment of obligations, 127
  highest point during Cairo visit, 103
  limitation of, 113, 154
  Syria, 199–200
  weaponry, 54–55, 59–61
military supply, U.S.-Israel, 75–76, 115
  as factor in Sadat's cease-fire request, 129
Minić, Miloš, 111, 140
Ministry of Defense (Soviet Union), xviii. *See also* Grechko, Andrei

Ministry of Foreign Affairs (Soviet Union), xviii. *See also* Gromyko, Andrei
Mitla Pass, 45, 66, 72
mobilization, Soviet, 180–81, 183
Moisov, Lazar, 161–62
Moorer, Ernest, 174, 175
Moroccan Communist Party ("Istiglal"), 101
Morocco, 67
Mukhitdinov, Nuritdin
  Arab unity, 68
  Assad communications, 199
  attempts for early cease-fire, 44, 45
  beginning of war, 18
  Brezhnev-Kissinger negotiations, 140
  Egypt-Syria relationship, 67
  expansion of military aid, 71, 72
  role in Yom Kippur War, 12–15
  Syrian military situation, 155–56

NAM (Non-Aligned Movement), 85. *See also* nonaligned states
Nasser, Gamal Abdel, 8, 29, 73
NATO, 97, 215
naval forces, Soviet, 191–92
*New Times*, 212
Nikitin, N., 212
Nixon, Richard M.
  Brezhnev and Israeli violations, 153
  Brezhnev and U.S. cooperation, 163
  Brezhnev communications, 37–38, 41, 116–20, 157
  Brezhnev negotiations, 2
  delegation of responsibility to Kissinger, 125
  guarantees and, 147, 148
  joint force opposition, 167–68
  letter to Dobrynin, 185–86
  message from Sadat on cease-fire guarantees, 155
  nuclear alert and, 182–83, 196, 197
  opposition to use of force, 187
  peace settlement, 161
  press conference, 202–5
  Soviet unilateral action, 169, 173–74
  U.S. supply to Israel, 75–76
  Watergate scandal, 94
Non-Aligned Movement (NAM), 85

234    INDEX

nonaligned states
   and cease-fire resolution, 82–83, 96–97, 120, 140, 141
   and Resolution 340, 201
   and superpowers-dominating-the-world, 161
nuclear alert. *See* Defcon III (Defense Condition III)
nuclear threat in Middle East, xvii

observers, military. *See also* troops, Soviet-American
   Brezhnev message to Nixon, 196
   sending and removing of, 210
   Soviet, 166–67, 172
   Soviet-American, 160–63, 184
   United Nations, 157–58, 165
"October Revolution Slogans of the CC of the CPSU," 77
Odeo-Jowi, Joseph, 161
oil embargo, 90, 97–98, 215
Okunev, Vasilii, 8–9, 72
Old Square, 5, 43. *See also* Central Committee of the Communist Party of the Soviet Union (CPSU)
Oleandrov, Vsevolod, 210

Palestine Liberation Organization (PLO), 61–62
Palestinians
   in Golan Heights and Sinai, 67
   involvement in peace settlement, 130
   "Palestine problem," 208
   rights of, 85, 104
Panama, 201
peace
   Brezhnev as supporter of, 51
   "guaranteed," 64
   Kosygin-Sadat talks, 105
   Kremlin outline for, 118
peace conference
   Brezhnev definition, 136
   continuing military support and planning for, 200
   Egypt's requirements for, 131
   Geneva Peace Conference, 218
   Kissinger's preliminary views on, 197
   preparations for, 210
   result of superpower policies, 217

peace process
   Brezhnev outline, 133
   delay due to Cold War, 219
   guarantee proposal by Brezhnev, 127
   meeting to gather ideas on, 209
   negotiations, 208
   as Politburo topic, xvii
   role of U.S. and Soviet Union, 135, 137, 161
   rumor of plan, 111
peaceful coexistence
   and evacuation from Egypt and Syria, 17
   goal of, 215
   as Politburo topic, xvii
People's Democratic Republic of Yemen, 63
Perez de Cuellar, Javier, 141
Peru, 201
Petrov, S., 212
PLO (Palestine Liberation Organization), 61–62
Podgorny, Nikolai
   and Arab unity, 61, 63, 64, 68
   assessment of Yom Kippur War, 211
   background, 23, 24, 26
   Boumedienne visit, 84
   Brezhnev-Kissinger negotiations, 134
   Cairo visit planning, 90, 91, 92
   cease-fire request by Sadat, 132
   cease-fire resolution, 95–97
   as formal head of Soviet Union, 212
   little knowledge of Middle East, 32
   military situation, 132–33
   military supply to Arabs, 58
   response to nuclear alert, 180, 183
   weakening of position, 216
   World Congress of Peace Forces, 195
Politburo
   Ad Hoc Commission. *See* Suslov Commission
   background, 23–30
   and joint military action, 160
   meetings, xi, 30–31, 57; October 6, 31–35; October 9, 54; October 10, 71; October 12, 76; October 15, 88–99; October 18, 109–10; October 21, 128–35; October 24, 166–67; October 25, 114, 178–84
   reaction to Nixon letter, 188

role in carrying out military decisions, 192–93
statement on Israeli retaliation, 68
Pompidou, Georges, 205
Ponomarev, Boris, 23, 29
  Arab-Soviet cooperation, 185
  Arab unity, 61, 63, 64
  cease-fire, 80
  oil embargo, 97
  as Politburo member, 31
  response to Nixon's press conference, 205
  response to nuclear alert, 180, 182
  Soviet propaganda, 77
  Syrian Communist Party, 74
  World Congress of Peace Forces, 164
Popov, Veniamin, 13, 15, 44
Popper, David, 152
*Pravda*, 5–6, 70, 76, 77
  Communist and Workers' Parties conference, 102
  and nuclear alert, 177
  propaganda and Kissinger visit, 145
  U.S. military support to Israel, 103
Presidium. *See* Politburo
prisoners of war, 199, 210
"progressive" countries, 215–16
"proletarian internationalism," 17
  Arab support and, 60
  and Brezhnev-Kissinger talks, 148
  and cease-fire resolution, 32
  Soviet-Arab cooperation and, 37, 185
  Soviet success in following, 213, 215
propaganda
  campaign against Israel, 5–6, 21
  Kissinger visit and, 145
  orchestration of, 219
  and Suslov Commission, 76–77
  and U.S. action as irresponsible, 206
  and U.S. imperialism, 214
  and World Congress of Peace Forces, 148–49
"propaganda insurance," 99–103
Pustov, N., 77
Pyrlin, Evgenii, 73, 143

Qadr, Y. A., 63, 65
Quandt, William, 60, 168

readiness, military, 180, 181, 192–93
Realpolitik, 32

Resolution 242
  Brezhnev and, 25, 119
  Brezhnev-Kissinger negotiations, 135–36
  establishing a durable peace, 32
  and guarantee of cease-fire, 130, 142
  implementation of, 185
  result of superpower intervention, 217
  and Soviet draft resolution, 87, 95, 96
  Syrian opposition to, 73, 80
  U.S. position, 83
Resolution 338
  "appropriate auspices," 197
  Brezhnev-Kissinger negotiations, 136–37
  Nixon view of, 188
  and sending of troops, 160
  vague language of, 163
  and violation of cease-fire, 152, 154–56
Resolution 339, 156–59
Resolution 340, 201
Richardson, Elliot, 94, 170
Rockefeller, Nelson, 9
Rogers, William, 123
RPG rockets, 54
Rubinstein, Alvin Z., 6
Ruckelshaus, Elliot, 94
Rumor, Mariano, 205

Sadat, Anwar al-. *See also* Egypt
  attitude toward Kosygin, 112–13
  beginning of war, 18
  Brezhnev-Kissinger negotiations, 139
  cease-fire, 45, 81, 82
  cease-fire opposition, 46–49
  cease-fire request, 129–31
  complaints on cease-fire violations, 154–55, 165–66
  Gromyko's opinion of, 29
  Israeli withdrawal and Assad, 140
  Kosygin talks, 87–114
  military observers, 158, 172
  reaction to nuclear alert, 198–99
  rejection of Jordan's involvement, 68
  and reopening of supply lines, 203
  and SCUD missiles, 60, 144
  Soviet relations, 6–10
  Soviet support, 71–72
  Soviet troop request, 167

U.N. forces, 200–201
Vinogradov talks, 39–41
sanctions against Israel, 172
satellite reconnaissance, 113, 115
Saudi Arabia, 67, 91, 98
Scali, John, 49, 79
  Resolution 339, 157, 158
  Soviet-American resolution, 138, 141
Schlesinger, James, 174, 190–91, 202–3
Scowcroft, Brent, 174
SCP (Syrian Communist Party), 63, 84, 101
SCUD missiles, 16, 59
  and Israeli targets, 143–45
  purpose and effect, 192
  Soviet use of, 60
"secrecy" of Kosygin's visit to Cairo, 103–6
Security Council. See United Nations Security Council
Semyenov, Vladimir, 147
Sen, Samar Ranjan, 141
Shaya, J., 63, 65
Shelepin, Alexandr, 29, 103
Shevchenko, A., 212
Shilka weapons, 59
Sinai Peninsula, 66, 67, 72
Sisco, Joseph
  activity with Arabs in New York, 5
  Kissinger-Sadat negotiations, 122, 126, 131, 136
Sixth Fleet (U.S.), 75, 191
Solidarity Committee of Peoples of Asia and Africa, 43
Sonnenfeldt, Helmut, 126
Soviet-American relations, 2, 17, 217–18. See also détente
  cooperation, 148
  dialogue, 35–39
  as Politburo topic, xvii
  Resolution 339, 156–59
  and Sadat, 40
  Soviet concern for, 51
  and unilateral action, 173
Soviet-Arab relations, xvii, 53–86
  Arab rejection of military cooperation, 53–56
  broadening of, 211–12
  cooperation, 90, 92, 184–85
  effect of Cairo visit on, 114

  lack of improvement, 213–14
  Syria, 140
  Vinogradov and Egypt, 8
Soviet Cultural Center (Damascus), 68
Soviet-Egyptian Treaty of Friendship and Cooperation (1971), 9, 26
Soviet Peace Committee, 69
Soviet Union. See also Central Committee of the Communist Party of the Soviet Union (CPSU); Politburo
  cease-fire role, 153–54
  collapse of, xvi
  détente and Arab cooperation, 215
  Egyptian contact, 6–10
  leadership style of, 65
  military actions, 190–93
  military involvement question, 33, 113–14, 148
  observers, 162, 167, 168, 172
  peace-process role, 135, 142, 161, 219
  Sadat's cease-fire guarantee, 131
  statement on war, 41–43
  troop intervention, 167
  U.S. cooperation, 160–64
  view of Kissinger's visit, 145–49
  view of results of war, 211
  view of U.S. action, 189
  warning to Israel, 159–60
Stepakov, Vladimir, 82, 120, 140
strategy of Arabs, 53–56
Strela rockets, 54, 59
Sudan, 91, 201
Suez Canal, 12, 21, 54
superpowers-dominating-the-world mentality, 151–54, 161, 171
Suslov, Mikhail, 23, 30
  and Arab unity, 61, 63, 64
  Israeli retaliation, 68
  little knowledge of Middle East, 32
  World Congress of Peace Forces, 164, 165
Suslov Commission (ad hoc commission), 31
  cease-fire discussion, 80
  discussion of sending troops, 160
  and Soviet propaganda, 77
  and U.N. Security Council, 159
Syria (Syrian Arab Republic). See also Assad, Hafiz al-; Soviet-Arab relations

beginning of war, xv
casualties and losses, 216–17
Egypt relations, 67
military losses, 46, 71–75
military operations, 54–55
military situation, 66–68, 132, 155–56
Resolution 242 opposition, 80
sample weapon delivery, 75
Soviet relations, 12–16, 73–74, 216
Soviet support, 185, 199–200
Suez Canal and Golan Heights attacks, 21–22
Syrian Communist Party (SCP), 84, 101
Syrian Community Party (SCP), 63
Sytenko, Mikhail, 2, 4, 35. *See also* "task force"
    joke on personal messages, 153
    as member of task force, 33, 35
    and Moscow's attitude to Assad, 73
    as under-secretary general of U.N., 212

T-62 tanks, 54, 61
tactics of Arabs, 53–56
Tanjug (Yugoslav press agency), 111
"task force"
    Boumedienne visit, 84, 86
    Brezhnev-Kissinger negotiations, 139
    Brezhnev's address to Nixon, 116
    cease-fire, 79, 81
    cease-fire violations, 151–53
    duties of, ix, 30, 33–35
    instructions for Cairo talks, 98–99
    message to Nixon, 41–42
    messages to Assad and Bakr, 185
    Resolution 340, 202
    statement on Israeli retaliation, 69
    Syria's cease-fire appeal, 44–45
    writing of documents, 190, 196–200, 202–6
Tass news agency
    end of blackout, 114
    and Israeli violations, 68, 69
    and Kissinger's visit, 145
    and Nixon's press conference, 205
    and nuclear alert, 177–78
    Soviet arms supply, 102
Tekoah, Joseph, 70, 142–43
    Resolution 339, 158, 159
time-zone differences, 2
*Times* (London), 155–56

Tito
    message from Brezhnev, 205
    nonaligned states and cease-fire, 82–83, 96, 140
Tomeh, Georges, 35, 73
trade relationships, 214
troops, Soviet-American, 140, 160. *See also* observers, military
    mobilization, 180–81, 183
    question of not deploying, 191–92
*Trud*, 70

"Understanding" (document), 197–98
    and diplomacy games, 218
    initialing by Brezhnev and Kissinger, 137–38
    interpretation by Kremlin, 161
    superpower intervention, 217
    vague language of, 163
unilateral Soviet action, 172, 173, 194, 196
United Nations
    observers, 152, 157–58, 165, 188
    Special Session on the Middle East, 25–26
    25th anniversary, 24
United Nations Emergency Forces. *See* Emergency Forces, U.N.
United Nations Security Council, 44, 46, 49–51. *See also* Resolution 242; Resolution 338; Resolution 339; Resolution 340
    Brezhnev and, 118–19, 136
    cease-fire, 79–80
    cease-fire resolution, 14–15, 38, 39, 43, 120
    Israeli violations, 70, 170–72
    nonpermanent members, 201
    Soviet-American resolution, 138, 141–43
United States
    cease-fire guarantees, 109, 131, 171
    cease-fire role, 153–54, 186
    cease-fire violations, 152–54
    Defcon III (nuclear alert), 174–75
    knowledge of Arab plans, 4–6
    military supply to Israel, 74–76, 90, 93–94, 115; and NATO crisis, 215; and Sadat's cease-fire request, 129
    opposition to joint force, 167–68
    peace-process role, 135, 142, 161, 219

## 238 INDEX

Resolution 242 support, 95
resolution drafts, 88
Soviet cooperation in Middle East, 160–64
Soviet relations. *See* Soviet-American relations
USSR. *See* Soviet Union
Ustinov, Dmitrii
  military supply to Arabs, 58, 71
  observer team proposal, 162, 168
  support for military readiness, 180, 181

victory, hollow, 213, 215
Vinogradov, Vladimir
  Brezhnev-Kissinger negotiations, 139
  cease-fire, 80–81, 82; request by Sadat, 129–31
  Egyptian firing of SCUD missiles, 143–44
  evacuation of Soviets, 3
  Kosygin and reconnaissance information, 113
  Kosygin's Cairo visit, 103, 104, 110, 112
  military aid expansion, 71–72
  military observers, 158, 172
  military situation, 203
  and nuclear alert, 197
  role during Yom Kippur War, 7–10
  Sadat and, 10–12
  Sadat and SCUD missiles, 60
  Sadat and time of planned attack, 18
  Sadat communications, 39–41, 45, 46–48, 67; cease-fire violations, 154–55
  Sadat complaints, 165–66
  Sadat reaction to nuclear alert, 198–99
  Sadat relationship, 72
  on Soviet airlift, 58
Vithana, Gunasena, 178
Volga (SA-5) missiles, 71–72
Vorontsov, Yuli, 123, 142, 197

Waldheim, Kurt, 132, 167
*Wall Street Journal*, 76

war
  casualties and losses, 46, 216–17
  Soviet avoidance of, 18, 190, 213
  Soviet possibility of, 179, 181
War Plan, 110
Warsaw Treaty Organization, 61
Watergate scandal, 94, 132, 197, 218–19
weapon sample confiscation, 75
weapon supplies. *See* military supply, Soviet-Arab; military supply, U.S.-Israel
West Bank, 115, 166. *See also* Suez Canal
Wilner, Meir, 102
withdrawal of Israeli forces
  Assad's view of cease-fire, 48
  as condition for cease-fire, 87–88, 104, 109, 111
  Sadat and, 129, 131
  Sadat-Assad interpretation of, 140
  Soviet-American communication, 117–20, 127
  Soviet-American resolution, 134, 136, 139
  Soviet resolution, 96
  Syria and Resolution 338, 156
Workers' Party, 102
World Congress of Peace Forces, 152, 164–65
  media coverage, 207
  opening of, 195
  schedule of opening, 177–78
World Federation of Trade Unions, 103

Yemen, 63
Yom Kippur (Day of Atonement), ix
"Yugoslav draft," 106
Yugoslavia, 81, 82. *See also* nonaligned states; Tito
  and nonaligned states, 120, 140
  as nonpermanent member of U.N., 201
Yugoslav press agency (Tanjug), 111

Zamyatin, Leonid, 68
Zayyat, Mohammed al-, 7, 35, 158, 170
Zergini, Hadj Mohammed, 84
Zionism, 93, 94, 142–43

# ABOUT THE AUTHOR

Victor L. Israelyan has had a rich and distinguished career as a physician, diplomat, scholar, and professor spanning more than five decades. Born in 1919 in Tbilisi, the capital of Georgia, Israelyan graduated from the First Moscow Medical Institute in 1941 and served as a military physician to the Soviet armed forces during World War II. As a result of his wartime experiences, he changed careers to specialize in international relations and studied at the Diplomatic Academy in Moscow, graduating in 1946. He was a fellow-commoner at Cambridge University in 1957–58 and earned his doctorate in historical science at the Moscow State Institute of International Relations in 1960.

After serving as a professor of international diplomacy during most of the 1960s, in 1968 he was assigned to a diplomatic position in the Permanent Mission of the Soviet Union to the United Nations. Over the next twenty years, he became one of the Soviet Union's leading diplomats, specializing in disarmament negotiations. Through years of multilateral diplomacy in New York and Geneva, he became personally acquainted with many leading world political figures and was entrusted with several special diplomatic missions. From 1968 to 1973 he served as First Deputy Permanent Representative to the United Nations and from 1973 to 1979 as Director of the Foreign Ministry's Department of International Organizations. He was granted the rank of Ambassador Extraordinary and Plenipotentiary in 1971. In Geneva, he headed Soviet delegations to the Conference on Disarmament, to the U.S.–Soviet negotiations on arms control (1979–87), and to review conferences on multilateral arms control treaties (1975–87). From 1975 to 1987 he was a member of the Collegium, the Foreign Ministry's principal advisory and decision-making body.

After retiring from the Foreign Ministry in 1987, Ambassador Israelyan rejoined the Diplomatic Academy in Moscow and remained a consultant to the ministry. His teaching and research include the history of international relations and diplomacy; the style, methods, and tactics of Russian and Soviet diplomacy; arms control; and the art of negotiation. Since 1958 he has lectured on these subjects in England, France, Germany, Austria, Italy, Sweden, Brazil, Mexico, Eastern Europe, and the United States. He has been a visiting lecturer at Stanford and Harvard universities and was a Visiting Fulbright Professor from 1991 to 1993 at The Pennsylvania State University.

Israelyan has authored more than ten books and over 300 articles, published in the Soviet Union, Eastern Europe, France, Canada, England, Switzerland, and the United States. Among his books are *The Anti-Hitler Coalition* (English, Russian, and French, 1964), *The United Nations and Disarmament* (Russian, 1981), *The Diplomacy of World War II* (Russian, 1985), and *Diplomats Face to Face* (Russian, 1990). He is currently writing a book on how the breakup of the Soviet Union has changed the diplomacy of Russia.

www.ingramcontent.com/pod-product-compliance
Lightning Source LLC
Chambersburg PA
CBHW031547300426
44111CB00006BA/211